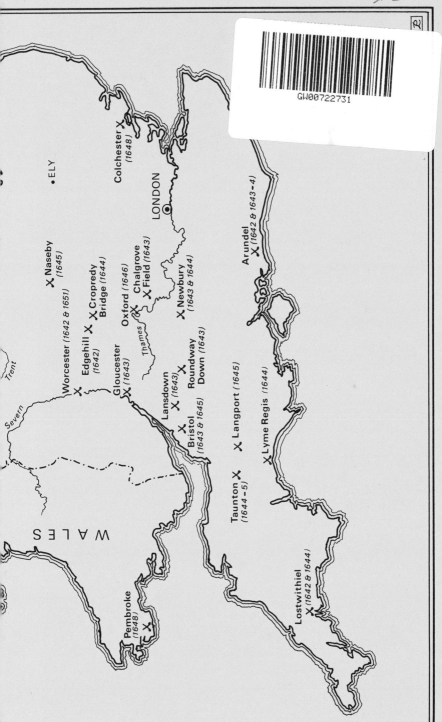

• ELY

Colchester ✗
(1648)

LONDON ⦿

✗ Naseby
(1645)

Worcester (1642 & 1651)
✗

Edgehill ✗
(1642)

✗ Cropredy
Bridge (1644)

Oxford (1646)

Chalgrove
✗ Field (1643)

✗ Newbury
(1643 & 1644)

Gloucester
✗ (1643)

Thames

Lansdown
✗ (1643)

Roundway
Down (1643)

Bristol
✗ (1643 & 1645)

Arundel
✗ (1642 & 1643-4)

Langport (1645)
✗

Lyme Regis (1644)
✗

Taunton ✗
(1644-5)

Trent

Severn

W A L E S

Lostwithiel
✗ (1642 & 1644)

Pembroke
(1648)
✗

The Roundheads

By the same author

Nicholas Ridley
Thomas Cranmer
John Knox
Lord Palmerston
Garibaldi

Oliver Cromwell, c.1649, by Robert Walker

JASPER RIDLEY

The Roundheads

CONSTABLE
LONDON

First published in Great Britain 1976
by Constable and Company Limited
10 Orange Street London WC2H 7EG
Copyright © 1976 by Jasper Ridley

ISBN 0 09 461230 7

Set in Monotype Garamond 11 pt.
Printed in Great Britain by
Ebenezer Baylis & Son Limited
The Trinity Press, Worcester, and London

To my wife

VERA

Contents

Illustrations

Oliver Cromwell, by Robert Walker   *frontispiece*
(*National Portrait Gallery, London*)

A*   ix

Acknowledgements

I wish to thank Mr Mark Bence-Jones and my publisher, Mr Benjamin Glazebrook, for their advice on the planning and form of this book; the staff of the British Museum (now the British Library Reference Division) and the London Library; Lady Antonia Fraser for lending me her books and allowing me to keep them for more than a year; Mr Peter Grant, for his encouragement and advice at the manuscript stage; the Hon. John Jolliffe, for his interest and suggestions; Mr Patrick Morrah, whose biography of Prince Rupert I was able to read in manuscript; my wife Vera, for her work on the proofs; Mr Christopher and Dr Margaret Small, for their hospitality in the course of my travels and research; and my agent Mr Graham Watson, for his help at all times.

Introduction

The 'Great Rebellion'—the Civil War and its aftermath in England, Scotland and Ireland between 1642 and 1660—has often been recognized as the great watershed in British history, dividing the distant past from the modern world. It was the last war in Britain in which the combatants fought in armour and besieged and defended medieval castles, and the first in which tobacco played an essential part in maintaining the morale of the troops. The men of the Civil War were inspired by religious beliefs and quoted Biblical texts like their predecessors in the previous century, but they also developed new ideas and arguments which are more commonplace to us today than they were to them. Some of them fought for the reign of King Jesus, some for the privileges of Parliament, and some—for the first time in English history—for political democracy and social equality.

The two sides are popularly known today as the Roundheads and the Cavaliers. Like most political labels, the names originated as terms of abuse applied to each party by their opponents and repudiated by themselves. The names were first used in a preliminary riot between the King's officers and the London apprentices who supported the Parliament, in Whitehall on 29 December 1641. The King's men called their opponents 'Roundheads' because the apprentices wore their hair cropped short, though not many of the soldiers who afterwards fought for Parliament on the battlefields, and none of their leaders, wore their hair short. The apprentices called the King's men 'Cavaliers', or 'Cavalleros', after the Spanish *caballeros*, because they considered them to be Spanish, foreign and 'Papist' in their sympathies. The Cavaliers, unlike the Roundheads, soon came to accept the name which their enemies gave them, after King Charles I himself had told them that they need not be ashamed of

1

it, because 'Cavalier' was a name 'signifying no more than a gentleman serving his King on horseback'.

In the Whig interpretation of history, the Civil War was a struggle for Parliament and freedom against royal tyranny. More recently the Marxists have interpreted it as a class war of the revolutionary bourgeoisie against the feudal monarchy and nobility. The Civil War was undoubtedly a phase in the social and economic development which took place during the sixteenth and seventeenth centuries, and as a result of which the country gentry and the merchant class emerged with much more power than they had had before; but the Civil War was not a class war. Of the 120 peers in England, ninety supported the King and thirty were either neutral or for the Parliament. The gentry were more committed to the Parliamentary cause than any other class, but many gentlemen fought for the King. The merchants in the towns usually supported Parliament, but some influential merchants supported the King. The independent yeomen and artisans who fought in Cromwell's army were the most revolutionary element in the country, but many yeomen and tenants followed their local squire and landlord into the ranks of the Cavaliers. Men aligned themselves more on religious lines than on any other basis. The more Protestant a man was, the more ardently he supported the Roundheads; if he was a High Church Anglican or a Roman Catholic, he supported the Cavaliers. Religious principles divided classes, and in many cases divided families, into the opposing camps. But social class played a part in deciding a man's allegiance. The higher the social class, the greater the proportion of Cavaliers; and though the King's men were not justified in despising the Roundheads as low-born up-starts, the fact that this accusation was made is in itself significant.

The conflict between the Roundheads and Cavaliers had its roots in the religious struggle which had divided Western Europe since the beginning of the sixteenth century. In 1517 Luther in Germany started the Reformation in a world where the medieval feudal society had broken down as a result of the extermination of the feudal nobility in wars, the discovery of America, and the development of trade. In 1533 Henry VIII repudiated the Papal supremacy over the Church of England because the Pope would not grant him a divorce from his first wife, Catherine of Aragon. For the first time the Protestants found a powerful protector who would support their attacks on the Papacy, and they became enthusiastic supporters of the doctrine of royal absolutism in its most extreme form. The great Protestant leader and martyr, William Tyndale, stated that it was the duty of the subject to obey the King in all things, even if he 'be the greatest tyrant in the world', and in his book *The Obedience of a Christian Man* asserted the doctrine of royal supremacy with such vigour that Henry VIII declared that 'this book is for me and all Kings to read'.

But the religious doctrines of the Protestants were subversive of authority, for they weakened the power of the clergy and the ecclesiastical hierarchy. In all the many subtle points of religious controversy between the Catholics and the Protestants, as well as in those between the various Protestant groups, it was in every case the Protestants, or the more extreme Protestants, whose doctrines weakened the status of the clergy as an instrument of salvation, and stressed the importance of the individual layman in the eyes of God. The Protestants denounced the celebration of Mass by the priest, placed great importance on sermons, in which the preachers expounded religious doctrines to the people, denounced ritual, church music, and anything which distracted the congregation from prayer and the sermons, and above all favoured the widest possible reading of the Bible, appealing from the authority of the church to the authority of the Word of God in Scripture.

To authoritarian monarchs like Henry VIII and Elizabeth I, these Protestant doctrines were subversive of the authority of both State and Church. Henry VIII approved of Tyndale's theories of obedience to tyrants, but not of his aim of making the simplest ploughboy as well versed in Scripture as the most learned clerk; and he burnt Protestants for heresy as well as executing Papal supporters for high treason. Elizabeth I adopted the same policy as her father, relying on the enthusiastic support of the Protestants against the Pope, but supporting the more orthodox and Catholic against the more Protestant position on all points of dispute as to doctrine and ceremonies.

Before Elizabeth became Queen, England had experienced the five-year reign of her sister Mary Tudor, which had had a traumatic effect on the English Protestants. Ninety years later, during the Civil War, the memories of Mary's persecutions were still very fresh, and they strongly influenced the political attitude of the Roundheads. For the seventeenth-century Protestant, Popery meant the fires of Smithfield and the dreadful years between 1555 and 1558, when a Protestant martyr was burnt, on an average, every five days. Within five years of Mary's death, John Foxe had published the first edition of his *Acts and Monuments*—or his *Book of Martyrs*, as it became known—and copies were soon to be seen in every cathedral and in most parish churches. In these massive volumes, which in their final form were nearly four million words in length, or five times as long as the Bible, Foxe told the story of the heroism and sufferings of his Protestant comrades. The Roundheads who fought in the Civil War in 1642 were the second and third generations who had been brought up on Foxe's *Book of Martyrs*, but it moved them as deeply as it had moved their fathers and grandfathers.

In Mary's reign, some of the Protestants for the first time rejected Tyndale's doctrine of obedience to sovereigns, and advocated revolution against their Catholic Queen. Although within six years they once again had a Protestant ruler on the throne, there were Protestant revolutions in Scotland, France and the Netherlands which Elizabeth I, for reasons of foreign policy, reluctantly supported. Many Protestants now believed that, in the last resort, it was justifiable for oppressed Protestant subjects to support revolution and civil war against their Papist kings. Another result of Mary's persecution was that a handful of leading Protestant divines took refuge in Geneva, where they imbibed the religious doctrines of John Calvin; and when they returned home in Elizabeth's reign, they introduced Calvinism into the Church of England. The Roundheads disagreed amongst themselves on many religious questions, but nearly all of them accepted the Calvinist doctrine of predestination, according to which mankind was divided into a small minority, the Elect, who would be saved, and the mass of the people, the Reprobates, who would be damned. Although Calvin was neither a democrat nor a revolutionary, his doctrine of predestination had a democratic and revolutionary effect. It led the Calvinists to believe that it was more important that a man was a member of the Elect— that is to say, a Calvinist—than that he was a king or a noble, and that the Calvinist Elect were entitled to impose their will, by armed force if necessary, on the people, on their kings and governments, and on their social superiors.

The Calvinists favoured the introduction of Calvin's new and democratic form of church organization, dispensing with bishops and substituting the presbyterian system. In the Presbyterian churches the minister (the priest) was elected by the congregation, and the church was governed by the minister and by elected lay elders subject to the supreme authority of the General Assembly, composed of representatives of all the local congregations. As the bishops in the Church of England were the nominees of the King and his agents in temporal as well as ecclesiastical government, neither Elizabeth I nor her successors would tolerate the Calvinist attacks on bishops or any move to weaken their authority.

The Protestant radicals in the Church of England in Elizabeth's reign, with their Calvinist and revolutionary doctrines, became known as 'Puritans'. The word was first used in 1564, and soon succeeded 'Lutheran' and 'sacramentary' as the general term of abuse applied indiscriminately to the more radical section of the Protestants. The Protestant extremists were called 'Puritans' because they wished to purify the church of Catholic practices and 'relics of Popery'. The word did not, at this time, have its modern meaning, and the Puritans were not then particularly 'puritanical' in the modern sense.

Although the Puritans had influential patrons at court and in the church, the Queen was decisively against them. Many of them were imprisoned or otherwise victimized, and in 1593 three Puritans were executed for writing pamphlets against bishops. The executions did not arouse much resentment, because of the Queen's great popularity and political skill, and her position as the leader of the nation in the struggle against Rome and Spain. The people had no sympathy for Puritans who caused trouble, as the Bishop of Winchester wrote in the year after the Armada, 'even now, when the views of the mightie Navie of the Spaniards is scant passed out of our sight'.

One result of this persecution was that some Puritans gave up their attempts to purify the Church of England and their public political activities, and became an isolated and introspective sect, concentrating on their personal purity. It was now that they developed their sabbatarian doctrines, condemning all activities on Sundays, and their hostility to sports and to the theatre. They also gave their children strange names, such as 'Free-love', 'Praise-God', or 'More-Fruit-and-Faint-Not', instead of 'John',

'Thomas', and such other traditional English Christian names.

The accession of James I in 1603 changed the situation. He had none of the old Queen's popularity, and soon made peace with Spain. He continued his policy of friendship with Spain even when the Thirty Years War broke out. His daughter Elizabeth had married Frederick, the Elector Palatine, whose principality was in the Rhineland but who was invited by the Czech Protestants to become King of Bohemia. Frederick and Elizabeth were driven out of Bohemia and the Rhineland by the Austrian Catholic troops and their Spanish allies. Despite the great sympathy in England for the beautiful English Queen of Bohemia* and the 'Protestant Cause' in Europe, King James refused to intervene in the Thirty Years War, apart from a brief and ineffective gesture of military support. This angered many people, and Puritan influence increased in the House of Commons and in the country. Although the Puritans in general repudiated the name of Puritan, by 1622 one of their supporters was prepared to define a Puritan as

A Puritan is he that speaks his mind
In Parliament: not looking once behind
To others' danger . . .
But for the laws and truth doth fairly stand . . .
His character abridged if you would have,
He's one that would a subject be, no slave.

But James I, by his political cunning, succeeded in postponing the storm until his death in 1625, when he was succeeded by his son Charles. Charles I not only continued his father's policy of friendship with Spain and neutrality in the Thirty Years War, but he also married a French Catholic Princess and appointed William Laud as Archbishop of Canterbury. Laud introduced a number of changes in the ritual of the Church of England which the Puritans considered to be Papist, and discouraged preaching as much as possible. He also encouraged the playing of games after church on Sundays, as a gesture against the Puritans.

Apart from the religious objections to the royal policy,

* Everyone in England considered Elizabeth of Bohemia to be an English princess, but in fact she was the daughter of a Scottish father and a Danish mother, and was born in Scotland before her father became King of England.

James I and Charles I fell foul of the lawyers. The common lawyers, in the four Inns of Court in London, had become increasingly important with the development of trade and the increase in the sale and exchanges of land which followed the breakdown of the feudal system; but until the end of the sixteenth century they had not played a prominent part in political life. The medieval and Tudor sovereigns had governed the country with the help of bishops and churchmen who were often canon lawyers, or who had studied the Roman civil law of the continent, which did not apply in England. The English common lawyers resented the domination of the canonists and civil lawyers, both out of professional rivalry and because the procedure of the civil law, unlike the common law, included the inquisitorial system in criminal cases, with the use of torture before trial. The common lawyers, with their close links with the country gentry and the merchants of the towns, became closely associated with the nationalist and Protestant feeling against the foreign Papists with their canon and civil law; and this Protestantism of the Inns of Court was assured when Elizabeth I in 1574 excluded Roman Catholics from membership of the Inns of Court.

The common lawyers, like the rest of the gentry, were prepared to overlook their dislike of the prerogative courts, the Court of Star Chamber, and the use of torture as long as Elizabeth was Queen; but as soon as James I became King they began to oppose the royal policy. Sir Edward Coke, who as Solicitor-General under Elizabeth had been a willing instrument of the Crown in the prosecution and torture of both Papists and Puritans, as James I's Lord Chief Justice gave a number of judicial rulings which limited the powers of the Royal Prerogative, and led to his eventual dismissal from the bench by the indignant King. Coke then became one of the leaders of the Opposition in the House of Commons. The common lawyers took over from the Puritan clergy the leadership of the struggle against the King and the government. Legal and constitutional arguments began to replace religious texts in the language of political controversy.

There was also opposition, especially among the merchants, to the King's economic policy of granting monopolies and imposing restrictions on freedom of trade. Here, too, the opposition to monopolies had first appeared in Elizabeth's reign, but was soft-muted because of the loyalty of the merchants to the Queen, and her skill in making concessions. James I and Charles I abused their power of granting monopolies to a much greater extent than Elizabeth I had done, and by the 1620s there was widespread criticism of monopolies, especially as the King sold grants of monopolies as a means of raising the money which he could not persuade his Parliaments to vote him.

As soon as Charles I came to the throne, the religious, legal, and economic opposition broke out in the House of Commons. For four years Charles struggled with three hostile Parliaments, and then for eleven years ruled without any Parliament. But matters came to a head in Charles's turbulent kingdom of Scotland.

Scotland was a poor country with a population of about 500,000 as compared with 5,000,000 in England. The power of the Crown and the government administration had always been much weaker, and the authority of the nobility in their districts much stronger, than in England; and there was a tradition of lawlessness and violence in Scotland which contrasted with the respect for law in England. In 1559 the revolutionary doctrines of John Knox inspired a revolution against the Queen and the Catholic Church, under the leadership of the Protestant nobility, which established a state church which was Calvinist and Presbyterian in doctrine and organization, and revolutionary in ideology. James I, who reigned in Scotland as James VI for fifty-eight years, succeeded, by his skilful policy, in curbing the power of the Kirk; but Charles I and Archbishop Laud, who considered the Kirk to be objectionable in its practices and subversive politically, decided in 1637 to suppress John Knox's prayer book in Scotland and introduce a new prayer book based on the Book of Common Prayer of the Church of England. This caused a riot in Edinburgh, and soon the whole country was in revolt. The Kirk, under the leadership of the nobility, organized the signing of a Covenant, as had been done before the revolution of 1559, and nearly every man in the country signed—the majority with enthusiasm, the minority through fear of the consequences if they refused.

The revolution in Scotland started a chain of events which led, five years later, to the outbreak of the Civil War in England. The object of this book is to present short studies of some of the men and women who played a leading part in the military and political events of the war on the Roundhead side.

John Hampden

John Hampden was born in London in 1594, but his family lived in their ancestral manor house at Great Hampden in Buckinghamshire. His father, William Hampden, like his grandfather, had been an MP as well as an influential figure in the county; he owned land in Buckinghamshire, Oxfordshire and Essex, and was said to be the wealthiest commoner in England. William Hampden's sister Anne was the mother of the Cavalier poet, Edmund Waller. His wife (John Hampden's mother) was the daughter of Sir Henry Cromwell of Hinchinbrook in Huntingdonshire and the aunt of Oliver Cromwell. When John Hampden was three, his father died, and John succeeded to the family home in Buckinghamshire and the rest of his father's estates.

Like most of the other gentlemen of the district, Hampden was brought up as a zealous Protestant and a fervent English patriot, devoted to the memory of the great Queen Elizabeth and firmly believing in the common law of England. He was educated at the free grammar school at Thame in Oxfordshire, and at the usual age of fifteen he went to university, to Magdalen Hall at Oxford. When he was nineteen he was admitted as a law student at the Inner Temple in London.

At the age of twenty-five he married Elizabeth Symeon, the daughter of the village squire of Pyrton in Oxfordshire. When she died after fifteen years of married life, she left him with three sons and six daughters. In 1640, when he was aged forty-six and was a leading political figure, he married Lettice Vachell, the daughter of Sir Francis Knollys and the widow of Sir Thomas Vachell. She survived him by twenty-three years, living on into the reign of Charles II.

In 1621 Hampden was elected an MP for the constituency of Grampound in Cornwall. He had no connection with the district, but there were many Parliamentary seats in Cornwall at the disposal of Protestant gentlemen who held the same political views as Hampden and knew some of his friends. He sat again for Grampound in the Parliament of 1624; but in the first three Parliaments of Charles I's reign he was elected for the newly-created constituency of Wendover near his Buckinghamshire home, and in the Parliaments of 1640 he sat for Buckinghamshire.

The majority of MPs were men like Hampden—country gentlemen who were convinced Protestants, who had been to university and the Inns of Court and who lived on their country estates when they were not attending to their Parliamentary duties in London. They were critical of James I for his neutrality in the Thirty Years War, for his failure to enforce with sufficient vigour the penal laws against Jesuits and other Roman Catholics, for his grants of monopolies in tobacco and other commodities, and for his dependence on his favourite, George Villiers, Duke of Buckingham, who owed his rise to his homosexual relationship with the King. Villiers was knighted when he was aged twenty-two, was created a Viscount at twenty-four and an Earl six months later, a Marquis at twenty-five, Lord High Admiral at twenty-six, and a Duke at thirty. He was also the second richest man in England, and he and his relations had been granted many monopolies. He was very friendly with the Spanish Ambassador, and was secretly considering becoming a Roman Catholic.

When Hampden first entered Parliament, King James and Buckingham were eager to gain the support of men of influence among the gentry, and a number of young gentlemen were given peerages in 1621. Hampden's mother was eager that Hampden should be granted a peerage, but he had no desire for this, and associated himself with the Opposition in the House of Commons. He was an active, though not outstandingly prominent MP; he spoke in favour of going to war in defence of Protestant Bohemia and its Queen; he spoke against the negotiations which were in progress for the marriage of Prince Charles to the Spanish Infanta; and he served on a Committee of the House to inquire into the enforcement of the laws against Catholics, because the MPs suspected that the King and Buckingham were winking at breaches of the laws and at Catholic activity in England in order to please the government of Spain.

In March 1625 King James died and Charles I succeeded him.

King Charles, who, to the distress of the Puritans, married the French Catholic Princess, Henrietta Maria, was not a homosexual like his father, but he was a close personal friend of Buckingham, and retained him in power. Buckingham tried to win popularity by declaring war on Spain and sending an expedition to attack Cadiz, while another expedition was sent to assist the King and Queen of Bohemia to regain their principality of the Rhineland; but as both expeditions were disastrous failures, Buckingham became even more unpopular. In the Parliament of 1625 a strong attack on Buckingham was launched in the House of Commons by Sir John Eliot, a fiery young Cornish gentleman who had formerly been a friend of Buckingham and had served under him as Vice-Admiral. Eliot had personal reasons for resentment against the King and Duke, because he had been dismissed from his office as Vice-Admiral after he had arrested a pirate who had a protector at court; but there is no reason to doubt the sincerity of his attachment to the law and constitution of England, the privileges of Parliament and the Protestant Cause.

Parliament voted for the necessary taxes to enable the King's government to be carried on, but the House of Commons then refused to vote further supplies until they had discussed the misconduct of Buckingham. The King dissolved Parliament but, being in need of money, summoned another Parliament in the spring of 1626. The House of Commons refused to vote supplies, and Eliot moved that Buckingham be impeached. Eliot was arrested by the King's orders, but as the House of Commons refused to proceed with any business while he was held in prison, Charles released him after a few months. After there had been further attacks on Buckingham in the House of Commons, Charles dissolved Parliament without having been voted supplies, and arrested Eliot and several other gentlemen who had played a prominent part in the attacks on Buckingham. One of these was Sir Edmund Hampden, John Hampden's uncle. Sir Edmund and four of his fellow-prisoners, all of whom happened to be knights, applied for a writ of *habeas corpus* in the Court of King's Bench, arguing that their imprisonment was illegal, as they had not been charged with any offence. The order for their arrest had been issued by the King himself. The case is known in legal history as the Five Knights' Case. The court held that the special

order of the King himself was sufficient to justify the imprisonment. The power of the sovereign to order the arrest of any
subject without assigning any cause had never previously been
challenged in an English court, and had often been exercised by
Elizabeth I and the Tudor monarchs.

As Charles I had been unable to obtain money from Parliament,
he tried to levy taxes on his own authority. Armed with the
decision of the Court of King's Bench in the Five Knights' Case
in his favour, he ordered wealthy landowners to contribute to a
loan to the Crown under threat of imprisonment if they refused.
Many of the more determined Protestant gentry refused to pay,
and suffered the consequences. John Hampden was summoned
before the Privy Council and ordered to pay; he replied that he
considered that the forced loan was illegal, as it was a violation of
Magna Carta. He was imprisoned, in somewhat rigorous conditions, in the Gatehouse prison in Westminster; and after a few
weeks he was again summoned before the Council and ordered
to pay up. As he still refused, he was sent as a prisoner to Hampshire, where he was held for a year in confinement under mild
conditions.

The King and Buckingham again tried to win popularity by
embarking on a war in defence of the Protestant Cause. Buckingham led a naval expedition to the Ile de Ré in support of the
French Protestants of La Rochelle, who had risen in revolt
against the Catholic government of King Louis XIII and
Cardinal Richelieu; but again the expedition was bungled, and
Buckingham returned to England defeated and humiliated. The
costs of the expedition had placed the King in even more urgent
need of money. In March 1628 John Hampden and the other
prisoners were released, and a new Parliament was summoned.
Hampden again played a supporting role when Eliot attacked
Buckingham in the House of Commons. The House refused to
vote supplies until the King had given his consent to the bill
which became known as the Petition of Right, which enacted that
the collection of taxes without the consent of Parliament was
illegal, that no one could be arrested without being charged with
an offence, and that martial law and the billeting of troops on
householders were illegal. Two months after the Petition of
Right became law, Buckingham was assassinated by a fanatical
Puritan. In nearly every town and village in England the people

celebrated the news by lighting bonfires, dancing in the streets and drinking the murderer's health. King Charles never forgave the Parliamentary leaders for this, as he believed that their attacks on Buckingham in the House of Commons had incited the assassin.

The House of Commons switched their attack to the King's religious policy. The new Bishop of London, William Laud, was certainly not a Roman Catholic as the Puritans suspected; but his authoritarian attitude made him further the adoption of ritual and ceremonies which elevated the status of the priesthood, and he was determined to restrict the preaching of sermons and discussion of religious doctrines, which the Puritans favoured. Eliot and his supporters attacked Laud and the bishops who supported him, and denounced the victimization of Puritans and the appointment of High Churchmen to positions of influence in the church and the universities. King Charles was as opposed to Popery as Laud was, but was equally eager to support high ritual and to suppress Puritan preachers. He regarded the intervention of the House of Commons in religious matters as an attack on the doctrine of the royal supremacy over the church, which Henry VIII and Elizabeth I had so rigorously enforced.

In March 1629, the King ordered the Speaker of the House of Commons, Sir John Finch, to adjourn the sittings of the House. When Finch, who supported the King's policy, announced that the House stood adjourned, the MPs refused to accept it. Eliot and his friends locked the doors of the House and held down the indignant Speaker in his chair; and with the King's officers battering at the door, and the Speaker struggling to rise from the Chair, Denzil Holles moved a resolution, which was carried by acclamation, denouncing taxation without the consent of Parliament and the recent Catholic innovations in the Church of England. The King arrested Eliot and Holles, and dissolved Parliament. Hampden and the other MPs returned to their homes.

Eliot and Holles were prosecuted for conspiracy against the King and his government and for their assault on the Speaker, and were heavily fined. Holles was released in October 1630, but Eliot remained a prisoner in the Tower, and his health suffered in his damp cell. He petitioned the King to be allowed to return to his home in Cornwall and to be detained there under house arrest, on account of his poor state of health. The King offered to grant his request if Eliot signed a document admitting that he had acted wrongly and acknowledging the justice of the King's proceedings; but as Eliot refused, he remained in his damp cell. In November 1632 he died of consumption, being only forty years of age. When his son petitioned to be permitted to bury Eliot's corpse in the family vault in Cornwall instead of in the Tower, the King refused, writing on the petition: 'Let Sir John Eliot be buried in the church of that parish where he died.'

The last letter that Eliot wrote from the Tower before he died was to his friend John Hampden; and Hampden, like the other Puritans, considered that Eliot had died a martyr's death. But there was nothing that they could do, as the King did not summon another Parliament, and Hampden lived on his country estates while Laud, who was appointed Archbishop of Canterbury in 1633, enforced the King's authority in the Court of Star Chamber, sentencing Puritan preachers to have their ears cut off and to be flogged, imprisoned and fined.

Hampden was a very popular figure in Buckinghamshire. His good looks and personal charm won him many friends. Unlike many of his contemporaries he was courteous to his social inferiors as well as to his equals, and was much loved by his tenants and neighbours. As a young man he was a keen sportsman, riding, hunting, and playing cricket and other outdoor games, and he was known for his joviality and gaiety; but he became more grave and pensive as he grew older and became involved in politics. He was generally regarded as a Puritan, though he never belonged to the more extreme Puritan sects.

Like all Puritans, he preferred listening to sermons to watching ritual in church. Attendance at church on Sundays had long been compulsory in England; but Puritans who lived in a parish where the vicar was a High Church ritualist preferred to go to church, not in their own parish, but in some neighbouring parish where they could hear a sermon from a Puritan vicar. In order to prevent this, regulations were issued compelling parishioners to attend service in their own parish church on Sundays. The Puritans tried to evade the order by arranging for Puritan vicars to hold their Sunday services at a different time from the neighbouring vicars, so that Puritans in other nearby parishes could comply with the law by attending service in their parish church and also come, earlier or later, to the service of a neighbouring Puritan vicar. Laud countered this by ordering that all services in all churches should be held at the same hour on Sundays, and that no sermons should be preached on any other days in the week. In 1634 Hampden broke the law by attending church in a neighbouring parish and not in his own parish church, and was prosecuted in the local ecclesiastical court; but he was let off with a warning.

Like other Puritans, Hampden was interested in emigration to America. In 1620 a number of Puritans had sailed for Massachusetts in *The Mayflower* in order to escape from religious persecution and build up a Puritan society in a free country. In 1629 Hampden discussed with Eliot the possibility of giving financial help to Puritans who wished to go to Massachusetts; and in 1632 the Earl of Warwick, who was a prominent Puritan, sold Hampden a large tract of land in Connecticut for development by emigrants. But Hampden never thought of going to America himself.

As the King's financial difficulties increased, he resorted to all sorts of expedients in order to raise money without having to summon a Parliament. In 1637 he levied the ancient tax known as Ship-Money—a word which future generations would always associate with the name of John Hampden. Ship-Money, like customs dues and other special taxes, could be levied under the Royal Prerogative power without the consent of Parliament. The tax had traditionally been imposed on many coastal towns and counties in times of emergency in order to pay the costs incurred by the navy in the defence of the realm. Charles now imposed the tax on all the counties of England. There was no precedent for levying the tax on the inland counties, and when Hampden was required to pay Ship-Money on his lands in Buckinghamshire and Oxfordshire, he refused, maintaining that the tax was illegal. A test case was brought in the Court of Exchequer on the assessment of twenty shillings on Hampden's property in the parish of Stoke Mandeville.

The hearing began in the autumn of 1637 at a time when public indignation was rising throughout England. News had reached England of the riot against the English Prayer Book in Edinburgh in the previous summer, and that the Scottish

Presbyterians were organizing a rising against the King's government; and a large crowd in London had acclaimed William Prynne and two of his fellow-martyrs when they were mutilated in the pillory for having published a pamphlet criticizing the bishops. At this juncture Hampden's stand against Ship-Money symbolized the defence of the rights of property against arbitrary royal tyranny, just as the resistance of the Scottish Covenanters and Prynne symbolized the struggle for religious freedom.

Hampden's case aroused the greatest interest throughout England, and the interest was prolonged by the fact that the court sat only one day a week to hear the arguments. Hampden had briefed his friend and political colleague, Oliver St John, as his counsel, and St John's speech to the court was as much a political appeal to the people as a legal argument to the court, though his plea that there could be no taxation without the consent of Parliament was phrased in legalistic language and strengthened with legal precedents. The speech was printed and distributed throughout the country; it was read, and read aloud to others, and discussed in the taverns, where it was accepted as an authoritative statement of the law of England, as if it were the final judgment of a supreme court, not merely the arguments of one of the parties in the case. Hampden became a national hero.

Sir John Finch, the former Speaker of the House of Commons, presided as Chief Justice of the Court of Common Pleas; but though Finch was an ardent supporter of the King, the twelve judges were not mere agents of the Crown, and considered the arguments on their merits. Eventually, after the hearing had lasted for seven months, judgment was given in June 1638. Nine of the judges ruled against Hampden's main argument that the King could not extend the levy of Ship Money to the inland counties without the consent of Parliament, but two of these held in Hampden's favour on the grounds that there was a technical irregularity in the wording of the notice of assessment; three judges upheld the arguments which St John had put forward on Hampden's behalf. The King's victory by nine to three on the vital issue was therefore misrepresented as being a victory of only seven to five; but in any case the nation at large had long since given its verdict in Hampden's favour, and the King and his government realized that Hampden and the Opposition had won a moral victory. The King's chief minister,

Strafford, wrote in a private letter that Hampden was a Puritan troublemaker, and that he and his colleagues should be 'whipped home into their right wits'.

In 1639 King Charles marched with an army against the Scottish Covenanters, but finding himself outnumbered by the Covenanters he made a truce with them. Next year he made extensive preparations for the second Scots War, and assembled a large army. Many of the officers in the army were Roman Catholics. Although the King was opposed to the Church of Rome, he persecuted Catholics far less eagerly than his opponents in Parliament wished, and he could therefore rely on the loyalty of his Catholic subjects. Many English Catholic gentlemen had served in the Catholic armies in the Thirty Years War, and as they had had experience of warfare they were useful officers to employ against the Scottish rebel commanders who had fought in the Thirty Years War on the Protestant side. But this appointment of Catholic officers aroused the greatest opposition among the English people, and was useful fuel for the Puritan propagandists.

Before starting the campaign, Charles summoned a Parliament —the first for eleven years—in the spring of 1640, and asked for a vote of supplies to pay for the war against the Scottish rebels. The House of Commons refused to vote supplies, and instead appointed a Committee of the House, on which Hampden served, to investigate the legality of the recent levy of Ship-Money. After three weeks the King dissolved Parliament, which became known as the Short Parliament, and marched against the Scots without having obtained the money. He was convinced that the English Puritan leaders were in secret communication with the Scottish Covenanters, and on the day after he dissolved the Short Parliament he ordered his officers to arrest Hampden and search his house in London to find evidence of his treasonable correspondence with the rebels. But no evidence could be found and Hampden was released after a few days.

As Charles marched to York, the Scots forestalled him and invaded England. For the first time in history they were welcomed as liberators by the people of Northumberland. They routed Charles's army at Newburn on the Tyne, and entered Newcastle. Many of Charles's soldiers deserted; some mutinied and murdered their Catholic officers. Charles was forced to sign a humiliating peace, by which he agreed to all the demands of the Covenanters for the preservation of the Presbyterian religion in Scotland, and also to pay an indemnity to cover the Covenanters' costs of the war. The treaty provided that the Covenanters' army should remain in occupation of the six northern counties of England until the money was paid, and that the additional costs of this occupation should also be paid by the King. Charles now capitulated completely. If he was to pay the indemnity to the Scots and find money to carry on the government of England, he must obtain supplies from Parliament. On 3 November 1640 a new Parliament met at Westminster. It became known as the Long Parliament, because it sat, in one form or another, for thirteen years.

The House of Commons began by impeaching Strafford and Archbishop Laud on charges of high treason for having advised the King to betray the liberties of the people. Strafford, as the more dangerous opponent, was dealt with first. As usual with the impeachment procedure, the leading members of the House of Commons conducted the case against him at his trial before the House of Lords. Hampden was one of the MPs engaged in the trial, though the leading part was played by his colleague, John Pym. Hampden believed that the public welfare required that Strafford should be convicted and executed, but he was determined that he should have a fair trial, and thwarted all attempts to prevent Strafford from speaking in his own defence. In the end the House of Commons, against Hampden's wishes, decided to abandon the impeachment and proceed by a Bill of Attainder, under which Strafford could simply be sentenced to death without trial by Act of Parliament. The King, under the pressure of public opinion, gave his Royal Assent to the bill, and Strafford was beheaded.

In August 1641 the King paid a state visit to Scotland. The House of Commons was suspicious of the King, and appointed a number of MPs, of whom Hampden was one, to accompany him to Scotland and keep an eye on him. Hampden's charm and courtesy made a favourable impression on the King, who himself knew how to exercise personal charm to good effect. Charles offered to appoint Hampden as one of his ministers, but Hampden declined.

When Hampden returned to London in the autumn, his tact came in useful in reconciling the differences which were developing among the Parliamentary leaders. They had all been united in getting rid of the hated Strafford; but when the more radical MPs, like Oliver Cromwell, proceeded to demand the abolition of bishops, this alienated the more moderate opponents of the King, particularly the peers in the House of Lords. Hampden was in his element in reconciling the differences between the House of Commons and the House of Lords, though he ultimately joined Cromwell and the 'Root and Branch' men in demanding the abolition of bishops.

At the beginning of January 1642, the King decided to carry out a *coup* against his opponents by arresting six of the Parliamentary leaders—one peer and five members of the House of Commons. He accused Lord Mandeville (afterwards the Earl of Manchester) and Hampden, Pym, Holles, St John and Sir Arthur Hazelrig of high treason for having 'traiterously endeavoured to subvert the fundamentall Lawes and Government of the Kingdom of England, To deprive the King of his Royall Power, and to place in Subjects an Arbitrary and Tyrannicall power over the Lives, Liberties and Estates of His Majesties leige people'. He also accused them of having incited his troops to mutiny and of having assisted the Scottish invasion of England. He marched into the House of Commons at the head of his guards, intending to carry out the arrest in person—a serious tactical blunder which laid him open to personal criticism if the attempt succeeded and to ridicule if it failed.

The MPs had been warned in advance, and had taken refuge in the City of London. When the King drove into the City to demand their surrender, he found the streets filled with hostile crowds, and someone threw a paper into his carriage containing the call for civil war: 'To your tents, O Israel!' The people of London built barricades to defend the city if the King's guards tried to force their way in and arrest the Five Members. When the news reached Buckinghamshire, four thousand of Hampden's neighbours and tenants marched to London to rescue him. On the night of 10 January the King and the royal family fled from Whitehall to Hampton Court, and next day Hampden and his colleagues returned from London to Westminster in triumph, travelling along the river by barge amid the cheers of the great crowds who lined the banks.

The King made an attempt to conciliate Parliament, but

failed. In August 1642 the Civil War began. London was in the hands of the Parliament; before the end of the year the King had established his capital at Oxford.

The attitude of the people throughout the country was determined chiefly by the decision of the local gentlemen, and the MPs hastened to rally the support of their tenants and the inhabitants of their localities. Hampden's personal popularity in Buckinghamshire was enough to ensure that the county supported the Parliamentary cause. The inhabitants enrolled enthusiastically in the regiment which Hampden, holding the rank of colonel, enlisted for the Parliament. He dressed his men in a dark green uniform.

The Commander-in-Chief of the Parliamentary forces was the Earl of Essex, who was appointed because he was the highest-ranking noblemen on the Parliament's side. By long-standing tradition, high military commands were always given to noblemen, so Essex's support was indispensable to the Parliamentary cause; but Essex did not submit readily to the instructions which he received from the House of Commons and from the Committee of Safety, which took over the government of the territory in Parliament's hands and the overall direction of the war. Hampden's tact and charm were once again in demand. He was usually successful in smoothing out the difficulties between Essex and the House of Commons and the Committee of Safety.

At the end of October, Essex engaged the royal army at Edgehill in Warwickshire in the first major battle of the war. Hampden arrived too late to play an important part in the battle, but rendered good service in covering the retreat when the Parliamentary army fell back towards Warwick. Charles marched on London, and his vanguard advanced as far as Turnham Green, less than ten miles from the capital. The London citizens were inspired to resistance by the sermons of the Puritan preachers, and turned out in their trained-bands to defend the city. The King's men, outnumbered by the defenders, retreated towards Oxford. Hampden, who was at Turnham Green with his regiment, was eager to pursue and engage the enemy, but Essex refused to do so.

During the winter an attempt was made to end the war by negotiation, and representatives of both sides met at Oxford in order to discuss peace terms. Hampden was eager to end the war by negotiation, but he believed that the only way to induce

Charles to compromise was to win a decisive military victory; and he therefore urged Essex to wage war more vigorously. A number of newspapers—the first ever to be published in England —had appeared in London during the early days of the meeting of the Long Parliament in 1641, and these newspapers now carried weekly reports of the progress of the war. Hampden was loudly acclaimed in the press, and was sometimes given the credit for purely fictitious military achievements. He became even more popular with his supporters.

In the summer campaign of 1643, the Parliamentary army under Essex advanced on Oxford. In the middle of June the Cavalier cavalry under the King's nephew, Prince Rupert—the son of Elizabeth, Queen of Bohemia—made a successful raid on Essex's outposts. While they were returning to Oxford, they were pursued by a Roundhead force, led by Hampden, who came into contact with Rupert on 18 June near the village of Chalgrove. Rupert charged the enemy, who broke before the sword-thrusts of his horsemen. Early in the engagement, Hampden was hit in the shoulder by a musket ball, and the wound was so serious that he had to leave the battlefield. He headed for the village of Pyrton, where his first wife's father lived; but finding that the road to Pyrton was in Cavalier hands, he went with the retreating Roundheads to Thame. There, in the town where he had gone to school, twelve miles from his Buckinghamshire home, he was put to bed in a house which later became the Greyhound Inn.

Soon it was known that his life was in danger. King Charles, who had always regarded him with respect, sent an envoy to Thame, offering to send his personal physician to care for Hampden; but six days after the battle, on 24 June 1643, Hampden died of his wound, at the age of forty-nine. He was buried in his family vault at Great Hampden.

His death was lamented by his supporters, who knew that they had lost a beloved leader. No one realized how greatly his qualities as a conciliator would be needed in the years ahead.

2

John Pym

At the beginning of the war, the less intelligent Cavaliers interpreted the situation very simply: the Civil War was caused by the ambition of one wicked man—John Pym. They considered that the issue at stake was whether England should be ruled by King Charles or King Pym.

John Pym was born at Brymore near Bridgwater in May 1583 (not in 1584, the date usually given). His father was a wealthy landowner in North Somerset, owning property in nearly every parish between Glastonbury and Exmoor. Thirty years before, the West of England had been solidly Catholic. In 1549, in Edward VI's reign, a formidable revolt had broken out in Cornwall and Devon against the abolition of the Catholic Mass and the establishment of the Book of Common Prayer; and during the Catholic reaction under Queen Mary, only one Protestant martyr had been burned to the west of Bristol. But during the twenty-five years before Pym was born, a great change had taken place. The struggle between Catholics and Protestants had been transferred from the divinity schools and heresy tribunals of England to the Spanish Main, where English Protestant seamen fought the Catholic Spaniards for Queen, country and the Protestant religion; and the little ports of Somerset, Devon and Cornwall provided the privateers who enriched themselves as well as the Queen's Exchequer by plundering the Spanish galleons. Every English captain who fought the Spaniards in the Atlantic and the Caribbean carried with him in his ship a copy of Foxe's *Book of Martyrs*, as well as the English Bible and the Book of Common Prayer. By 1583 the south-west of England was a Protestant and Puritan stronghold. The concept of a Puritan pirate did not seem as strange in the sixteenth and seventeenth centuries as it would today.

When Pym was sixteen, he went to Broadgates Hall (today Pembroke College) at Oxford, and three years later, in November 1602, a few months before Queen Elizabeth died, he was admitted to the Middle Temple in London. After this usual education of a Puritan gentleman of university and the Inns of Court, he returned to Somerset to manage his country estates. He married the daughter of a neighbouring gentleman, but within a few years, when he was thirty-six, his wife died. He never remarried, nor is he known to have had any further love affairs during the rest of his life. He was not of a romantic disposition; in private life, as in his political career, he was cool, efficient and unobtrusive.

He was not associated with extreme Puritan sects or practices, but was sober and godfearing, a devout Protestant and a determined enemy of Popery. Like his seafaring neighbours of the West Country, he objected even more than most other Englishmen to King James's policy of friendship with Catholic Spain. His opponents had no hesitation in labelling him a Puritan, though he himself on one occasion condemned those who called their enemies by 'that odious and factious name of Puritans'.

In 1614, when he was thirty-one, Pym was elected as MP for Calne in Wiltshire, and he represented Calne in the last two Parliaments of James I's reign in 1621 and 1624. In 1625 he changed his constituency, being elected for Tavistock in Devon, and he sat for Tavistock in all the subsequent Parliaments during his lifetime. He naturally attached himself to the Opposition in the House of Commons under the leadership of Coke and Eliot, and was particularly active in demanding the strict enforcement of the penal laws against Papist priests.

In the Parliament of 1621 he distinguished himself by his intervention in the case of Edward Floyd, an old Papist barrister who was imprisoned in the Fleet prison in London. News had reached England that the Austrian Catholic armies had defeated the forces of the King and Queen of Bohemia at the Battle of the White Hill outside Prague, and had forced Frederick and Elizabeth to flee from their kingdom. Public opinion in England was outraged at the disaster that had befallen the popular Queen of Bohemia; but it was reported to the House of Commons that Floyd, in the Fleet, had openly rejoiced when he heard about the Catholic victory at Prague. Some of the MPs demanded that

Floyd should be whipped, that hot bacon fat should be rubbed into his wounds in the Spanish style, that his tongue should be bored through, or that his ears should be cut off. Pym moved that he should be whipped, unless he could pay a fine of £1,000. But the House of Lords intervened with a claim that the peers alone had the right to exercise the judicial powers of the High Court of Parliament, and that the House of Commons had no authority to try anyone except its own members. King James upheld the House of Lords' contention, and referred the case to the Lords. They sentenced Floyd to be branded, whipped, imprisoned for life, and fined £5,000. After he had been branded, the King remitted the rest of the sentence.

The MPs who criticized Buckingham in the House of Commons became known as the 'Country Party', as opposed to the 'Court Party', and for the first time in history a kind of political party organization appeared in the House of Commons. If Eliot can be called the first political party leader, Pym was the first Chief Whip. He occasionally spoke in the House, making unemotional statements which contrasted with Eliot's fiery oratory; but most of the time he worked behind the scenes, organizing the support for Eliot, and planning tactics. He was not of the stuff of which martyrs are made, and when his enemies had the upper hand he thought it wiser to lie low and wait patiently for better times. Unlike Eliot, Holles and Hampden, he was not one of those MPs who was arrested in 1627 for refusing to pay the taxes which Charles I imposed without the authority of Parliament or for resisting the adjournment of the House of Commons in 1629; nor did he make any gesture of resistance to authority, or suffer any persecution, during the eleven years when Charles ruled without a Parliament.

He found scope for his organizational ability during this time by becoming the secretary of the Providence Company. Puritans continued to go to Massachusetts throughout the 1630s; but there were other possibilities for emigration and colonization. A number of wealthy Puritans, among whom were the Earl of Warwick and Oliver St John, contributed large sums of money to finance the emigration of Puritans to Providence Island in the Caribbean, where they could establish a godfearing Puritan society, cultivate the island with the labour of African slaves, spy on the Spanish ships in the area, and perhaps attack and rob these ships if a suitable opportunity arose. Lord Warwick was the President of the company, but Pym attended the meetings of the Board more often than any other member, and was chiefly responsible for the organizational work. A colony was established but their piracy was too successful, and in 1640 the Spaniards attacked and sacked Providence Island.

The revolt of the Scottish Covenanters and their successes in the wars of 1639 and 1640 revived the hopes of the English Puritans. The King believed that the Puritans were in secret touch with the Scots, and that the board meetings of the Providence Company were an excuse for conspiratorial gatherings at which Pym and his colleagues discussed their treasonable communications with the rebels. When the King dissolved the Short Parliament before leaving London for the second Scots War, he ordered that Pym's lodgings, along with Hampden's, should be searched, but no correspondence with the rebels could be found. After the treaty with the Scots, the King was forced to summon the Long Parliament; and when Parliament met on 3 November 1640, Pym at once assumed the leadership of the King's opponents in the House of Commons.

The first object of the Puritans was the impeachment and execution of Strafford, and Pym took charge of this operation, planning each move in his cat-and-mouse game with great skill. Although everyone expected Strafford to be impeached as soon as Parliament met, Pym waited for eight days, while routine business was dealt with, before taking any action against Strafford; then he denounced him as a traitor, and the officers of the House of Commons took him into custody and soon afterwards conveyed him to the Tower. Pym accused Strafford of having attempted 'to subvert the Fundamental Laws and Government' of the realm and 'to introduce an arbitrary and tyrannical Government, against Law', and of 'giving His Majesty Advice, by Force of Arms, to compel His loyal Subjects to submit therunto'. The charges against Strafford were published in pamphlet form and widely circulated in London and elsewhere, with the result that Strafford was judged guilty by the public before his trial in the House of Lords had begun.

Pym spent six months collecting the evidence and conducting the case. He knew that the evidence against Strafford was weak, and he had to use everything that he could find. Almost immediately he was approached by the younger Sir Henry Vane, the son of Sir Henry Vane, the King's Secretary of State. The elder Vane had taken home from his office in Whitehall a copy of the minutes of a meeting of the Privy Council on 5 May 1640; and his son, who was an ardent Puritan, had looked through them and found an entry which he thought might constitute deadly evidence against Strafford. The elder Vane had noted in the minutes that at this meeting Strafford had proposed that Irish troops should be brought into 'this kingdom'. The younger Vane made a copy of the entry and gave it to Pym, pledging him to secrecy as to how he had obtained it. The weakness of the evidence, from Pym's point of view, was that the minutes did not show which of King Charles's two kingdoms—England or Scotland—was meant. If 'this kingdom' meant Scotland, then Strafford was making the not unreasonable proposal that Irish troops should invade Scotland in order to assist in suppressing the Scottish rebels who were fighting against the King. If 'this kingdom' meant England, then he was suggesting that Irish troops should be brought into peaceful England in order to overawe the Parliament and the people.

Pym kept the evidence secret when he began the case against Strafford. Instead of producing the entry which the younger Vane had given him, he thought it would be better if the elder Vane were called to give evidence as to what was said at the meeting of the Privy Council on 5 May 1640. The King, after protesting that Privy Councillors should not be asked or permitted to disclose what had been said at Council meetings, gave way and allowed the evidence to be given; but the elder Vane, though he testified that Strafford had said that Irish troops should be brought into 'this kingdom', would give no indication as to which kingdom was meant. Eventually Pym produced the entry in the minutes which the younger Vane had given him; but as the case against Strafford was obviously too weak to induce the House of Lords to convict him, Pym decided on 10 April 1641 to proceed against Strafford by Bill of Attainder and sentence him to death by Act of Parliament.

At this point a number of courtiers, including the poet Sir John Suckling, entered into a rash and clumsily-organized plot to carry out a military *coup d'état*. The Tower and other strongpoints were to be seized by army officers who were loyal to the King and

Strafford, with the object of overthrowing the Parliament and saving Strafford's life. One of the plotters talked too freely, and information about the plot reach Lord Mandeville, who was the leader of the Opposition in the House of Lords. Mandeville told Pym. Pym again kept the secret to himself in order to be able to reveal it at the best tactical moment.

The House of Commons passed the Bill of Attainder. Pym managed to get it through the House of Lords by inducing the peers to accept a ruling, for which there was no precedent at all, that the bishops could not vote on an issue involving life or death; but on 1 May the King announced that he would never give his Royal Assent to the bill which condemned his loyal minister to death. On 3 May Pym revealed the military plot to save Strafford, and on the same day, as the MPs and the people were aroused to fear and fury by the prospect of a military *coup*, the London apprentices marched from the City to Westminster and demonstrated in front of the King's palace in Whitehall, demanding that the King should assent to the Bill and that Strafford should be put to death. The demonstrations continued every day until 10 May, when the King, who was afraid that his wife's life was in danger from the mob, gave way and gave his Royal Assent to the bill, after Strafford himself had advised him that this would be his wisest policy. Strafford was beheaded next day.

Strafford was so intensely hated that even the more moderate of the King's opponents were prepared to approve of his execution; but the moderates were shocked when the more extreme Puritans in the House of Commons proceeded to introduce the 'Root and Branch' Bill for the abolition of bishops. Pym was placed in a difficult position. He did not wish to lose the support of the moderates, who were the majority in the House of Lords; but he knew that not only the Puritans in the House of Commons, but also the Scottish Covenanters, were eager for the abolition of bishops, and that the Covenanters might withdraw their support if this proposal were rejected. He managed to postpone the question, and at the same time to intensify the popular resentment against the King, by drawing up the Grand Remonstrance. In this lengthy document, all the King's acts of misgovernment since he came to the throne were described at length; but moderate opinion in Parliament was now rallying to the King, and the Grand Remonstrance passed the House of Commons by only eleven votes in November 1641.

In January 1642 the King attempted to arrest Lord Mandeville and the five members of the House of Commons, of whom Pym was one. Pym had several spies at court, including Lady Carlisle who was an intimate friend of the Queen. There is probably no truth in the rumour that she was the mistress, first of Strafford and then of Pym, but she was intimate with both of them, and seems to have acted as a double-agent for the court and the Opposition. Pym learned through her and his colleague the Earl of Essex of the King's plan to arrest the Five Members, and was therefore able to warn his colleagues and escape with them to the City before the King arrived at the House. When Charles left London and prepared for civil war, the government of the country was in effect taken over by Pym. A Committee of Safety was set up in July 1642 to govern during the King's absence. Pym was the leading figure on the Committee.

In August the war began. Parliament had declared that the objects for which they stood were the defence of the Protestant religion against Popery, the freedom of Englishmen and the rights of property, and the privileges of Parliament. They proclaimed their loyalty to the King, and disclaimed any intention of harming his royal person or restricting his Royal Prerogative, but asserted that as the King had been induced by evil advisers to attack his Parliament, the Parliament was lawfully entitled to wage a defensive war for its own protection and in defence of the laws of England. They claimed that during the King's absence from London the two Houses of Parliament were entitled to make laws and levy taxes without the Royal Assent, and proclaimed that any taxes levied or authority exercised by the King's supporters were illegal. They proclaimed that the motto of their armies should be 'For King and Parliament'.

Pym did not join the army, like so many of his Parliamentary colleagues—at the age of fifty-nine he was older than most of them—but remained at Westminster, and acted as the Prime Minister of the territory under the control of Parliament. After the first campaign of the war and the abortive peace negotiations at Oxford, the Parliamentary cause suffered a series of disasters in

the summer of 1643. Hampden was defeated and killed at Chalgrove. An army of Cornishmen, under the command of Sir
Ralph Hopton and Sir Bevill Grenville, drove the Roundheads
out of the whole of the south-west and held Cornwall, Devon and
Somerset for the King. In July Sir William Waller, who had
hitherto been one of the most successful of the Parliamentary
generals, was defeated at Roundway Down near Devizes, and the
important seaport of Bristol fell to the Cavaliers. In Yorkshire,
the Parliamentary army under Lord Fairfax was defeated at
Adwalton Moor, and the Cavaliers held the whole of the north of
England except for a few isolated strongholds. The picture was
lightened only by Essex's success in relieving Gloucester, which
held out successfully against a long siege by the King's army, by
his victory at Newbury in September, and by Colonel Oliver
Cromwell's local successes in East Anglia.

Pym had some difficulty in maintaining the morale of the people
of London, where a movement for peace arose, particularly
among many of the more moderate peers in the House of Lords.
At the same time he came under attack from an extremist group,
under the leadership of Henry Marten, who disapproved of the
official line that they were fighting for King and Parliament, and
wished to proclaim a republic. They also demanded that Waller
should replace Essex as Commander-in-Chief. Essex had been
criticized for some time by many MPs for his dilatoriness in
marching to the relief of Gloucester, and in July Pym responded
to Marten's pressure by sending a letter to Essex in which he
sharply criticized his generalship. Essex thereupon issued a
statement that he was in favour of opening new peace negotiations with the King.

This encouraged the mood of defeatism and pacifism in
London. The women of London demonstrated in favour of
peace, and much resentment was caused when a young girl who
was watching the demonstration was accidentally killed by the
Parliament soldiers. But Pym did not lose control of the situation.
He patched up his quarrel with Essex, who publicly withdrew his
support for the peace party; and the House of Commons imprisoned Marten for having stated that the King and the royal
family should be put to death.

Pym was very conscious that it was vital to the Parliament that
the Scottish Covenanters should enter the war, for the whole

situation would be transformed if a Scottish army could attack the Cavaliers in the north in the rear. But the Covenanters were prepared to fight only for Presbyterianism. The Presbyterian Kirk of Scotland believed as firmly as the Church of Rome that it was the only true Church of Christ, that no salvation could be found outside its fold, and that it was under a duty to suppress heresy and to force all persons under its control to join the Kirk and adopt its Calvinist doctrines. They believed that the Book of Common Prayer of the Church of England contained dregs of Popery, and that they must not only prevent it from being introduced into Scotland but must also suppress it in England, where it should be replaced by John Knox's Book of Common Order.

On 1 July 1643 a body which became known as the Westminster Assembly opened its sessions in Westminster. It consisted of representatives from the House of Commons and the House of Lords, a number of English Puritan ministers and preachers, and Scottish Presbyterian ministers who had been sent to London as the representatives of the Kirk of Scotland. Next month Pym sent Henry Vane the younger to Edinburgh to negotiate directly with the leaders of the Scottish Covenanters, who were in complete control of Scotland. The Scots demanded, as a price of their intervention in the war, that England should become a Presbyterian country, and that the Church of England should be completely remodelled in the image of the Scottish Kirk.

The Scottish proposals shocked the moderates in London, especially those in the House of Lords. Anglicans who were opposed to Charles I's arbitrary methods of government would not support the forcible conversion of England to Presbyterianism, and many English Puritans were also opposed, for different reasons, to Presbyterianism. But Pym was convinced that it was essential to accept the Scottish terms. Although he was a sincerely religious man, his approach to the problem was completely pragmatic. He disliked many features of Presbyterianism and was aware that many of the Parliament supporters would be alienated if it were adopted in England; but he believed that if the Scots did not enter the war, the King would win. Charles would then impose an arbitrary despotism, and would execute all the Parliamentary leaders for high treason. In a speech in the House of

Commons, Pym compared their position to that of a man lying ill in bed who has been told by his doctor that he must rest, but found that an armed enemy had entered his room and was seeking to kill him; whatever the doctor had said about resting, the patient had better jump out of bed and seize his sword to fight the intruder.

It was chiefly because of Pym's efforts that Parliament agreed to accept the Scots' conditions. Every peer and MP, and everyone in a position of authority in England, was to sign the Solemn League and Covenant, by which they undertook to maintain the Kirk of Scotland as a Presbyterian Church and to bring the Church of England into line with the Scottish Kirk. In return, the Scots entered the war on the Parliament's side, and agreed to send an army into England. The Westminster Assembly then set about making the Church of England Presbyterian. Bishops had already been abolished in January 1643, and by the spring of 1645 the Book of Common Prayer was replaced by the Directory of Worship, a new Presbyterian prayer book. It was made a criminal offence to use the Book of Common Prayer in any religious service.

Fifteen days after the treaty with the Scots was signed, Pym died, on 8 December 1643. The Cavaliers spread the rumour that he had died of syphilis; the Roundheads said that it was the result of overwork and the strain of his exertions on behalf of his country. Modern medical knowledge has established that he died of cancer of the bowel. He was aged sixty. He was given a great state funeral; his body lay in state for two days before being buried in Westminster Abbey. After the Restoration of 1660 it was removed and thrown into a pit.

3

Robert Devereux, Third Earl of Essex

The third Earl of Essex in the Devereux line was born in 1591. His father, the second Earl, was only twenty-four years old but was already the favourite of the aged Queen Elizabeth I, the darling of the nation, and the hero of the war against Spain. His mother was the daughter of Sir Francis Walsingham and the widow of Sir Philip Sidney. The second Earl's romantic and successful career ended in 1601 when his attempted rebellion in London was defeated, and the Queen reluctantly authorized his execution. His son at the age of ten found that his title and lands had been forfeited for high treason; but James I, who had been in contact with his father and may even have been a party to the Essex rebellion, restored the title and estate to the thirteen-year-old boy in 1604. He also appointed the young Earl to be a page to his son Henry, the Prince of Wales. •

One day when Essex and the Prince were playing tennis, the two boys quarrelled and the Prince called Essex the 'son of a traitor'. Essex struck the Prince on the head with his tennis racket, and drew blood. The matter was reported to the King, but James pardoned Essex and told his son that if Essex could strike him so hard now, he would be sure to strike his enemies even harder in time to come.

In January 1606, when Essex was not yet quite fifteen years old, King James arranged an advantageous marriage for him with Lady Frances Howard, the daughter of the Earl of Suffolk, the Lord Chamberlain. Frances was a year older than her husband, and was rapidly becoming one of the leading beauties of the court. She took a violent dislike to Essex, and refused to allow him to consummate the marriage; and when Essex, perhaps with official encouragement, went abroad for two years to complete his education in France and Italy, Lady Essex became the mistress of the Prince of Wales, and after a short liaison with the Prince formed a more lasting attachment with the King's Scottish favourite, Robert Ker. In 1613 Lady Essex petitioned for a divorce on the grounds that Essex was impotent. Essex contested the case. Ker's intimate friend, Sir Thomas Overbury, who disliked Lady Essex, was in possession of evidence which would have won the case for Essex; but Lady Essex arranged for him to be imprisoned in the Tower, and poisoned him. Ten days after Overbury died, the divorce commissioners gave judgment in Lady Essex's favour; and a few weeks later she married Ker, who had been created Earl of Somerset.

The murder was hushed up for two years, but in 1615 the truth came out and caused a scandal which touched the King and the whole court. The Earl and Countess of Somerset were convicted of murder and sentenced to death, but the King commuted the sentence; and though the lesser agents in the murder were executed, Lord and Lady Somerset were released from the Tower after six years. Essex was in no way involved in the crime of his former wife, and emerged from the scandal as the innocent but slightly ridiculous dupe of a wicked woman.

Essex was completely different in character from his dashing, flamboyant father. He was sober, cautious, and had no vices except smoking his white clay pipe. He was patient, courageous, upright and shrewd, and a sincere Protestant. In 1620 he joined a number of English gentlemen who, being disgusted at King James's failure to help his daughter and son-in-law in the Thirty Years War, went as volunteers to help defend their principality of the Rhineland from the Austrian Catholic armies; but Essex returned home before he could take part in any fighting, being summoned to take his seat in the House of Lords when Parliament met in 1621.

Essex was still in favour with James I, and was appointed Vice-Admiral under Buckingham. In this capacity he took part in his first military campaign in 1625, when he sailed in the expedition against Cadiz. Thanks to Buckingham's mismanagement, the expedition was a fiasco. The English landed at Cadiz, but re-embarked a few days later and sailed away in an unsuccessful attempt to find the Spanish treasure-fleet. No arrangements had been made to provide them with provisions or money. Discipline collapsed, the hungry and unpaid troops looted and maltreated the local inhabitants, and eventually Essex and the military commanders were ordered to return home, having failed to achieve anything.

His disgust with Buckingham's incompetence, and his Protestant indignation at King Charles's home and foreign policy, made Essex join the Country Party in Parliament, and he became one of Eliot's leading supporters in the House of Lords. When the King called on his subjects to contribute to the forced loan in 1627, Essex refused to pay on the grounds that taxation without the consent of Parliament was illegal; but he was not imprisoned along with Hampden and Eliot, perhaps because of his high rank. After again supporting Eliot in the House of Lords during the Parliament of 1628-9, he withdrew into private life when Parliament was dissolved, living in London and on his estates at Chartley in Staffordshire.

In 1631, when he was aged forty, he married again, but once more the marriage was a failure. The new Countess, who was the daughter of Sir William Paulet, bore him a son but the child died almost immediately; and soon afterwards Essex petitioned for a judicial separation on the grounds of his wife's adultery. Divorce, as opposed to a decree of nullity for non-consummation, did not exist in English law, as it did in Presbyterian Scotland. Lady Essex strongly denied the charge, and said that she was the victim of a conspiracy by Essex's friends who feared the extent of her influence over him because he was so much in love with her; but the court found the charge proved, and awarded Essex a decree of judicial separation.

In 1639 King Charles recalled Essex to court and offered him the post of Lieutenant-General of the infantry in the campaign against the rebel Scots. Like all the English Puritans, Essex sympathized with the Covenanters but he did not think that they were justified in revolting against the King, and he accepted the offer of the military command, hoping to use his influence in favour of conciliation and peace. He was loyal to Charles, and when the Covenanters wrote to him secretly, in a bid to gain his support, he handed the letter to the King with the seal unbroken. After Charles and Essex and the army had reached Berwick, they found that the Scots across the border were in much greater strength than they had expected, and the King agreed to a truce and returned to London to prepare for a second campaign next year. He did not offer Essex a military command in this second war, and when Charles marched against the Scots Essex remained in London, in close touch with Pym and the Puritan leaders. The King was sure that he was in secret communication with the Covenanters.

When the Long Parliament met in November 1640, Essex was one of Pym's chief supporters in the House of Lords, and energetically pressed the proceedings against Strafford. He was convinced that Strafford's execution was necessary, and rejected the compromise proposal put forward by some peers and MPs that Strafford should be convicted, but that he should only be banished from the realm and not executed. When Edward Hyde put this proposal to him, Essex dryly replied: 'Stone-dead hath no equal.' But he deprecated the attacks on the bishops by the 'Root and Branch' men, being sincerely attached to the Church of England and the Book of Common Prayer. He did not allow political differences to interfere with personal friendships. His half-brother, the Earl of Clanricarde, who was the son of Essex's mother by her third marriage, supported the King. When Clanricarde entrusted Essex with his proxy vote in the House of Lords, Essex regularly cast Clanricarde's proxy against the resolutions for which he voted himself.

Pym was determined to take the control of the armed forces out of the hands of the King. None of the lawyers who supported him could find any legal precedent for removing the army from the control of the sovereign; but in November 1641 Pym directed a back-bench MP, Oliver Cromwell, the member for Cambridge, to propose a motion in the House of Commons that the Earl of Essex should be appointed commander of all the trained-bands in the south of England. It was the first step in setting up a Parliamentary army against the King. Essex was still in attendance at court, because Charles was pursuing a conciliatory policy and hoped to win over the more moderate Opposition leaders. By frequenting the court, Essex was able to discover some of Charles's secret projects; it was Essex who first warned Pym of the King's plan to arrest the Five Members, passing on the information that he had received from Lady Carlisle. After the failure to carry out the arrest, Essex tried to dissuade the King from leaving London; but Charles no longer trusted Essex, and Essex's intervention merely persuaded him to hasten his departure.

In July 1642 Essex was appointed a member of the Committee of Safety, and when war broke out in August he was appointed Commander-in-Chief of the Parliamentary armies, with the title of Lord General. He had had very little experience of warfare, but his rank and his political reliability made him the only possible choice for the post. He joined the army at Northampton on 13 September. With his usual prudence he was prepared for the worst, and took with him his family escutcheon and his winding-sheet to be used, if necessary, at his funeral. In accordance with Pym's official policy, he told his troops that they were fighting, not against the King, but for King and Parliament, to rescue the King from his evil advisers who were forcing him to make war against his loyal Parliament. His commission from Parliament ordered him 'to rescue His Majesty's person, and the persons of the Prince and the Duke of York, out of the hands of those desperate persons who were then about them'. His army, consisting of nearly 15,000 men, was substantially larger than the King's forces.

On 23 October the first major battle of the war was fought at Edgehill, with Essex in command of the Parliamentary forces. In accordance with the accepted military tactics of the day, Essex placed his infantry in the centre, with his cavalry on both wings, and was embarrassed to find that the enemy infantry facing him was commanded by the King himself. Essex had the best of the fighting in the centre, but Rupert's cavalry charge routed the Parliamentary horse, and Essex fell back in some disorder. Later he was in command of the defence of London at Turnham Green, but when the Cavalier forces, who were outnumbered, withdrew to Oxford, Essex disappointed his supporters by refusing to pursue and attack.

As Lord General, Essex was nominally Commander-in-Chief of all the Parliamentary forces, but in practice his position was far from strong. The tendency in all armies for generals to quarrel with each other was made much worse in the Civil War by the fact that the Parliamentary side was politically divided, and that the political factions tried to make use of the personal rivalries between the generals. Essex himself took command of the army in the South Midlands between the two capitals of London and Oxford. Waller commanded the army operating in Sussex and Hampshire. Lord Mandeville, now Earl of Manchester, commanded in East Anglia, with Cromwell in effect acting as his second-in-command; Lord Fairfax and his son, Sir Thomas Fairfax, were in command in the north. Waller, Manchester and Fairfax were in fact independent commanders.

Essex's campaign of 1643 opened successfully with the capture of Reading; but in June Hampden was defeated and killed at Chalgrove, and immediately in Parliament and in London criticism of Essex's generalship began to be heard. Pym supported Essex, but Marten and the extremists attacked him, even hinting that he was reluctant to fight and win the war. Marten and the republicans praised Waller in comparison with Essex. After a temporary estrangement between Pym and Essex, when Pym criticized Essex's dilatoriness and Essex responded by supporting the peace party, they composed their differences, and Essex, after issuing a statement in favour of continuing the war, marched to the relief of Gloucester, where the Parliamentary garrison, under the command of the twenty-three-year-old Edward Massey, was gallantly holding out against the Cavalier army. Essex succeeded in relieving Gloucester. On his way back to London he encountered a Cavalier army under King Charles which barred his passage at Newbury; but after a fierce day's fighting the Cavaliers, who were short of ammunition, withdrew with heavy losses. Essex marched on to London, and was justified in claiming that he was the victor of Newbury.

In December 1643 Pym died, after concluding the treaty with the Scots under which the Covenanters entered the war on the Parliament's side and Parliament established Presbyterianism as the only lawful religion in England. The Committee of Safety was replaced by a new body which took over the task of governing the country in the Parliament's hands and assumed the supreme direction of the Parliamentary armies. This was the Committee of Both Kingdoms, in which the Scots were represented. The Committee consisted of fourteen English representatives, members of the House of Lords and House of Commons, including some, like Essex, Manchester and Waller, who were generals, and others, like Cromwell, who were subordinate commanders. Four Scottish commissioners, who had

taken up residence in London, were members of the Com-
mittee, and it was agreed that no decision of the Committee could
be taken unless at least two of the Scottish members were present.
The Committee met at Derby House in Cannon Row, the former
London home of the Earl of Derby, who was fighting for the
King, and it was popularly known as the Derby House Com-
mittee. The dominant personality on the Committee was Sir
Henry Vane the younger, who, after a political struggle with
Denzil Holles, had in effect succeeded Pym as the chief of the
Parliamentary government. This was a setback for Essex, because
Vane, unlike Holles, had no confidence in Essex as a general.

As the military campaign of 1644 began, a new religious and
political controversy developed in London. The newly-established
Presbyterian state found itself attacked by more radical religious
opponents, who became known as the sectaries, or Independents.
They took the Presbyterian docrine of the abolition of bishops a
stage further by demanding the abolition of the national Church
itself, and its replacement by independent Protestant congregations worshipping under their own elected ministers, or even
without a minister, for some Independents went so far as to hint
at the abolition of the priesthood as well as of episcopacy. In the
summer of 1644 Roger Williams, who had emigrated to America,
returned to England for a short visit. He had been expelled from
the Presbyterian settlement in Massachusetts because he favoured
liberty of conscience and complete religious toleration, and had
gone to Rhode Island to establish another colony there. During
his brief stay in England in 1644 he published a book, *The Bloody
Tenent of Persecution*, in which he condemned all religious persecution and advocated complete religious toleration, even for
Jews, Turks and pagans. Not all the Independents went as far as
this, but they demanded religious toleration for all Protestant
sects. The Presbyterian preachers, egged on by the Scottish
delegates in London, condemned this doctrine as heresy and
demanded that the Independents be muzzled and punished. In the
sermons on Sundays and on the monthly fast days, the Presbyterian preachers called for the suppression of heresy and the
Independent preachers for liberty of conscience.

The result was that Presbyterianism, which had hitherto

always been regarded as a revolutionary doctrine, now became the bulwark of established society against the Independents, and all the more conservative sections of the community supported the Presbyterians. The House of Lords, including those peers who had been devout Anglicans a few months earlier, was firmly Presbyterian; but Independent influence increased in the House of Commons, where Vane began to rely on Independent support and Holles became the leader of the Presbyterians. When the Covenanters entered the war, the Presbyterians hoped that a Scottish military victory over the Cavaliers in the north would strengthen their influence at Westminster against the Independents; but Manchester's army in East Anglia was thoroughly infiltrated by Independents. The Scottish Covenanter, Major-General Crawford, who had been appointed as Manchester's second-in-command, complained about Colonel Cromwell's habit of appointing 'Anabaptists' and other Independents to military commands in Manchester's army. In July 1644 a combined force consisting of the Scots, Manchester's army, and Fairfax's, defeated the Cavaliers under the hitherto-invincible Prince Rupert at Marston Moor, and captured York. To the great indignation of the Scots and the Presbyterians, the Independent preachers in London and most of the newspapers gave the credit for the victory entirely to Cromwell.

Essex, like the moderate politician that he was, overcame his attachment to the Book of Common Prayer and became a Presbyterian supporter. The Presbyterians acclaimed him as the military genius who would win the war and prove that the God of Battles favoured Presbyterianism. But the campaign of 1644 did not go well for the Roundheads in the south. The Derby House Committee decided that Essex and Waller should operate jointly against the Cavaliers in the west. Essex was to advance against the Cavaliers who had marched from Cornwall to Wiltshire in the previous summer, and drive them back into Cornwall, while Waller's army hemmed in the King's main force in the West Midlands and prevented it from breaking out and attacking Essex in the rear.

Essex advanced into Dorset and prepared to go to the relief of Lyme Regis, where Colonel Robert Blake was valiantly defying the besieging Cavaliers; but at Waller's request, the Derby House Committee ordered Essex to turn back and join Waller in a campaign against Charles's army in Warwickshire. Essex, believing that he had the Cavaliers' western army on the run, refused to obey orders, and insisted on going to the relief of Lyme Regis. He raised the siege with the help of the navy, which had been under the control of Parliament since the beginning of the war, and then beseiged Exeter, where Queen Henrietta Maria had just given birth to a daughter; but the Queen escaped by sea to France, and the King and his army set out in pursuit of Essex and cut off his retreat to the east. Essex then called on Waller to come to his assistance; but it was now Waller's turn to refuse to go to the help of his brother-general. Parliament had recently enacted that any Irish Papist who fought for the King in England was to be punished by death. Essex consequently hanged seven Irish Papists who had been captured fighting for the Cavaliers. The Cavaliers retaliated by hanging twelve of their Roundhead prisoners as a reprisal.

King Charles raised the siege of Exeter, and Essex, who was outnumbered by the King's army and was reluctant to fight against the King in person, marched on into Cornwall, having nowhere else to go, and relying on the Parliamentary navy for his supplies. By the end of August he was completely surrounded at Fowey by the King's army. He refused Charles's invitation to abandon the Parliamentary cause and join the Cavaliers, but decided that he could neither fight nor hold out at Fowey. He ordered his cavalry to try to cut their way through the King's army, and they succeeded in doing this at night, and made their way to the east. He himself then escaped in a small boat to the Parliamentary fleet, after handing over the command of the infantry to Major-General Skippon and ordering Skippon to arrange the surrender to the King. Charles allowed the infantry to depart after they had handed over all their equipment and ammunition.

The Presbyterians in London, who had hoped that their cause would be bolstered up by Essex's victory in the west, had to console themselves by claiming that the disaster was a Divine punishment inflicted on Parliament for its failure to suppress the heresy of the Independents. Meanwhile fresh dissensions had broken out among the Parliamentary generals. In August, when the Derby House Committee first heard of Essex's danger in Cornwall, they ordered Manchester, who had established his headquarters at Lincoln after his victory at Marston Moor, to march at once to Abingdon, link up with Waller, and go to Essex's assistance. Manchester was a Presbyterian and a friend of Essex, but he was slow in moving, and claimed that he could not march until he had recruited more men and obtained the necessary money and provisions. When Essex's army surrendered at Fowey on 2 September, Manchester had not yet left Lincoln.

A week later Manchester's subordinate commander, Cromwell, appeared at a meeting of the Derby House Committee and denounced Manchester, virtually accusing him of treachery for failing to march sufficiently rapidly to Abingdon. Major-General Crawford also attended the meeting; he repudiated Cromwell's allegations against Manchester, and accused Cromwell of disobeying Manchester's orders and of planning the subversion of the state by Independents and Anabaptist heretics. The Committee ordered them to patch up their quarrel, and sent Manchester, with both Cromwell and Crawford serving under him, to join Waller at Basingstoke. Essex and his defeated army also reached Basingstoke, but Essex fell ill and retired to a sick-bed at Reading, taking no further part in the campaign.

On 27 October Manchester and Waller met King Charles's army at Newbury. The Roundheads had the best of the fighting, but they allowed the Cavaliers to withdraw with all their equipment, making no attempt to pursue them until it was too late, and a fortnight later failed to prevent the King from raising the siege of Donnington Castle. Cromwell denounced Manchester in the House of Commons. He stated that when he and Waller had urged Manchester, at a council of war at Newbury, to press forward with the attack on the King's army, Manchester had said that this was pointless, because 'if we beate the King 99 times he would be King still, and his posterity, and we subjects still; but if he beats us but once we should be hang'd, and our posterity be undonne.' Crawford alleged that these words had been spoken, not by Manchester, but by Cromwell's ally Sir Arthur Hazelrig; he stated that Cromwell had been guilty of cowardice at Newbury and had taken no part in the battle, and that it was because of Cromwell's refusal to advance with the cavalry that the King's army had escaped and had relieved Donnington Castle. At the meeting of the council of war, according to Crawford, no man spoke so much against fighting as Cromwell.

Essex had not been involved in the controversies about Newbury, but on political grounds he supported Manchester against Cromwell. He invited Manchester, Crawford, and other Presbyterian leaders to a meeting at his house in London on the evening of 3 December, at which it was decided to impeach Cromwell for sedition, because Cromwell was supporting the demand for religious toleration and had appointed Anabaptists and Independents to positions in the army. Like in other civil wars—for example, the Spanish Civil War of 1936–9—accusations of military incompetence and treason were made against generals who adhered to opposite factions, and victories and defeats in the field were regarded primarily according to their effect on the political struggle in the rear. Cromwell was winning the propaganda war in London, and the Independent preachers and the newspapers presented his image as that of the only successful general on the Roundhead side, who, unlike the incompetent Essex and Waller, had never been defeated and was responsible for all the successes of Manchester's army.

Cromwell was supported by Vane. Thanks largely to Vane's skilful handling of the Derby House Committee and the House of Commons, the impeachment proceedings against Cromwell were shelved, and a bill was introduced in the House of Commons, which soon became known as the Self-Denying Ordinance. It provided that no member of either House of Parliament could hold a military command in the army or navy; he must resign either his command or his seat in Parliament. This proposal was ostensibly put forward merely on the grounds of military efficiency, to ensure that commanders should not be distracted by their Parliamentary duties; but the opponents of the measure realized that it was also a far-reaching attack on the established social order. Although MPs, if they wished, could resign from the House of Commons and retain their military command, no peer could resign from the House of Lords, and the nobility were thus deprived of their traditional position as military leaders in time of war. The House of Lords threw out the bill. But Vane and Cromwell reintroduced it, and worked out a compromise with the Presbyterians: the Independents in the House of Commons would withdraw their opposition to the Presbyterians' attempts to introduce the Presbyterian Prayer Book and ordinal for the appointment of ministers in the church, with its restrictions on the right of laymen to preach, if the House of Lords would pass the Self-Denying Ordinance. They also accepted an amendment to the Self-Denying Ordinance which would make it possible for those peers and MPs who had resigned their commands to be reappointed to them. In April 1645 the House of Lords passed the bill.

The only consolation for the peers was that Cromwell himself would have to give up either his military command or his seat in the House of Commons. But in fact he gave up neither. He was reappointed to his command, at first temporarily and then permanently, under the provisions of the amendment which the House of Lords had favoured in the hope that Essex and Manchester would be reappointed. Cromwell was thus the only commander who was also an MP.

On 2 April 1645, the day before the House of Lords passed the Self-Denying Ordinance, Essex and Manchester resigned their military commands. Parliament rewarded them for their past services with a 'golden handshake'; Essex was voted a pension of £10,000 a year for the rest of his life. In September 1646, three months after the war had ended with the final defeat of the King's armies and the victory of Parliament, he went hunting in Windsor Great Park. He caught an 'ague', from which he died four days later, at the age of fifty-five. He was buried in Westminster Abbey. A few days later his grave was desecrated and his effigy and escutcheon torn down. The guilty man was apparently not a political opponent, but a crazy hooligan.

The time had passed when men like Essex—upright, moderate men who sincerely believed that they were fighting for King and Parliament—could lead the Roundhead movement. He had lived too long for his peace of mind. In December 1644 he had seen the demonstrations in the streets of London, when the City apprentices and the people had protested at the reluctance of the House of Lords to pass the Bill of Attainder which condemned Archbishop Laud to death. 'Is this the liberty which we claim to vindicate by shedding our blood?' asked Essex. 'Our posterity will say that to deliver them from the yoke of the King we have subjected them to that of the common people.'

4

Sir William Waller

Sir William Waller had all the virtues of a knight of the Middle Ages—bravery in battle, respectful gallantry to ladies, a high regard for his own honour, and a religious devotion which led him to place his sword and his life at the service of his faith. But his faith was not medieval Christianity: it was seventeenth-century Puritanism.

His grandfather was the owner of the ancestral manor house at Groombridge on the Sussex–Kent border; but as his father was the second son, Groombridge passed to the elder brother, and it was there that William Waller's cousin, Hardress Waller, was born in 1604. William Waller's father went into the army and became Lieutenant of Dover Castle and the Cinque Ports, and the King's Butler under James I. William Waller was born in 1598 at Knole in Kent, where his mother's father lived, and spent his childhood with his father in Dover Castle. A distant cousin, Edmund Waller of the Hertfordshire branch of the family, was born in 1606.

When William Waller was fourteen, he went to Magdalen Hall at Oxford, and on leaving Oxford he went to Paris and Italy. In Friuli he had a narrow escape from drowning in the River Isonzo. He had an escape of a different kind at Bologna, where a priest denounced him to the Inquisition as a Protestant heretic. 'I was searched, my trunke, wherein I had nothing but clothes, was rifled to the bottome, but itt pleased God to so order itt, that they lett alone a box, wherein I had some papers, which might have exposed me to question; when they had itt in their hands ready to open it.'

With a number of other English volunteers, he enlisted in the Venetian army. Though Venice was a Catholic state, an English Protestant could serve in her army with an easy conscience because the Venetians, pursuing their traditional foreign policy of alliance with France against the Habsburg Emperors, had intervened on the Protestant side in the religious war in the Valteline. Waller went into action for the first time against the Austrian forces at the siege of Rubia, where he had several narrow escapes from death.

Waller's next campaign was in a cause that was dear to English Protestants' hearts—the defence of Elizabeth, Queen of Bohemia, and her husband Frederick, the Elector Palatine, from the attacks of the Emperor's armies in Bohemia and the Rhineland. In November 1620 Waller fought in the Battle of the White Hill outside Prague. The Austrian army, under the command of the old General Tilly, was composed of mercenaries from many countries, including Irish Catholic exiles. Waller had another narrow escape when his troop was charged by a body of Polish Cossacks. His horse was killed under him, and he fell with his foot caught in the stirrup, but managed to escape from the surrounding enemy and reach the Protestant lines.

After the defeat at the White Hill, Prague fell to Tilly's army, and the King and Queen of Bohemia, with their one-year-old son, Prince Rupert, were forced to flee through the bitter winter cold. Waller and the English officers escorted the royal family, and when their coach could go no further through the snow, a Cornish gentleman, Ralph Hopton, placed the Queen, who was pregnant with the future Prince Maurice, on his horse. The Catholic armies occupied the whole of Bohemia and the Rhineland, and drove Frederick and Elizabeth into exile in Holland. Waller and his comrades returned to England, and Waller was knighted by King James I for his services to the Protestant Cause in Europe.

Having won his spurs and his knighthood by the time he was twenty-four, Waller decided to abandon his military career, perhaps because he had married a wife with whom he was deeply in love. She was Jane Reynell, the daughter and heiress of Sir Richard Reynell, who was an eminent lawyer and a wealthy Devonshire landowner. Sir Richard handed over the management of his Devonshire estates to Waller, who settled down with his wife at Forde House at Walborough near Newton Abbot. Waller lived here for thirteen years as a country gentleman, serving as a Justice of the Peace in the county, studying somewhat desultorily at the Inns of Court in London, sometimes dining at his old college in Oxford, and once entertaining King Charles I when the King was on his way to Plymouth. He became a close personal friend of two gentlemen in Cornwall, Sir Bevill Grenville and Sir Ralph Hopton, who had served with him in Bohemia.

Waller was a devoted husband and father. When his wife, seven years after their marriage, gave birth to their first child after a difficult pregnancy, he was beside himself with anxiety; and he was deeply unhappy when his wife died in 1633 after giving birth to a daughter. This second child survived, but the eldest child, a son, died next year at the age of five. Again, as on the occasion of his wife's death, Waller accepted the tragedy as being the will of God. He was a very religious man, and like many of his West Country neighbours was sufficiently Protestant to be considered a Puritan by the High Church supporters of Archbishop Laud.

Soon after his wife's death, Waller married Lady Anne Finch, the daughter of the Earl of Winchelsea. Lady Anne was an ardent Puritan, although her cousin, Sir John Finch, was the Lord Chief Justice who sentenced Prynne and other Puritans to cruel punishments and held against Hampden in the Ship-Money case. At Lady Anne's suggestion, she and Waller spent the whole day before their wedding in fasting and prayer. Despite her religious opinions, she remained on good terms with her Royalist family, and after the wedding King Charles gave Waller Winchester Castle as a residence, as well as other lands and privileges.

In November 1640 Waller stood at Andover in the first by-election after the meeting of the Long Parliament, but the eighteen electors divided equally for him and his opponent, and the Mayor gave his casting vote against Waller. Waller petitioned Parliament to unseat his opponent, and after a lengthy dispute between the Court and Country parties in the House of Commons, Waller was finally able to take his seat in May 1642, on the eve of the Civil War. His friend Sir Bevill Grenville, whose political and religious doctrines were close to Waller's, discussed with Waller where their duty lay in the event of war between King and Parliament; but though Grenville, like Waller's old comrade in Bohemia, Hopton, joined the Cavaliers, Waller sided with the Roundheads. His opponents blamed Lady Anne Waller for this, and jeered at Waller for being under his wife's thumb. Though this is certainly a slander on Waller, there can be no doubt that Lady Anne's Puritanism reinforced Waller's and played a part in Waller's decision.

His military experience made him an obvious choice for a high command, and he was appointed a colonel and given the command of the Parliamentary forces on the south coast, under the supreme authority of Essex as Lord General. Waller was the most successful of the Roundhead generals during the first winter of the war: he captured Portsmouth, Farnham, Winchester, Arundel and Chichester after short sieges in December and January. Neither Essex in Warwickshire, Manchester in East Anglia, or Fairfax in the north had had comparable successes, and the newspapers in London acclaimed Waller as 'William the Conqueror'.

In May 1643 the poet Edmund Waller, who was living in London as a professed Roundhead, took part in a Cavalier plot to seize the Tower, kidnap Pym and the Parliamentary leaders, and surrender London to the King. Though Edmund Waller was only a distant cousin, Sir William Waller used his influence on Edmund's behalf in order to save him from the death penalty. Edmund Waller betrayed his fellow-conspirators and escaped with fifteen months in prison.

In the new campaign which began in the spring of 1643, Waller, who had been promoted to the rank of Major-General, won a number of successes in Gloucestershire, Monmouthshire and Herefordshire. But his old friends Hopton and Bevill Grenville enlisted the support of their tenants and neighbours in the south-west; they drove the Roundhead forces out of Cornwall and Devonshire and advanced to the Somerset–Wiltshire border. Waller was sent to stop them. After winning a number of local engagements, he received a letter from Hopton proposing an exchange of prisoners and inviting Waller to meet him for a talk. Waller agreed to the exchange, but refused to meet Hopton. He wrote from Bath to his 'noble friend Sir Ralphe Hopton' at Wells: 'Certainly my affections to you are so unchangeable, that hostility itselfe cannot violate my friendship to your person, but I must be true to the cause wherein I serve . . . Wee are both upon the stage and must act those parts assigned us in this Tragedy: Lett us do it in a way of honour, and without personall animosities, whatsoever the issue be, I shall never willingly relinquish the dear title of your most affectionated friend and faithfull servant, Wm Waller.'

On 5 July Waller met the Cavaliers in the battle of Lansdown. The Cornishmen, disregarding all orthodox military teachings, charged Waller's strong defensive position and drove his men off the field; but they suffered heavy losses, including Sir Bevill Grenville who was killed, while a few days later Hopton was severely injured when some Roundhead prisoners, who were lighting their pipes, caused some gunpowder to explode. Eight days after Lansdown, Prince Maurice routed Waller at the battle of Roundway Down, near Devizes. The Cavaliers made great play with the defeat inflicted on 'William the Conqueror'. Sir John Denham, the poet, wrote a rhyme:

> Great William the Con
> So fast did he run
> That he left half his name behind him.

But 'my dismal defeat att Roundway Down', as Waller was honest enough to call it, did not lessen Waller's popularity with the people of London. When he arrived in London they acclaimed him as a hero and demanded that the city should enroll a new army of volunteers to serve under him. The Independents and Henry Marten's republican supporters tried to make use of this popularity for political purposes. They denounced the incompetence of Essex in order to discredit Pym, who supported him, and demanded that Waller should be given a command independent of Essex's authority. But though Waller admired the energy of the Independents in the struggle against the King, he did not agree with them politically. They demanded that he should appoint only 'godfearing' men to be officers in his new army, which meant that he should do what Cromwell was accused of doing in East Anglia and pack the army with Independent officers. Waller agreed to appoint a committee under the Independent colonel and MP, Sir Arthur Hazelrig, to vet the characters of all applicants for officers' commissions; but he refused to make the appointments solely on political grounds. 'I wished them to consider,' he wrote, 'that there went more to the making up of an officer than single honesty . . . A good man might make a good souldier, but there must go the good man and the good soldier to the composition of a good officer.' He pointed out that he owed a duty to his soldiers to appoint efficient officers, as the men's lives might depend on their officers' actions.

He campaigned throughout the winter of 1643-4, capturing Alton, and Arundel Castle for the second time, and winning a hard-fought victory at Alresford. In the summer of 1644 he was sent to hold Charles's army in Warwickshire while Essex advanced in the west, but after being defeated at Cropredy Bridge in June, he remained inactive while the King pursued Essex. At Cropredy he received a letter from a lady with whom he had been in love many years before. She was on the King's side, and asked Waller to leave the Roundheads and join the Cavaliers. 'Before this lady's marriage,' he wrote, 'I had been her suitor, and did dearly love her, and she remembered me of this, and of some soft passages . . . but I returned for answer, that as I had never been traitor to my love, so would I not to my cause, which I should be, if I did as she would advise, and after this I heard no more.'

In the disputes between the Parliamentary generals after the second battle of Newbury, Waller supported Cromwell against Manchester, and soon afterwards he was appointed as commander of the Parliamentary forces against the Cavaliers in Dorset with Cromwell as his second-in-command; but as an MP he was caught by the provisions of the Self-Denying Ordinance and resigned his military command in April 1645. A year later the war was over, and the political struggle between Presbyterians and Independents intensified. The English Presbyterians, with the ardent support of the Scottish Covenanters, were determined to crush the heresy, as they termed it, of the Independent sects. The Independents demanded religious toleration. The political influence of the Independents was greatly strengthened by having the support of Cromwell, who had emerged as the most successful general in the war.

Waller had supported Cromwell against Manchester in the military disputes of 1644, but he supported Manchester and the Presbyterians against Cromwell and the Independents in the political arguments of 1647. He wrote afterwards that at the beginning of the war the Independents 'were remarqued for their extraordinary diligence and activity to advance and promote the service, which knitt my heart to them'; but later they became 'incendiaries, putting the whole state into combustion and confusion; and this alienated me from them . . . I used them as Moses did his rod: so long as they were of aid and support to the Publique I inclined to them, and rested in some measure upon them.' But he abandoned them when he saw their 'impious, disloyal, antimonarchical ends'. His sense of military discipline, which had been shocked at the mutinies and looting which he had seen in his armies during the war, made him fear the consequences of religious toleration, 'which is no other in plain English but that any man might hold any opinion, though never so impious, as long as he used a good trade, and kept the peace: by which rule the church would come to be governed, like Fryer John's Colledge in Rabelias, by one general statute, Do what you list.' Freedom in religion would inevitably lead to atheism and anarchy. Waller became, with Denzil Holles and Prynne, the leader of the Presbyterians in the House of Commons. His cousin, Sir Hardress Waller of Groombridge, who had fought for the Parliament in the war, was an Independent.

The Presbyterians controlled Parliament. They had the support of nearly all the peers in the House of Lords and of all except about sixty of the 300 MPs in the House of Commons. But the army who had fought and won the war were not impressed by the Presbyterians' argument that they should submit to a Parliament for which most of the soldiers were not entitled to vote, because only landowners and property-holders had the right to vote at Parliamentary elections. The army rank-and-file came under the influence of the party which was known as the Levellers. Their leader, John Lilburne, had been imprisoned by the Presbyterian House of Lords; but his agents, the Agitators, had set up revolutionary organizations in the army. They demanded that the army, having fought for the freedom of the people against the King, should now defend this freedom against Parliament. On this issue they won the support of Cromwell and the army leaders, who did not agree with the Levellers' demand for almost universal manhood suffrage, but were prepared to stand with them against the Presbyterian Parliament on the issue of religious toleration.

In March 1647 Parliament sent Waller and two other Presbyterian MPs to the army headquarters at Saffron Walden to convey Parliament's orders to the army. A limited number of

soldiers were to enlist for a campaign in Ireland against the
Irish Papist rebels, and the rest of the army was to be disbanded.
Waller's mission to Saffron Walden precipitated a political crisis.
The army refused to obey the orders of Parliament.

Parliament made preparations for an armed struggle against
the army. Waller and two other Presbyterians who had distinguished themselves in the Civil War—Major-General Massey,
the hero of the siege of Gloucester, and Major-General Browne
—took steps to organize the Parliamentary forces. They formed
a new militia in London, which only Presbyterians were allowed
to join, and brought artillery from Oxford for use by the militia.
They also apparantly decided to arrest Cromwell, but he escaped
from London just in time and sent Cornet Joyce to fetch the
King from Holmby House near Northampton, where he was
under the control of Parliament, and bring him to the army
headquarters.

In the middle of June the army moved towards London.
From their headquarters at St Albans they issued a manifesto
impeaching Waller, Denzil Holles and nine other Presbyterian
MPs for having tried to create hostility between Parliament and
the army and to instigate a new civil war. They demanded that
these eleven MPs be suspended from the House of Commons.
When the House rejected this demand, the army moved forwards
to Uxbridge. Waller and his colleagues then offered to withdraw
from the House for an indefinite period, and the House agreed.
Cromwell persuaded the army to withdraw to Bedford.

The army's retreat encouraged the Presbyterian supporters.
A few weeks later, the London apprentices rose in support of
the eleven MPs. The apprentices were an unruly class who
played an important part at every crisis of the Civil War period.
It was chiefly because of their threatening demonstrations in
Whitehall that King Charles had agreed to Strafford's execution
and to the revolutionary legislation of the Long Parliament.
Many apprentices were the sons of rich merchants and even of
gentlemen. They can perhaps best be compared to students in
the twentieth century—a tempestuous and enthusiastic body
who were capable of rioting in support of either revolutionary
or counter-revolutionary causes.

On 26 July 1647 the apprentices marched to Westminster and
invaded the House of Commons, demanding that Waller and

his ten colleagues should resume their place in the House. The eleven MPs returned in triumph, while the Speaker and fifty-seven Independent MPs fled from Westminster to the army headquarters. The army then marched on London, and on 6 August occupied the City and Westminster. The fifty-seven Independent MPs returned to the House, and the Presbyterian leaders went into hiding. On the night of 12 August, Waller and his friends rode to a secret rendezvous on the Essex coast, because they believed that they would be arrested if they went to Gravesend. They embarked on a ship bound for France, and though they were stopped by a naval warship and brought back to the Downs and questioned, they were allowed to proceed and reached Calais. From there Waller travelled to Holland to pay his respects to the exiled Queen of Bohemia. Many of the officers in the Cavalier army had gone to Holland at the end of the Civil War, and some of them greeted Waller warmly as a respected ex-enemy. In England the House of Commons, in fear of the army in London, expelled Waller and the other ten Presbyterian leaders from the House.

Meanwhile King Charles had entered into secret negotiations with some of the Scottish Covenanters and agreed to establish Presbyterianism temporarily as the state religion in England if they would reinstate him in power and crush the army and the Independents. In the spring and summer of 1648 the Scots invaded the north of England, and a band of Cavaliers seized control of Colchester and Pembroke and organized a rising in Kent and a mutiny in the Parliamentary navy in the Downs. The Independents, hearing that Waller had been fraternizing with the Cavaliers at The Hague, believed that it was he who had planned the Scottish invasion and the outbreak of the Second Civil War. Waller denied this, and explained his conduct in Holland. 'I could not choose but pay my homage to that queen of women, the Queen of Bohemia, whom I had the honour to serve at Prague, in the first breaking out of the German warr. I could do no less than return civilities, when I received them from gentlemen, and I could not refuse to receive them from some, that had born arms for the King, except I would have denounced a warr with the whole party, and have made them mine enemies upon no other ground, but because they shewed an inclination to be my friends.'

John Hampden

Master *PYM*
HIS SPEECH

In *Parliament*, on *Wednesday*, the
fifth of *January*, 1 6 4 1,
Concerning the Vote of the House of *Commons*,
for his discharge upon the Accusation of High
Treason, exhibited against himselfe, and the
Lord *Kimbolton*, Mr. *Iohn Hampden*, Sr.
Arthur Haslerig, Mr. *Strowd*,
M. Hollis, by his Maiesty.

The true Effigies of Mr. *Iohn Pym*, Esquire

London Printed for I. W, 1641.

Robert Devereux,
Earl of Essex,
with Prince Henry

Countess of Essex

(*Left*) John Pym,
from a 1641 engraving

Sir William Waller

Lady Anne Finch
by van Dyck

(*Right*) William Prynne

Mr WILLIAM PRYNNE Barister
at Law, &c.

John Lilburne, print by Glover

(*Left*) Henry Ireton, attributed to Robert Walker

Robert Blake, miniature by Samuel Cooper

The army, after denouncing King Charles for his treachery and promising to bring him to justice for his crimes, marched off to fight the enemy in Kent, Essex, South Wales and the north of England, leaving London denuded of troops. The Presbyterians in Parliament thereupon felt free to act, and took charge again. Waller returned to England, and with the other ten expelled MPs took his seat in the House of Commons. Parliament entered into negotiations with the King, who was a prisoner at Newport in the Isle of Wight, for an alliance against the army and the establishment of a Presbyterian monarchy. But contrary to the Presbyterians' expectations and hopes, the army, though outnumbered, were everywhere victorious. The mutiny in the fleet was suppressed, Colchester and Pembroke surrendered, the Scots were defeated at Preston, and only Pontefract still held out for the King.

Cromwell was in the north besieging Pontefract; but his son-in-law, Henry Ireton, was in command of the army in the south under the nominal authority of Fairfax. On 20 November 1648 the Army Council at Windsor presented a remonstrance to Parliament, demanding that Parliament break off their negotiations with the King. When Parliament refused, Ireton sent a troop of soldiers to bring the King from Newport to Windsor, and the army marched on London. On 2 December they occupied London and Westminster. The Independent MPs moved a resolution in the House of Commons demanding that negotiations with the King should be broken off; but on 5 December, after an all-night sitting, the Presbyterian majority defeated the motion.

Next day, when the MPs arrived at the House at the usual hour of 8 am, they found the precincts surrounded by soldiers under the command of Colonel Pride and Sir Hardress Waller. Pride stood at the door with a list of names of MPs in his hand. He allowed some eighty MPs—the Independents and a few Presbyterians and neutral members—to take their seats, but the rest were turned away, and forty-one of the leading Presbyterian MPs, including Sir William Waller, General Massey and Prynne, were placed in custody in a building in Queen's Court. They were kept there all day, and taken in the evening to a victualling-house known as 'Hell', where they were confined in two rooms. The rooms became very cold, as there was no fire. The forty-one MPs, who had had no food all day, were given some biscuits to eat, and seven of them, who were elderly men, were told that they could go home for the night if they promised to return next morning. They refused to leave their colleagues, all of whom spent the night in 'Hell', singing psalms and discussing the political situation.

Next morning they were taken to Whitehall Palace where they were told that the Army Council would meet them; but after waiting there till the evening they were informed that the army leaders could not see them that day, and they were marched through the streets under an armed guard to the *Swan* and the *King's Head* in the Strand. They were lodged for the night in these two taverns, with armed sentries posted at their bedroom doors. Next morning they were all released, except Waller, who was imprisoned in St James's Palace. Meanwhile the thirty Presbyterian MPs who had been allowed to take their seats in the House of Commons had proposed that the House should refuse to sit until their colleagues were released and allowed to take their seats; but this motion was defeated by the fifty Independent MPs, and the thirty MPs withdrew in protest. The House of Commons was thus reduced to about fifty Independent MPs, who became known as 'the Rump'.

The Rump passed a resolution declaring that it alone held sovereign legislative power, abolishing the House of Lords and setting up a High Court of Justice to try the King for high treason against his people. On 27 January 1649 the King was condemned to death by the High Court, and three days later he was beheaded. The Rump proclaimed the republic, and set up a Council of State, which was dominated by Cromwell, to govern the country. Waller remained in prison. After being held for nearly twenty months in St James's, he was removed to Windsor Castle in July 1650, and in April 1651 to Denbigh Castle in North Wales. He was well treated by his jailers, his only complaint being that at Denbigh, unlike at St James's and Windsor, the prison governor refused to allow him to attend church. In November 1651 he was comforted by a secret visit from his wife, who walked over the mountains in disguise to reach Denbigh.

At the beginning of 1652 Waller was brought back to St James's, and in March, after he had petitioned the Council of State for clemency, he was released from prison. It was a tragedy that his loyal wife should have died a few months earlier; but within a fortnight of his release from St James's he married his third wife, Lady Anna Harcourt, the daughter of Lord Paget and widow of Sir Simon Harcourt. She had been brought up as a Puritan in her father's household, but her first husband had fought for the King in the Civil War.

Waller himself, like the other Presbyterian leaders, had become a Cavalier in his sympathies. In his *Vindication*, which he wrote in prison, he bitterly denounced the murder of Charles I as a crime which cried out to Heaven for vengeance. The regicides, 'contrary to all example among Protestants, and beyond all example of Papists, or Heathens, have presum'd with wicked hands to seize upon and imprison his Royal Person, to try him without law, and to execute him without conscience.' Waller stated that his object in the Civil War was 'That GOD might have had his fear; the King his honour; the Houses of Parliament their priviledges; the people of the kingdome their liberties and properties.' He now wished to see 'that government restored again, by King, Lords and Commons, under which we, and our forefathers for many ages have happily flourished'. It was a 'Democratical Aristocratical monarchy' in which neither King, Lords nor Commons could dominate.

After his release from prison he was approached several times by Cavaliers and invited to take part in their plots against Cromwell; but he gave them no help beyond expressions of sympathy. He turned his attention, like so many other people at the time, from politics to business speculation, buying up land which was constantly on the market as a result of the expropriation of Cavaliers and the subsequent sales by speculators. He sold Winchester Castle and bought Osterley Park in Middlesex, where he resided, and also bought several other manors and properties.

In March 1658 Cromwell, who was constantly on the alert against Cavalier plans for insurrections and their assassination plots, ordered that Waller's house should be searched and that Waller should be brought before the Privy Council. Here Waller was examined by the councillors, with Cromwell himself presiding. Cromwell's attitude was correct and formal towards his former comrade-in-arms, under whom he had served for a brief period as his second-in-command. 'He did examin me as a stranger,' wrote Waller, 'not as one whome he had aforetime known and obeyed, yet he was not discourteous, and itt pleased the Lord to preserve me, that not one thing objected could be prooved against me.'

After Cromwell's death, the republican regime collapsed in less than two years. In the summer of 1659 a Cavalier rising took place under the leadership of Sir George Booth, but it was easily suppressed. Waller and his wife were both arrested for complicity in the rising and were imprisoned for a few months in the Tower before being released. The tide of public opinion was now strongly set in favour of a restoration of Charles II, and General Monck marched from Scotland to London and decided to restore Charles II to the throne. Monck's first step was to recall the Presbyterian MPs who had been excluded from Parliament by Pride's Purge eleven years before. In February 1660 Waller took his place in the House of Commons, and voted for new elections which, as everyone knew, would result in the election of a Cavalier Parliament which would invite the King to return. Waller's hour of triumph was marred by only a minor mishap. As he walked into the House of Commons for the first time since 1648, immediately behind his colleague Prynne, Prynne's long sword got entangled in Waller's short legs, and Waller was thrown to the ground.

Waller, like the other Presbyterians, welcomed the Restoration. He had been close enough in recent years to the Cavaliers to be sure of being granted a pardon for his Roundhead past; but he made no effort to obtain any benefits from the King, or to join the hue-and-cry for vengeance against the Cromwellians and Independents. He withdrew into private life at his house at Osterley. His cousin Sir Hardress Waller, who had been one of Charles I's judges and had signed the death warrant, was exempted from the Act of Indemnity and Oblivion at the Restoration, and in October 1660 he was tried, with the other regicides, for high treason for his part in the murder of King Charles the Martyr. He pleaded guilty and was sentenced to be hanged, drawn and quartered. Sir William Waller used his influence with his Cavalier friends on Sir Hardress's behalf, and this, combined with Sir Hardress's submissive and repentant attitude at his trial, caused the death sentence to be commuted to imprisonment for life. Sir Hardress died in prison in 1666.

Sir William Waller spent his last years quietly at Osterley. In 1661 he became a widower for the third time, and several of his children and grandchildren also died soon afterwards. He sought consolation in his religion, writing several books of reminiscences and reflections which show the deep sincerity of his faith. He died at Osterley on 19 September 1668, at the age of seventy, and was buried with military honours in the New Chapel at Westminster.

5

Oliver Cromwell

The people who fought on the Roundhead side in the Civil War were animated by a number of different motives. The lawyers stood for the rule of law and constitutional government; the country gentry in the House of Commons for the privileges of Parliament; the merchants for the abolition of monopolies and for freedom of trade; the Scottish Covenanters and English Presbyterians for the suppression of Popery and Anglicanism, and the imposition of a Calvinist and Presbyterian state and church; the Levellers for political democracy and social equality. Oliver Cromwell fought for freedom of religious worship. Even in the early days of the struggle, as an MP, he did not show much interest in the privileges of Parliament, and he always opposed the social and political aims of the Levellers. It was freedom of conscience which inspired him.

Cromwell was born in Huntingdon in 1599, the son of a local gentleman and the nephew of Sir Oliver Cromwell of Hinchinbrook, a wealthy Huntingdonshire magnate who had often entertained the royal family and high government officials. The stories told many years later about the younger Oliver Cromwell's youthful escapades—his stealing apples from orchards and forcing kisses on young women in the street—may be disregarded. The Cavalier pamphleteers who published these stories resorted not merely to exaggerations but also to the crudest inventions about their opponents; one of them went as far as to invent a story that Cromwell's son was hanged at Tyburn as a highwayman. Nor do Cromwell's own statements about his sinful youth and his conversion mean very much, because his Puritan contemporaries were in the habit of expressing their penitence in similar language when they had been guilty of nothing worse than a few sensuous thoughts in adolescence. Cromwell was brought up as a typical

Puritan gentleman, going to his local grammar school at Huntingdon, to Sidney Sussex College, Cambridge, and the Inns of Court. At the age of twenty-one he married Elizabeth Bourchier, the daughter of Sir James Bourchier, a wealthy London furrier, and had a very happy family life, being devoted to his children. In 1631 he moved from Huntingdon to the neighbouring town of St Ives, and in 1636 to Ely.

When he was twenty-nine he was elected to the House of Commons as MP for Huntingdon in the Parliament of 1628. He supported Eliot on all the issues between the Opposition and the King, but it is significant that it was only on the religious question that he spoke in the House, making his maiden speech when he denounced the victimization of his old Puritan schoolmaster by Bishop Neile, who supported Laud's policy. Cromwell did, however, concern himself with other matters, and after the dissolution of Parliament in 1629, when he withdrew to his estates like the other MPs, he championed the cause of the local commoners against the Mayor of Huntingdon who was threatening their privileges, and against the attempts of the Earl of Manchester to enclose the Fens. He advocated both these causes with such intemperance that he twice incurred the censure of the higher authorities, and on one occasion was summoned before the Privy Council and reprimanded.

Cromwell was a passionate man, possessed of great energy. He was fond of outdoor sports, playing cricket and football in his youth and riding and hunting all his life, thus acquiring a thorough knowledge of horses which he used to good effect during the Civil War. He would sometimes indulge in horseplay and practical jokes, especially at moments of personal or political tension. He was liable to fits of depression, and periodically suffered from boils and other ailments which may have been partly caused by psychological factors. The emotional side of his character also showed itself in his great love of music. He was a deeply religious man, with a devotion to the Protestant Cause and a firm belief that God would ensure its triumph. He happened also to have a gift which first manifested itself when he was middle-aged—the capacity to be a brilliant military commander. This military genius was a product of his energy, unorthodoxy and imaginative flair, combined with careful planning and his natural gifts of leadership.

In 1640 he was elected first to the Short and then to the Long Parliament as MP for Cambridge. He supported Pym in the impeachment and attainder of Strafford, but only became prominent in the arguments on the Root and Branch Bill, when he and the other Root and Branch men introduced a bill for the abolition of bishops. When the Civil War began he believed that God had hardened the King's heart, and joined the army as a captain. He showed great energy and fearlessness in his actions against the King's men. Hearing that the principals of the Cambridge colleges were about to sell their plate in order to raise money for the King's cause, he seized the plate for Parliament. After serving at Edgehill, he was promoted to the rank of colonel and served in the Earl of Manchester's army in East Anglia. He won a number of minor victories in Cambridgeshire, Norfolk and Lincolnshire, and in October 1643 a more important battle at Winceby. In January 1644 he was appointed Lieutenant-General and second-in-command under Manchester.

Cromwell's military genius, combined with his Puritan religious zeal, made him the perfect military leader in a revolutionary war. He was fighting for liberty of conscience and freedom of worship for the extremist Protestant sects, which were threatened by his Church of England and Presbyterian allies as well as by his Cavalier enemies. He wanted victory in the field not only for its own sake but also for the political leverage which it would give the Independents against the Presbyterians; and he believed that the best way to win victory in the field was by forming an army of devoted Independents who would be inspired by their religion to fight with a far greater determination than the ordinary soldier who had enlisted only for his pay, or had been pressed reluctantly into the Parliamentary armies. When the Independent and republican leaders in London, in the summer of 1643, turned to Waller, hoping to find in him a military leader whom they could back against the Presbyterian leadership of Pym and Essex, Waller regarded the position as a professional soldier. He told them that he wanted his officers to be godfearing men, but that he would choose them for their ability as officers, not because they were Independents. Cromwell, on the other hand, looked at the situation as a revolutionary leader. He chose reliable Independents as officers and then trained them to be militarily efficient, relying on their revolutionary *élan* and morale to make up for any technical weaknesses. Unlike Waller and all the professional soldiers on both sides, he never lost a battle.

The Scottish Covenanter, Major-General Crawford, who, like many other Covenanter commanders, had fought for the Protestant Cause in the Thirty Years War, was attached to Manchester's army in East Anglia. Crawford became alarmed at the way in which Cromwell was infiltrating Anabaptists and Independents into the army. When Crawford dismissed for disobedience an officer whom he called a 'notorious Anabaptist', Cromwell protested on the ground that the officer was 'a Godly man', and insisted that he should be reinstated. Another Presbyterian complained that Cromwell had told him 'that it must not be souldiers nor Scots that must doe this worke, but it must be the godly to this purpose'. He objected that Cromwell did not appoint gentlemen to be officers in his regiment, but that whenever 'some new upstart Independent did appeare ther must be a way mayd for them by cashiering others'.

Parliament appointed Cromwell to be military governor of the Isle of Ely, and he immediately set about making it, not only a very strong military defence zone, but also 'a place for God to dwell in'. He marched into Ely Cathedral and drove out the officiating Anglican clergyman who was conducting a service in which a choir was singing, because Cromwell, despite his love of music, believed that, music like ritual, was improper in church where the congregation ought to be listening to godly sermons. He outraged the Presbyterians as well as the Anglicans when he encouraged preaching by godly men who had not been ordained as ministers. The Presbyterians complained that 'in the chefest churches on the Sabbath day the souldiers have gonn up into the pulpitts both in the forenoon and the afternone and preached to the whole parish, and our ministers have satt in their seatt in the church, and durst not attempt to preach'.

Although Cromwell was often accused of being an ambitious man seeking personal power, this accusation was unjust. He had no personal vanity, and wished only to advance the cause in which be believed. He knew his own abilities, and for this reason insisted on playing a leading part in military and political affairs; but he was much readier than the other Parliamentary generals to subordinate his personal prestige and serve under the command of other generals, even though he knew that they were less able than himself. His method of using other leaders as a cover and getting rid of his opponents one by one recalls the so-called 'salami tactics' by which the Communists in twentieth-century Europe have used 'front organizations' to destroy their enemies. Cromwell realized that if the war was to be won and religious toleration for the sects was to be achieved in England, it was necessary to break the long-established tradition that the nobility were the natural military leaders in wartime, because the noblemen who commanded the Parliamentary armies were militarily incompetent, were reluctant for political reasons to fight the King to a finish, and were opposed to the Independent sects and religious toleration.

Cromwell used his position as a member of the Committee of Both Kingdoms and as an MP to achieve this step by step. He began by accusing Lord Willoughby of incompetence. The Earl of Manchester was in command of the six counties of the Eastern Association, but in Lincolnshire Lord Willoughby exercised an independent command. Cromwell demanded that Willoughby be dismissed and that Lincolnshire should be included in the Eastern Association and the Roundhead forces there placed under Manchester's command. Having achieved this success, he next accused Manchester of incompetence, having already weakened discipline in Manchester's army by organizing petitions of officers and soldiers in support of freedom of conscience.

In the summer of 1644 a combined Parliamentary army of Scottish Covenanters under Lord Leven and David Leslie (two veterans of the Thirty Years War), Fairfax's army in Yorkshire and Manchester's forces, laid siege to the Cavalier stronghold of York. On 2 July the relieving Cavalier army under Prince Rupert met the Roundhead armies on Marston Moor. Rupert had heard of Cromwell's successes as a cavalry leader, and was eager to meet him in battle; in every engagement in which he had taken part in the war, Rupert had led a cavalry charge which had routed his frightened and demoralized enemies at the first assault. At Marston Moor at 7.30 pm on a rainy summer evening he realized, like all professional soldiers, that it was too late in the day to start a battle, and was having supper in his tent. Cromwell ordered his cavalry to charge Rupert's horse, catching the Cavaliers completely by surprise. The Cavaliers quickly recovered, and were holding their own in the hand-to-hand fighting with Cromwell's men when the Scots under Leslie joined in, and Cromwell, after routing Rupert's cavalry, attacked the other wing of the Cavalier army in the rear. The battle ended in the total defeat of the Cavaliers and the surrender of York, after which nearly the whole of the north of England came under the control of Parliament.

The Presbyterians, who had been hoping that the military intervention of the Scots would silence the opposition of the Independents in London and their demands for religious toleration, claimed for Leven and Leslie the credit for Marston Moor. The Independents claimed the credit for Cromwell. It was only because of Cromwell's military reputation that the campaign for religious toleration was able to gain ground in London. In Cromwell's first report of Marston Moor, he wrote that 'The Left Wing, which I commanded, being our own horse, saving a few Scots in our rear, beat all the Prince's horse.' The Independent preachers and the London newspapers succeeded in presenting Cromwell as the victor of Marston Moor, and on 13 September Parliament voted congratulations to him. On the same day Cromwell took his seat in the House and spoke for the Independents against the ordinal in the new Presbyterian prayer book.

Meanwhile he had struck a blow both for military efficiency and for religious toleration by pursuing his campaign against the Presbyterian generals. He attacked his commanding officer, Manchester, in the Committee of Both Kingdoms, accusing him of being dilatory in obeying the orders of the Committee to march to the relief of Essex's armies in Cornwall. After the battle of Newbury in October 1644, he denounced Manchester in the House of Commons for his failure to capture Donnington Castle and to prevent the relief of Basing House. Waller supported Cromwell's criticisms of Manchester; and Cromwell, although he had been much more successful than Waller as a general in the Civil War, agreed to serve under the Presbyterian Waller in the campaign in Dorset in the winter of 1644-5.

Cromwell was one of the most eager supporters of the Self-Denying Ordinance, by which all peers and MPs were disqualified from holding military commands. The passage of the bill compelled Essex, Manchester and Waller to resign their commands. Cromwell himself would also have been compelled to resign if he had not been specially reappointed to his command for a short period which was subsequently extended. But Cromwell did not use this opportunity to obtain the position of Lord General and the supreme command of the Parliamentary forces. He was very willing that the office of Lord General should be given to Sir Thomas Fairfax, who was not an MP and was not affected by the Self-Denying Ordinance. Cromwell served as second-in-command under Fairfax, although Fairfax was inferior to him as a general.

It was chiefly thanks to Cromwell that the Parliamentary armies, under the command of Fairfax, won the decisive battle of the war at Naseby, where they defeated King Charles and Prince Rupert in June 1645. By the summer of 1646 the war was over. When the conflict between Parliament and the army broke out in 1647, Cromwell, after some hesitation, supported the demands of the Agitators and Levellers in the army. Using Fairfax as the figurehead, he marched on London and ousted Waller and the other ten Presbyterian leaders from the House of Commons. But he came down firmly against the Levellers' demands for universal suffrage and their social demands. In the debates with the representatives of the rank-and-file soldiers at Putney in November 1647 he argued in a vague and rambling way against the Levellers, taking the view, as he expressed it on a later occasion, that the nobleman, the gentleman and the yeoman would always have their separate stations in society. At this time he was adopting a conciliatory attitude towards the King, whom he had removed from the control of Parliament into army custody. In view of the fact that Parliament was refusing to agree to religious toleration for the Independent sects, Cromwell proposed to Charles I that the army should restore him as King and the Church of England as the official Church, if Charles and the Anglicans would agree to grant religious toleration.

Charles rejected Cromwell's proposal, and instead entered into a secret agreement with one section of the Scottish Covenanters, who promised to invade England and reinstate him in power, impose Presbyterianism as the state religion, and suppress the army and the Independents. In May 1648 the Scots crossed the Border, and Cavalier revolts broke out in Kent, Essex, South Wales and elsewhere, while the Parliamentary fleet mutinied. Cromwell and the army believed that the King had betrayed them and was responsible for the bloodshed in the Second Civil War. Before marching against the Cavaliers, the Army Council held a meeting at Windsor, and passed a resolution that 'It was our duty, if ever the Lord brought us back again in peace, to call Charles Stuart, that man of blood, to an account for the blood he had shed, and mischief he had done to his utmost.'

The army was greatly outnumbered by the Cavalier rebels and the Scots. But the mutiny in the fleet was quickly suppressed, and while Fairfax besieged Colchester, Cromwell marched into Wales and besieged Pembroke. After a six weeks' siege, Pembroke surrendered. Cromwell ordered that the Presbyterian commander of Pembroke—a former Roundhead soldier—should be exempted from mercy, and he was tried by court-martial and shot. He then went to the north, where Colonel Lambert with a small force was harrying the flank of the invading Scots. Joining forces with Lambert in Yorkshire, Cromwell marched his 8,600 men quickly across the Pennines into Lancashire to deal with the Scottish Covenanter army of 20,000 who were marching to the south. He unexpectedly attacked the Scottish army in the rear, and the Scottish rearguard stampeded in panic into their comrades in the vanguard, thus enabling Cromwell to win one of his most brilliant victories at Preston. By November Colchester had surrendered to Fairfax, and Cromwell was besieging Pontefract, the one remaining town held by the enemy forces.

Cromwell did not play an active part in the opening stages of the events which led to the trial and execution of Charles I. He was still in the north when the army brought Charles from Newport to Windsor and marched on London, and he only returned to London on the day after Pride's Purge. But he had already indicated his general approval of the army action, and as soon as he reached London he directed each step in the proceedings, overruling the hesitations of the waverers and putting pressure on them to take part in the King's trial and to sign the warrant for the execution. Although he is said, on doubtful authority, to have declared that the King's execution was a 'cruel necessity', he regarded it, not as an expedient step, but as an act of justice and a fulfilment of the will of God. From a political point of view, it turned out to be a great blunder, and anyone with any experience of seventeenth-century politics and ideology would have realized that it would have been far wiser either to have kept Charles alive as a prisoner or to have had him surreptitiously murdered. Cromwell declared that 'we will cut off his head with the crown upon it', and, like his fellow-regicides, boasted that they had acted openly in the light of the sun when they killed the King. They believed that God required them to kill Charles as He had required Jehu to kill Joram and Ahaziah, because evil kings, like other evil men, should be brought to justice for their crimes.

The Levellers had pressed for justice on Charles Stuart, but as soon as the King was dead Cromwell destroyed them. He told the new republican government that 'you have no other way to deal with these men but to break them or they will break you'. He crushed a Leveller mutiny in the army at Burford, executing three of the ringleaders, and prosecuted the Leveller leader, John Lilburne, for sedition. He stamped out a rebellion in Ireland, where he treated his enemies with a cruelty which was probably justified by the contemporary laws of war, but which he would not have adopted against English Protestants. Like nearly all the English he had been inflamed against the Irish Catholics by the true and false allegations of the atrocities which they had committed against English Protestant settlers during the Irish Catholic rebellion of 1641.

After the execution of Charles I, the Scottish Covenanters proclaimed Charles II as King. Charles came to Scotland, where he became a Presbyterian. Cromwell marched into Scotland at the head of an English army. For the first time he had to act officially as Commander-in-Chief, because Fairfax refused to serve in this capacity despite Cromwell's efforts to persuade him to do so. Cromwell himself therefore became Lord General. For once he was outmanoeuvred in the campaign by his old comrade-in-arms of Marston Moor, General Leslie, the Covenanter commander, and he allowed himself to be cooped up at Dunbar, where he was in danger of being starved out; but when the Presbyterian leaders of the Kirk forced Leslie, against his better judgment, to come down from his strong position on the hills and engage Cromwell's army in battle, Cromwell's tactical skill allowed him to retrieve the situation by winning one of his greatest victories against a force nearly twice as large as his own.

He spent the next eleven months in Scotland, trying unsuccessfully to make peace with the Scottish Covenanters whom he regarded, unlike the Catholic Irish, not as wicked enemies but as misguided friends.

As the Scots refused his offers, he led them on to destruction by advancing north across the Forth and deliberately leaving the road into England open. Charles II and his Covenanter allies, believing that the Cavaliers in England would rise in their support, marched for London through Lancashire and the West Midlands. Cromwell timed his movements to a nicety. He spent another twenty-four hours bombarding Perth into submission, and then set out in pursuit of the enemy, marching by way of Leith, Kelso and Durham through Yorkshire and Nottinghamshire to Warwickshire, covering nearly thirty miles a day in the heat of a very warm August, and stopping every five or six days to give his men a day's rest. He caught Charles II and the Scots at Worcester, and with his superior forces destroyed the enemy on 3 September 1651, the anniversary of his victory at Dunbar a year before.

Since the proclamation of the republic in January 1649, England had been ruled by the Rump Parliament and the Council of State under the chairmanship of John Bradshaw, who had presided at the trial of Charles I. Cromwell was a member of both these bodies. The House of Commons had consisted of about 500 MPs when it was elected in 1640. Some of these had been killed in the war, and others who had joined the Cavaliers had gone into exile after their defeat. At the end of the war, these vacancies had been largely filled at a number of by-elections in 1645 and 1646. Pride's Purge had turned out all except eighty of these MPs, and as another thirty had withdrawn in protest, all that was left after 1648 was about fifty zealous Independents. The army officers— the 'Grandees', as the Levellers called them—had no intention of being dominated by the fifty MPs of the Rump, and by 1653 a conflict had developed between them, not on any religious or ideological issue, but simply on the question as to whether the army Grandees or the Rump should rule.

The army demanded that the Rump should dissolve itself, and that a new Parliament be elected to replace the remnants of the Long Parliament which had sat for thirteen years. The republicans in the Rump feared that if the Rump were dissolved, it would be replaced either by military rule or by a new Parliament in which Cavaliers or Presbyterians might dominate. In April 1653 Sir Henry Vane and the republicans introduced a bill providing that the Rump should continue permanently in being, and that vacancies caused by death or resignation should be filled by co-option of new members nominated by the MPs. Cromwell marched to the House with a troop of musketeers. He took his seat in the chamber, but only to order the Speaker to dissolve the Parliament, and when the Speaker and the MPs refused to leave, the soldiers entered and drove them out at the sword-point, Cromwell declaring: 'You have sat long enough.'

Cromwell was now hated by the Cavaliers, the Presbyterians, the Levellers and the republicans of the dissolved Rump. He had to look for the support of other groups and classes. He turned first to the extreme radical wing of the Independent sects in the army. These were the Independent zealots who had been denounced as Anabaptists by the Presbyterians and who had won the two civil wars. They had supported Cromwell against the Levellers because of their personal loyalty to him, and because their radical and egalitarian religious doctrines had not led them to the point where they demanded political and social equality as well. They had supported him against the Rump out of their contempt for civilians, and because of the lack of religious zeal and the lax moral standards which many of the Rump leaders, like Marten, showed in their private lives.

Cromwell replaced the Rump by a Parliament of 140 MPs nominated by him, who met in July 1653. It became known as the Barebones Parliament from the name of one of its active MPs, the Puritan extremist Praise-God Barebones. The Cavaliers and other critics noted that the MPs came from a lower social class than the MPs in ordinary Parliaments, and that only about half of them were gentlemen. The Barebones Parliament passed a number of measures which gave protection to tenants, reformed the law, and in other ways alarmed the gentry, the lawyers and the merchant class, who united with the Grandees in the army and persuaded Cromwell to dissolve the Barebones Parliament and assume the title of Lord Protector in December 1653.

Cromwell's failure to take the title of Lord Protector in the previous April, after the dissolution of the Rump, is another proof of his lack of personal ambition; but now he allowed himself to be persuaded to take the title, to be addressed as 'Your Highness', and to live in state in the former royal palaces, in order to present the image of traditional authority which the army Grandees and the gentlemen and merchants expected from their head of state. In 1654 he summoned a Parliament in which MPs from Scotland and Ireland were represented for the first time, and which was elected on a wider franchise than had ever been known in England and would not be known again until the nineteenth century. It was composed of MPs of a higher social class than the members of the Barebones Parliament, and several republicans and former members of the Rump were elected. But Cromwell grew tired of their criticism and constitutional discussions, dissolved the Parliament in January 1655, and arrested some of the republican leaders.

In March a Cavalier revolt broke out in Wiltshire and the south-west. Cromwell suppressed the revolt, and in the summer of 1655 established a military dictatorship. England was divided into eleven districts and one of his Major-Generals was appointed governor of each district, Scotland and Ireland remaining as before under the rule of the English army of occupation. The Major-Generals governed their areas by decree, being responsible only to Cromwell and his Council in London.

Cromwell aroused the resentment of the country gentlemen and the merchants of the boroughs by submitting them to the dictatorship of the Major-Generals instead of leaving the country to be governed by the local JPs—that is to say, by the gentry in the countryside and by the mayors and corporations in the towns. He also became unpopular with the common people because he suppressed fairs, race-meetings and other assemblies. He did this more for reasons of security than out of Puritan zeal. He and his Major-Generals were no more intolerant than the Rump or the Presbyterians in enforcing the Puritan code of morals, but Cromwell's fear of Cavalier revolts and plots drove him to ban all kinds of public gatherings which might have been used as a cover for conspiracies and risings against his government.

In September 1656 Cromwell summoned a new and elected Parliament in order to obtain money for his war with Spain. He abolished the rule of the Major-Generals in order to please the gentry and merchants, and, relying on the support of these classes, tried to govern as a constitutional King. He seriously considered taking the title of King in 1657, which would have been the best way of ensuring stability and the support of the middle classes on whom he now relied; but the opposition of the army Grandees, including some of his closest officers, prevented him from doing so. The Grandees were still distrustful of the monarchical principle, and realized that King Oliver I would be less dependant on military support than His Highness the Lord Protector. Cromwell reverted as far as possible to the traditional forms of government which the middle classes preferred, and in 1658 he created an Upper House of Parliament, in which his nominees sat as peers. This was the first time since 1648 that Parliament had consisted of more than a single chamber. But the Parliament of 1658 was critical of his policy, and he dissolved it in disgust.

He pursued his cherished ideal of religious toleration for all Protestant sects, though he found it impossible to prevent the local JPs and gentry from persecuting Quakers. He allowed the Jews to return to England after an exile of 365 years. He had never intended to apply religious toleration to the Papist enemies of the Protestant Cause; but Roman Catholics—in England if not in Ireland—were persecuted much less savagely under Cromwell than they had been by the Presbyterians in the early days of the Civil War, or than they would be in the future, after the Restoration, by Charles II's Anglican governments. The Presbyterians often accused Cromwell, without the least foundation, of being a secret sympathizer with Papists and Jesuits.

Cromwell's foreign policy was a combination of religious zeal and national interest. In Cromwell's case, as with other revolutionary governments, ideology played a more important part than it does in the foreign policy of normal governments. He made peace with Holland partly at least because of his reluctance to go to war with a Protestant state; he worked for a grand Protestant alliance with Sweden, Denmark and Holland; he reacted violently to the persecution of the Protestant Vaudois by the Duke of Savoy—in a region where English national interests were in no way involved; and when he went to war with Spain and captured Jamaica, he was very conscious that he was waging war against a Papist state and that he would liberate the oppressed Indians of the Caribbean from the cruelties of the Spanish Inquisition. But he vigorously upheld the honour and prestige of England. He forced the foreign powers who had denounced the regicide English republicans in 1649 to reopen diplomatic relations with him and to treat his over-touchy ambassadors with respect; and his foreign policy furthered the development of English trade and led to the first steps in the acquisition of the British overseas colonial empire. He did not hesitate to make an alliance with Papist France, and acquired Dunkirk as the price for his military assistance to France against Spain.

It is sad, but not surprising, that Cromwell, one of the most high-principled and well-meaning of English rulers, was hated more bitterly than any of his predecessors or successors. All his enemies denounced him as a tyrant, though except in the period of military government he never ruled as an absolute dictator. He was in constant fear of assassination. He appeared in public as little as possible, and never left London except to go to Hampton Court. He personally supervised the selection of his guard every day, and is said to have slept in a different bedroom in his palaces every night in order to foil any attempt on his life. When he died at the age of fifty-nine on 3 September 1658—the anniversary of his victories at Dunbar and Worcester—he appointed his son Richard to succeed him as Lord Protector. He was given a great state funeral, but the official mourning was not an expression of the feelings of the majority of the people.

6

Henry Ireton

After the Restoration the Cavaliers, remembering with horror the murder of King Charles the Martyr, thought that the arch-regicide was Henry Ireton. They considered him to be even worse than Oliver Cromwell, and the guiltiest man of all those who had shed the royal blood. Throughout the critical years 1647-9, when Cromwell acted against both the King and the Levellers, his son-in-law Ireton was his right-hand man. They formed a closely allied, but strongly contrasting, pair—Cromwell the emotional, extrovert genius, passionate and ebullient; Ireton, the dark, ice-cold, taciturn, ruthless intellectual.

Ireton was born in the autumn of 1611, the son of a gentleman of Attenborough in Nottinghamshire. He was not connected either with the Hampdens and Cromwells of Buckinghamshire and Huntingdonshire, or with the Puritans of Devon and the south-west, but his upbringing was the same—the English Bible and Foxe's *Book of Martyrs*, university and the Inns of Court. He went to Trinity College, Oxford, at the age of fifteen, and to the Middle Temple in 1629, and then returned to Attenborough to manage his country estate.

He was thirty when the Civil War began. When it was clear that war was inevitable, he and his younger brothers raised a troop of his tenants and neighbours to fight for Parliament; but on 22 August 1642 the King raised his standard and declared war on Parliament at Nottingham and occupied the area with his army. Ireton got away to the south with his men, and joined Essex's forces in time to fight at Edgehill. He was then sent to join Manchester's army in East Anglia. Here he met Cromwell, who immediately spotted him as one of those 'godly men' on whom he was relying to win the war and to stand for Independency against Anglicanism and Presbyterianism. When

Cromwell was appointed Governor of the Isle of Ely, he chose Ireton as his Deputy-Governor. Ireton had his first political experience here. He actively seconded Cromwell's steps to purge Ely of Anglican and Presbyterian influence, and to encourage preaching by soldiers who had never been ordained as ministers.

Ireton served under Cromwell in Lincolnshire in 1643 and at Marston Moor and Newbury in 1644. He strongly supported Cromwell in the disputes with Manchester, whom he accused of dilatoriness and lack of will to fight the enemy. At Naseby in June 1645 he led a damaging raid on the King's position on the evening before the main battle was fought, and next morning Cromwell persuaded Fairfax to appoint him to the rank of Commissary-General and to entrust the command of the left wing of the Roundhead army to him in the battle. Here Ireton had to bear the brunt of Rupert's cavalry charge. His men broke, but Ireton rallied them and led them against the King's infantry in the centre, setting the example by charging into the thick of the fighting. His horse was killed under him, he was wounded in the thigh by a pike and in the face by a halberd, and was taken prisoner. Next day, hearing that the Roundheads had won a decisive victory in the battle, he persuaded the Cavalier soldiers who were guarding him to allow him to escape by convincing them that they themselves would shortly be captured by the Roundheads, and that he would then show his gratitude by ordering them to be released. Despite his wounds, he managed to find his way to the Roundhead lines.

He served with distinction during the last year of the war, and played a leading part in the final siege and capitulation of Oxford. Ten days before Oxford surrendered, Ireton married Cromwell's daughter Bridget at Cromwell's headquarters at Holton outside Oxford. In their five years of married life, Bridget bore him a son and three daughters.

By the time that the political conflict with Parliament broke out in 1647, Ireton had become one of the highest officers in the army and had also been elected MP for Appleby in Westmorland during the by-elections of 1645-6. He soon showed himself to be the ablest and most clear-thinking politician among the army leadership. He drafted most of the manifestos, issued in the name of the Lord General Fairfax and the officers and soldiers of the army, in which the army's grievances against the Presbyterians

at Westminster were stated and the demand for religious toleration for the Independent sects was put forward. He was active in
organizing the army's march on London in August 1647 and the
expulsion of Waller and the other ten Presbyterian leaders from
the House of Commons.

When the disputes arose between the army officers and the
Levellers and Agitators, Ireton was again the chief political
adviser and representative of the officers. He was the leading
spokesman for the Grandees against the Levellers in the debates
at Putney in November 1647. He put the case for the preservation
of the different social classes and the political privileges of the
gentry against the arguments of Rainsborough, Sexby, and
Wildman. He was the only participant on the Grandees' side
who was capable of meeting the Leveller leaders in argument.
While Cromwell rambled on in the inconclusive and almost
incoherent style which he often adopted when it was a question
of speaking as opposed to acting, Ireton was concise and crystal-
clear: the Levellers' demand that all men except servants and
wage-earners should have the vote would destroy the privileged
position of property-owners, whereas it was only through holding
property that a man acquired the interest and the right to take
part in governing the country.

At the outbreak of the Second Civil War in the summer of
1648, Ireton did not accompany Cromwell in his campaigns in
South Wales and in the north against the Scots, but helped
Fairfax suppress a Cavalier rising at Maidstone and besiege
Colchester. Many people thought that Cromwell had sent him to
keep an eye on Fairfax. When the Cavaliers at Colchester at last
surrendered, Fairfax sentenced two of their leaders to be shot.
The condemned men accused Fairfax of violating the surrender
terms by carrying out these executions; but Ireton, who attended
the execution, coolly argued with them in the last few minutes of
their lives, pointing out that when they surrendered 'at mercy'
they must have known that this meant that mercy would be
shown to some of them, but not to others.

By the autumn of 1648 only Pontefract still held out for the
Cavalier rebels. Cromwell was in Yorkshire at the siege of
Pontefract, and Ireton at the army headquarters at Windsor was
second-in-command, under Fairfax, of the army in the south.
With Fairfax a reluctant figurehead and Cromwell absent, Ireton

became the leader of the army and the Independents in the struggle against the Presbyterians in Parliament. He decided, probably after consulting Cromwell, and in collaboration with the Levellers, to carry through a military *coup d'état*, to put the King on trial and execute him, and to establish a republic. It was Ireton who began the final chain of events by drafting the Remonstrance of 20 November in which the army demanded that Parliament should break off its negotiations with the King; it was he who sent 200 soldiers on 30 November to bring the King from Newport in the Isle of Wight to Hurst Castle in Hampshire; and it was he who ordered the army to march on London on 2 December. His first idea was to turn out Parliament altogether and resort to direct army rule, but at the suggestion of Ludlow and other Independent MPs he modified his proposal and ordered Colonel Pride and Sir Hardress Waller to carry out the purge of 6 December by which forty-one leading Presbyterian MPs were detained, and all except fifty Independent and thirty other MPs were excluded from the House of Commons.

On the day after Pride's Purge Cromwell arrived in London, and took over the direction of events; but Ireton was his chief lieutenant and perhaps his prompter. Cromwell and Ireton moved into Whitehall Palace, and there, sitting in the King's chairs, or more often reclining on his beds, they planned every move. First they broke with the Levellers. In December discussions were held between representatives of the Grandees and the Levellers in Whitehall. The Levellers demanded that before any steps were taken against the King, a political constitution should be adopted and a Parliament elected by almost universal manhood suffrage, after which this new people's Parliament could decide to proceed against the King. The Grandees had no intention of waiting for this before executing the King, and indeed did not wish that such a constitution and Parliament should ever be established. Ireton was again the chief spokesman against the Levellers. In the course of the discussions he grew more intolerant, and eventually the Levellers walked out after complaining of the bias which Sir Hardress Waller showed as chairman at the talks.

After the Rump of the House of Commons abolished the House of Lords and set up the High Court of Justice to try the King, Ireton seconded Cromwell's efforts to force everyone to proceed to the end and cut off the King's head. Ireton sat as one of the seventy-eight judges at Charles's trial and signed the death warrant. There can be no doubt that, in putting the King to death, Ireton, in his cold, silent way, acted like Cromwell from a sense of justice and service to God, not from political expediency.

Ireton accompanied Cromwell on the expedition to Ireland in the summer of 1649. Like Cromwell and all the soldiers in the army, he was not disposed to show mercy to the Irish Papist rebels. As an Englishman and a Protestant he despised and hated the native Irish and the Papists, and he had been as outraged as all his fellow-countrymen and fellow-Protestants by the stories which he had heard of the Irish atrocities against the English Protestant settlers during the rebellion of 1641. But, like Cromwell, he sometimes showed mercy as well as severity, and on one occasion executed two of his soldiers who had murdered an Irishman.

When Cromwell returned to England in 1650 to undertake the campaign against Charles II and the Covenanters in Scotland. Ireton was left in command of the forces of the republic in Ireland. He successfully conducted the war and the pacification of Ireland, stamping out the last traces of resistance, capturing Carlow, Waterford and Duncannon, and invading Connaught. In the summer of 1651 he besieged Limerick. He summoned the Irish rebel garrison to surrender, but was pleased that they refused, as this gave him the excuse to wreak vengeance on the Papists when they surrendered after a four-month siege. He said that this was desirable 'in point of freedom for prosecution of justice, one of the great ends and best grounds of the war', as well as 'in point of safety to the English planters'. He hanged seven of the garrison on the spot, and sent another nineteen of them for trial by court-martial and the civil courts.

Limerick surrendered on 27 October 1651. There was plague in the town, and Ireton caught it and died on 26 November. He was just forty years of age. He was given a state funeral and buried in Westminster Abbey. His widow Bridget married another of her father's generals, Major-General Fleetwood.

At the Restoration, Ireton's corpse was removed from the Abbey and, along with the bodies of Cromwell and Bradshaw, was drawn on a hurdle to Tyburn, where it was hung up all day. The heads were then cut off and exhibited at Westminster Hall, where they remained for at least twenty-four years. Ireton was one of the twenty-four regicides who had died before the Restoration, and to whom the Cavaliers could do nothing worse than outrage their corpses. He escaped the agonizing death or the incarceration for life which was the fate of most of the surviving regicides. One is inclined to consider that the twenty-four who died before 1660 were lucky to have died in time; but perhaps these congratulations are misplaced in Ireton's case. He was probably the only one of them all, apart from Cromwell, who, had he survived, might have prevented the Restoration. If Ireton had been living in 1658–60, he might have ended his days in peace as Lord Protector.

7

John Lilburne

During his lifetime John Lilburne was one of the most prominent and controversial of the Roundhead leaders. He was shamefully neglected by the nineteenth-century historians, but has been acclaimed by the Left-wing writers of the twentieth century as the most important figure of the Civil War, and as the forerunner of modern Radicalism. He was the link between John Foxe's Marian martyrs and the Chartists, the suffragettes, the conscientious objectors, the passive resisters, and the hunger-strikers of the nineteenth and twentieth centuries. He began his career as a martyr for Puritan doctrine, and became a champion of political democracy before ending his days as a Quaker and pacifist.

He was born in 1615 in Sunderland, some twenty-five miles from the family home in the village of Thickley Punchardon near Bishop Auckland in Durham. It was still a predominantly agricultural area, though there were many small coal mines where indentured miners dug out the coal in some cases as much as sixty feet beneath the surface of the fields. His father was the village squire of Thickley Punchardon; his mother was the daughter of the Master of the Wardrobe at the King's palace at Greenwich, where the Lilburnes sometimes resided when John Lilburne was a small child. In later life, Lilburne on several occasions emphasized that he was a gentleman, not a yeoman, by birth—a piece of snobbery in a popular leader which was more excusable in the seventeenth century, if only on tactical grounds, than it would be today. Like most other Englishmen of his generation, he was brought up on Foxe's *Book of Martyrs*; but in his case the book aroused in him, not merely indignation against the Papists who had sent these martyrs to the stake, but an urge to follow in their footsteps and suffer for God's truth as they had done.

When he was fifteen he was sent to London and apprenticed to Thomas Hewson, a Puritan clothier. Hewson, like most other employers of the period, sometimes browbeat and insulted his apprentices. Lilburne resented this, and adopted the very unusual course of bringing an action against his master in the Court of the Lord High Chamberlain. Hewson, as a Puritan, could respect a young man who stood up for his rights in the face of what he considered was oppression; the dispute was settled amicably, and Hewson thought none the worse of Lilburne because of it. Within a few years Lilburne was acting as Hewson's ally in a nobler cause against a more formidable enemy. Hewson took him to the Gatehouse prison in Westminster to visit John Bastwick, a physician who had been imprisoned for writing pamphlets against bishops. Lilburne joined Bastwick's Puritan group, and was soon busily engaged in smuggling illegal Puritan pamphlets from Holland into England, and secretly circulating them in London.

In the summer of 1637 proceedings were brought in the Court of Star Chamber against Bastwick, William Prynne and Henry Burton for writing and preaching against bishops. Archbishop Laud, Chief Justice Finch and the other judges sentenced the three men to stand in the pillory, to have their ears cut off, to be imprisoned for life, and fined £5,000 each. Prynne was also to be branded in the face with the letters 'S L' for 'seditious libeller'. The sentence was carried out in Palace Yard at Westminster on 30 June before a large crowd who openly demonstrated in favour of the victims. The pillory, which was supposed to be a disgraceful humiliation, was a triumph for the three Puritans; the crowd cheered them, and rushed forward to dip their handkerchiefs in the blood as the ears were cut off, and the martyrs declared that they were proud to undergo such torments for the truth. Lilburne, standing with Hewson at the foot of the pillory, nearly fainted with horror when the ears were cut off, and had to be comforted by the suffering Bastwick himself.

In December 1637 Lilburne was arrested, having been betrayed by a member of his Puritan group who was an agent of the government. He was brought before Laud and other judges in the Court of Star Chamber and charged with smuggling illegal books from Holland into England. The Star Chamber, like the other conciliar courts which had been introduced into England under the Tudors, adopted the inquisitorial procedure which was unknown in the English common law courts. The defendant was required to take an oath, swearing to speak the truth, and then to reply to the questions put to him by the court. Lilburne, like other Puritans before him, refused to take the oath on the grounds that it was illegal—a point on which he had the support of many common lawyers, though it had been regularly administered in the conciliar courts for many years. He was sentenced to be whipped at the cart-tail from the Fleet prison in Fleet Street to Palace Yard in Westminster, where he was to stand in the pillory, and then to be imprisoned until he conformed and admitted his guilt. He was also to be fined £500—the equivalent of about £25,000 in today's money.

The sentence was carried out on 18 April 1638. As he walked at the cart-tail from Fleet Street to Westminster, he was whipped every three or four paces with a three-pronged whip; one of the bystanders reckoned that he received three times five hundred lashes on the journey. Another observer described the wounds on his back as being as big as tobacco pipes. As he received each blow of the lash, he cried out: 'Hallelujah, Hallelujah, Glory, Honour and Praise be given to thee O Lord for ever!' and declared that he had committed no crime against the law, the King, or the state, but was a victim of the bishops' cruelty. His punishment, like that of Bastwick and his colleagues ten months earlier, turned into an anti-government demonstration. Cheering crowds escorted him at the cart-tail and surrounded him in the pillory, where he made a speech attacking the bishops. An official ordered him to be quiet, and when he refused, he was gagged so violently that blood spurted from his mouth; but he then produced a number of pamphlets which he had hidden on his person, and distributed them to the crowd as he stood in the pillory.

When he arrived back at the Fleet prison, a surgeon dressed his wounds; but to punish him for his conduct in the pillory, he was placed in solitary confinement and was not permitted to receive any visitors or any further medical treatment. He was given very little to eat, and as he was not allowed to receive any visitors, his friends could not adopt the usual course of supplementing his prison rations by sending him food. But despite the closeness of his imprisonment, he somehow succeeded in writing a number of pamphlets in which he described his sufferings, and in smuggling them out of prison to his friends who published them illegally. In these pamphlets he proclaimed that he was a loyal subject of the King, but denounced the bishops, whose 'delight is only in the blood of the Saints . . . therefore doe they tortour my poore weake body, with vnparaleld Paganish and Heathenish cruelty'. He did not minimize the sufferings that he had undergone. He stated that he would prefer to die at Tyburn or Smithfield than to endure 'my Constant Extraordinarie bodily paines and torments', and added: 'I have read a great part of the Booke of Martyrs, with some Histories of the like kinde; and J will meantaine it, that such an vnparaleld Act of crueltie and barbarous tiranie, as haue been exercised vpon mee, is not to be found in them all. Yea wicked bloodie Bonner himselfe, never did the like to any of the Saints as have been done vnto mee.'

He remained in prison for nearly three years until Charles I, having been defeated by the Scots, was forced to summon the Long Parliament in November 1640. Six days after Parliament met, the MP for Cambridge, Oliver Cromwell, addressing the House of Commons for the second time in his career, drew attention to the case of Lilburne, speaking with passion about the bishops' cruelty. On 11 November the House ordered that Lilburne be released, and he was set free; four weeks later, Archbishop Laud was taken into custody by the officers of the House of Commons. As the revolutionary fervour of the Londoners developed, Lilburne played an active part, haranguing the crowds at Strafford's execution and leading the apprentices in the riot with the King's guards in Whitehall on 29 December 1641. Soon afterwards he married Elizabeth Dewell, a Puritan admirer who had apparently first met him when she comforted him during his whipping or in the Fleet prison. She became a most loyal wife and fellow-fighter for the cause.

On the outbreak of the Civil War, Lilburne joined the army as a captain, and fought under Essex at Edgehill. During the Cavalier advance on London he was given the duty of holding off Prince Rupert's attack on Brentford while the Roundheads evacuated the artillery. He succeeded in doing this and in rallying the fleeing Roundhead soldiers, but his troop suffered heavy losses, and he himself, after being nearly drowned in the river, was taken prisoner by the Cavaliers and sent to Oxford.

He was the first prominent Roundhead to be taken prisoner
in the war, and the Cavaliers had to decide how to treat him. At
first he was treated with kindness, and offers were made to him
to join the Cavaliers; but after he had indignantly rejected them,
his captors began to threaten to treat him as a traitor because he
was undoubtedly guilty of high treason, having waged war
against the King. He was examined by Prince Rupert, Mr Justice
Heath, and other leading Cavaliers at Oxford, and eventually it
was decided to put him on trial for high treason. In view of
Lilburne's past and future career, it cannot have been coincidence
that it was he, the born martyr, who was singled out for this
fate. Edward Hyde, afterwards Earl of Clarendon, wrote in his
History of the Rebellion that Lilburne 'behaved himself with so
great impudence in extolling the power of Parliament, that it
was manifest he had an ambition to have been made a martyr
for that cause'.

On Tuesday 13 December 1642 Lilburne smuggled out of
his prison at Oxford a letter to his wife, telling her that his trial
for high treason was due to begin in a week's time, on Tuesday
the twentieth. Elizabeth Lilburne received the letter in London
on Friday the sixteenth, and immediately informed the Speaker
of the House of Commons. The House, after an emergency
debate the same afternoon, published next day a letter to Mr
Justice Heath at Oxford, threatening to execute their Cavalier
prisoners in reprisal if Lilburne was put to death as a traitor.
Elizabeth Lilburne undertook to carry the letter to Oxford in
time to stop Lilburne's trial. She arrived in time, the threat of
reprisals was effective, and Lilburne was not put on trial.

After a five-months' imprisonment at Oxford, during which
he alleged that he was maltreated, he was exchanged for a Cavalier
officer in Roundhead hands. He joined Manchester's army in
East Anglia, and was soon promoted to the rank of Lieutenant-
Colonel. He became friendly with Cromwell, who had championed his cause in Parliament in 1640, and was one of the officers
whom Cromwell considered to be 'godfearing' men who knew
what they were fighting for, and whom Manchester's Presbyterian
commanders stigmatized as Anabaptists or sectaries. He served
with Cromwell in Lincolnshire and at Marston Moor, where he
distinguished himself in the initial charge against Rupert's
position, and soon afterwards, at the instigation of Cromwell and

Ireton, captured Tickhill Castle in Yorkshire in defiance of orders from Manchester forbidding him to do so. He then went south with Cromwell and Manchester, and took part in the Newbury campaign. He outspokenly supported Cromwell in the disputes with Manchester.

As the controversy between the Presbyterians and the Independents developed, Lilburne became a leading supporter of the Independents and of religious toleration, sticking his neck out at a time when Cromwell and Vane and the wiser Independent leaders were adopting more cautious tactics. In the summer of 1644 the Presbyterians in Parliament ordered the burning of Roger Williams's *The Bloody Tenent*, with its plea for religious toleration, and in the autumn they likewise suppressed Milton's *Areopagitica*, in which Milton had pleaded for the abolition of censorship. In January 1645 Prynne, in his *Truth Triumphing*, demanded the vigorous suppression of every deviation from Presbyterianism and the crushing of the Independents. Lilburne replied with his *Letter to Prynne*, a defence of liberty of conscience which he published without the consent of the censor, in defiance of the licensing laws. This brought Lilburne into conflict with his former heroes and collaborators, Prynne and Bastwick, who were too zealous for the cause of Presbyterianism to be deflected by any feeling of gratitude for the support which Lilburne had given them in the days when they were the victims, not the instigators, of persecution. Prynne attacked Lilburne for publishing illegal and seditious pamphlets, and Bastwick denounced him to the Speaker of the House of Commons. A few days after Lilburne's *Letter to Prynne* was published, Lilburne nearly lost an eye in an accident when he was injured by a pike, which permanently damaged his eyesight. A Presbyterian preacher thanked God, in his sermon, for having inflicted this punishment on Lilburne.

In April 1645 Lilburne resigned from the army. As he was not an MP he was not caught by the Self-Denying Ordinance, but he had been required to subscribe to the Presbyterians' Solemn League and Covenant. Cromwell and the other Independent officers had been able to reconcile the wording of the document with their consciences, and had subscribed and retained their military commands; but Lilburne would not subscribe, although Cromwell tried hard to persuade him to continue in the army.

In the summer of 1645 Lilburne published a pamphlet in which for the first time he raised social as well as religious issues. In his *Copy of a Letter from Lieutenant-Colonel John Lilburne to a friend* he denounced the MPs who had lived in comfort during the Civil War and were now wealthy, while the soldiers who had risked their lives and lost their limbs on the battlefields were penniless and hungry, as were the starving widows and orphans of those who had died fighting for Parliament. Prynne denounced this pamphlet as the most seditious writing ever published.

In August 1645 Lilburne was arrested by order of Parliament for having published the *Letter from Lieutenant-Colonel John Lilburne*, but he was released on 14 October. He was at liberty for exactly six months, which he spent in writing pamphlets in which he advocated an extension of the Parliamentary franchise and the payment of MPs. These pamphlets were illegal, as they were published without the consent of the censor. This was a typical example of high-principled obstinacy on Lilburne's part, because the censor, John Bachiler, strongly sympathized with the Independents, and to the indignation of the Presbyterians licensed nearly every pamphlet by Independent propagandists which was submitted to him. Lilburne also reopened the old quarrel between Cromwell and Manchester, although Vane and Cromwell, who had got rid of Manchester under the Self-Denying Ordinance, were very happy that he should rusticate in peace in the House of Lords. Lilburne now accused Manchester of having been a traitor and sympathizer with the Cavaliers during the campaign of 1644.

On 14 April 1646 Lilburne was arrested for having committed contempt of the House of Lords by his attack on Manchester. In prison he wrote and published another pamphlet in which he again denounced Manchester as a traitor, and wrote that 'His Lordship's Head hath stood, it seemes, too long upon his shoulders'. When he was brought before the House of Lords he refused to acknowledge their jurisdiction to try him, a commoner, and he appealed to the House of Commons. He refused to take off his hat in the House of Lords, or to keep quiet when he was told to stop speaking, and he put his fingers in his ears when the clerk read out the charge. The Lords sentenced him to be imprisoned in the Tower during the pleasure of the House, to be fined £2,000 and to be disqualified from holding any military or political office. He refused to return to the Tower and had to be dragged through the streets by force.

Lilburne the martyr, the former victim of the tyranny of the King and the bishops, now became the victim of the tyranny of the House of Lords and the Presbyterians. He wrote one pamphlet after another in the Tower, and smuggled them out to sympathizers who published them. In order to stop him from doing this, the House of Lords gave orders to the officers at the Tower that he was not to be allowed to receive visitors, and his wife was denied access to him. She rented a room in a house opposite his prison window and communicated with him by signs, but when the prison officers discovered this, they boarded up Lilburne's window. Lilburne pulled down the boards, and threatened to set fire to them if they were put up again, even if this were to set his room and the whole of the Tower on fire. He wrote at length about these attempts to prevent him from seeing his wife, and about all his other sufferings, in the pamphlets which he somehow still succeeded in writing and publishing.

At first he appealed from the tyranny of the House of Lords to the House of Commons. The House of Commons appointed a committee to investigate the case under the chairmanship of Henry Marten, the Independent and republican who had himself been imprisoned by the House in the days of Pym's ascendancy; but the Presbyterian majority in the House of Commons prevented the committee from taking any action to help Lilburne. Even the Independent MPs were not too eager to upset their strategy in their struggle against the Presbyterians in order to espouse the cause of Lilburne, whom they were beginning to regard as more of a liability than an asset to Independency.

As the House of Commons would not hear his appeal from the House of Lords, Lilburne appealed from Parliament to the people of England and to the army. When the struggle between Parliament and the army broke out in 1647, he added fuel to the flames by his pamphlets from the Tower, in which he appealed to His Excellency the Lord General Sir Thomas Fairfax and the officers and soldiers of the army. These pamphlets were circulated in the army by Lilburne's friends, who at this time were first called Levellers. Edward Sexby, a private soldier who was in touch with Lilburne's Levellers, organized committees of Agitators elected by the soldiers. The Agitators discussed

Lilburne's pamphlets and supported his ideas. The central theme of his doctrine was that the army must become the champion of the people against the tyranny of Parliament. While Prynne and the Presbyterians argued that the Civil War had been fought to defend the privileges of Parliament from the King's tyranny, and that these privileges were now threatened by the greater tyranny of the army, Lilburne turned the arguments of the Parliamentarians in 1642 against themselves: if, he argued, the army had been justified in resorting to armed force to defend English freedom against the King, how much more were they justified in resorting to a similar use of armed force to defend it against the tyranny of Parliament, as it was surely as justifiable to fight against Parliament as to fight against the King.

The Levellers and the Agitators, and Lilburne from prison, played a leading part in the events of the summer of 1647 which led to the expulsion of Waller and the other ten Presbyterian leaders from the House of Commons and the army's march on London. But though the release of Lilburne had been one of the demands of the Agitators, he remained in the Tower even after the army occupied London and Westminster on 6 August. Cromwell and Ireton were preparing for their showdown with the Levellers, and they did not wish to give their opponents the benefit of Lilburne's presence and leadership. In October, when the debates between the Grandees and the Levellers on the question of the Parliamentary franchise took place at Putney, the Levellers had to argue their case without Lilburne's assistance; but on 9 November, two days before the Putney debates ended, he was partially released on bail. The House of Commons ordered that he was to be permitted to leave the Tower during the daytime in order to prepare his arguments for the House of Commons committee which was considering his case, provided that he returned to his prison in the Tower every night. He used his liberty not only to prepare his case but also to build up a party organization of Levellers, and after two months, in January 1648, he was arrested on a new charge of sedition and confined once again, day and night, in the Tower by order of the House of Lords.

In May 1648 the Second Civil War broke out, and with the army away fighting the royalist rebels and the invading Scottish Covenanters, the Presbyterians in Parliament took charge again, recalling Waller and the expelled Presbyterian MPs and opening negotiations with the King. Lilburne obtained from the Presbyterians what he had been unable to obtain from Cromwell and the Independent Grandees of the army. On 2 August Parliament ordered that he be released from the Tower unconditionally, and that the fine imposed upon him be remitted. If this was an attempt to win his support against Cromwell, it was unsuccessful. The Levellers in the army were demanding that Charles Stuart be brought to trial for his treachery and for having planned the Second Civil War, and Lilburne associated himself with the demand. He opened negotiations with Ireton, who was directing the political campaign of the Army Grandees during Cromwell's absence at the siege of Pontefract.

During these negotiations in the autumn of 1648, Lilburne for the first and last time in his life was in a position to exercise a real influence on political events. He demanded that before the King was tried and executed, the Grandees should agree to accept the Leveller manifesto, *The Agreement of the People*, which Lilburne had drafted in the autumn of 1647. In it he demanded a complete redistribution of Parliamentary seats, and drew up a list of new constituencies, including many which were not given representation in Parliament until the Reform Bill of 1832. He also demanded a reform and simplification of the law to end its delays and complexities; that laws should be written in English, not in Latin or Norman French, and be available for all to read; and that the death penalty should be abolished for petty theft.

Lilburne was insistent that the Grandees should accept the *Agreement of the People* before they executed the King; otherwise the King's death would be seen as an arbitrary act of military government, not as an expression of the people's justice. Ireton said that they must overthrow the Presbyterian Parliament and deal with the King without delay, and that they could not afford to wait until they had reached agreement about the *Agreement of the People*. After the army marched on London and excluded the Presbyterian MPs in Pride's Purge, a number of meetings between the Grandees and the Levellers were held in Whitehall Palace in December 1648. Lilburne, who attended for the Levellers, complained bitterly of the bias shown by the chairman, Sir Hardress Waller, who interrupted Lilburne and the Leveller representatives and would not let them argue their case. Eventually Lilburne and the Levellers walked out in protest. Ironically enough, the final split came on the point on which the two sides appeared to be most in agreement—religious toleration. Lilburne demanded that a clause be inserted in the manifesto declaring that the state would not interfere with any man's religious worship or teaching. Ireton objected: he favoured freedom of conscience for the Protestant sectaries, but could not agree that the state should relinquish the right to interfere with religious practices which might endanger public peace and the safety of the state. He thought that religious toleration, carried to this extreme, would mean anarchy.

When Lilburne walked out of the Whitehall conference, he ended his career as a political leader; henceforth he could only resume his traditional and congenial role as a martyr. He left London for the north in order to deal with a dispute which had arisen in connection with his family estates in Durham, and did not return until after the King's death. There was nothing that he could have done to influence events if he had stayed in the south. The Grandees, not the Levellers, were to have the honour, or the shame, of executing the King, and Lilburne could neither have joined the Presbyterians in denouncing the execution nor have played any part in carrying it out.

As soon as he returned to London in February 1649, he attacked the new republican government in a number of pamphlets. He had been imprisoned by the King and by the Presbyterians, and now it was his turn to be imprisoned by Cromwell and the Grandees. He was, in the words of Lucy Hutchinson, the wife of Ireton's kinsman, Colonel Hutchinson, 'a turbulent spirited man that never was quiet in aniething'. Other contemporaries commented on the fact that he was always in opposition to those in power, and compared him to a rainbow that was never on the same side as the sun; people said 'that if John Lilburne were left alone on the earth, John would quarrel with Lilburne, and Lilburne with John'. On 28 March he was arrested, and was safely in the Tower when the Leveller mutiny in the army broke out and was crushed by Cromwell at Burford in May.

After the Levellers had been defeated, Lilburne was accused

of having incited the mutiny with his pamphlets and he was prosecuted for high treason against the republic. In his bitterness he wrote that he 'had rather chuse to live seven years under old King Charles his government (notwithstanding their beheading him as a Tyrant for it) when it was at the worst before this Parliament, then live one year under their present Government that now rule.' But his treatment in the Tower in 1649 was far more lenient than that which he had received in the Fleet under Charles I. When his wife and some of his children fell ill with smallpox, he was released on bail to be allowed to visit them, and was with his two sons when they died; and when he was put on trial for high treason, his judges treated him with great patience. After he had harangued the jury at the Guildhall with his usual vehemence, they returned a verdict of Not Guilty.

He was released from prison in October 1649 and for a time withdrew into private life. Cromwell treated him with the leniency which he usually showed to his political opponents, and re-established friendly personal relations with him, which were helped by the fact that Lilburne's brother Robert was one of Cromwell's most prominent colonels. But John Lilburne soon came into conflict with the government. He became involved in a private dispute with Sir Arthur Hazelrig, who had been one of the Five Members whom Charles I had tried to arrest in 1642, and was now one of the leading Independents and a member of the Council of State. Lilburne alleged that Hazelrig had used his authority as a member of the government to confiscate a colliery in Durham in which Lilburne's relatives had an interest, on the grounds that it was the property of a Royalist, and that Hazelrig had then taken a lease of the colliery from the government at a nominal rent. When Lilburne obtained no redress from Parliament, he published his accusations against Hazelrig in a pamphlet, and in January 1652 he was charged by the House of Commons with criminal libel. He was sentenced to a fine of £7,000 and banished from England on pain of death if he returned.

He first went to Amsterdam, and after travelling in the Netherlands settled in Bruges. Here he was in danger both from Roundheads and Cavaliers. The English government sent secret agents to spy on him. The Cavalier exiles refused to believe that he had really fallen out with Cromwell and thought that the sentence of banishment imposed by the Rump Parliament was a ruse to hide the fact that he had been sent abroad as an English agent; and as the Cavaliers considered him to be morally responsible for the death of Charles I, some of them planned to murder him in Bruges as they had murdered Dr Dorislaus and Ascham, the Commonwealth Ambassadors at The Hague and Madrid. But there was talk in the air of collaboration between Cavaliers and Levellers, if only because the Commonwealth authorities in England were accusing the Levellers of being in touch with Charles II. George Villiers, Duke of Buckingham (the son of the hated minister of Charles I), who was one of the closest and most profligate of Charles II's friends, entered into negotiations with Lilburne and had several talks with him. Lilburne became friendly with Sir Ralph Hopton, now Lord Hopton, who after the Civil War had gone into exile and lived in Bruges; but the more conventional Cavaliers, especially Edward Hyde, Charles II's chief political adviser, did not trust Lilburne, and refused to accept his offers of an alliance against the English government.

In April 1653 Cromwell turned out the Rump. When Lilburne heard the news, he returned to England, and was promptly arrested. Under the sentence imposed by the Rump in January 1652 he was liable to be executed if he returned from banishment; but he argued that the sentence was made void by the dissolution of the Rump. Cromwell had overthrown the Rump with the assistance of Major-General Harrison and the most extreme section of the Puritan sectaries in the army, and in the summer of 1653 he summoned his nominated Parliament—the 'Barebones Parliament'—which was the most radical Parliament that ever met under the Commonwealth; but it was not radical enough to repeal the sentence which the Rump Parliament had passed against Lilburne. On 13 July, nine days after the Barebones Parliament met, Lilburne was put on trial for his life at the Guildhall in London.

He could still command a great deal of sympathy in England, especially in London. His supporters thronged to the Guildhall to demonstrate in his favour, as they had done at his trial in 1649. The Levellers distributed leaflets containing the rhyme:

And what, shall then honest John Lilburne die!
Three-score thousand will know the reason why!

Lilburne's guilt was self-evident, as all that the prosecution needed to prove was that he had returned to England in defiance of the Rump's order; but once again, as had happened four years before, the jury stood by Lilburne, and returned a verdict of Not Guilty. Cromwell then ordered that Lilburne should be detained in prison indefinitely—as arbitrary an imprisonment as any that had been imposed by Charles I.

After being held in the Tower for eight months after his trial, Lilburne was transferred in March 1654 to Mont Orgueil in Jersey, where he remained until October 1655. He was then brought back to England and imprisoned in Dover Castle. But though Cromwell, beset by Cavalier and Leveller plots, thought it safer to have Lilburne in custody, Lilburne was no longer a danger to the government. For the first time in his life he did not spend his time in prison writing political propaganda and smuggling it out for his friends to publish. Instead, he turned to a new religion which was beginning to spread in England, and became a Quaker. The Quakers preached that God would continue to punish England by civil wars and unrest until Englishmen became better human beings, and believed that the individual should renounce the use of force, abandon politics, and concentrate on his personal purity and kindness. They were encountering a good deal of persecution from JPs who imprisoned them and put them in the stocks, and from mobs who assaulted them and wrecked their meeting-houses; but Lilburne was attracted by the religion of this new, introspective sect. He corresponded with the Quakers from Dover Castle and embraced their doctrines.

In the spring of 1656 he was given a degree of liberty, being allowed to leave the castle during the daytime to visit his wife and children, who had settled in Dover. Later he was given leave of absence for longer periods and was permitted to stay away from prison for several days at a time. On these occasions he often visited the Quaker settlements in Kent, and sometimes preached in their meeting-houses. In May 1656 he published the last of his eighty-three pamphlets, *The Resurrection of John Lilburne now a Prisoner in Dover Castle*, in which he proclaimed himself a Quaker. 'I confidently now believe,' he wrote, 'I shall never hereafter be an user of a temporall sword more, nor a joyner with those that so do.'

In the summer of 1657 he was given leave of absence from

prison because his wife was expecting her tenth child. He visited her at Eltham, but fell ill of a fever and died there on 29 August, the day on which he was to have returned to captivity at Dover Castle. He was only forty-two. During the last twenty years of his life, he had spent more than twelve years in prison.

8

Edward Sexby

No two men could have been more different than the two Leveller leaders, John Lilburne and Edward Sexby. Lilburne, a gentleman by birth, a martyr by temperament, high-principled in politics, spending most of his adult life in prison, his pamphlets burning with indignation at his own sufferings and at the injustices inflicted on the people, ending his days as a Quaker pacifist; Sexby, low-class by birth, an adventurer by temperament, unscrupulous in politics, always avoiding arrest until the final capture, his pamphlets gay, laughing in the face of danger, ending as an assassin employed by the Cavaliers.

Sexby's place and date of birth and parentage are unknown, but he was born somewhere in Suffolk, probably about the year 1615, and he was not a gentleman by birth. By 1643 he had enlisted in the Roundhead army, serving in Cromwell's regiment in East Anglia. He served under Cromwell throughout the Civil War, though by the end of the fighting in 1646 he had been transferred to Fairfax's regiment. He ended the war as he had begun it, as a private soldier, which is surprising in view of the energy and ability which he afterwards showed. His failure to become an officer may be partly explained by his low birth, but this would not have been an insuperable obstacle in Cromwell's regiment, and his lack of religious zeal was perhaps a more serious drawback. He was a man of too practical a turn of mind to be the type of 'godly' soldier who leapt into the pulpit and preached to the congregation in church on the spur of the moment. Unlike almost all the other Roundheads, he never referred to the Lord or the will of God in the letters in which he discussed his political tactics.

Like many other soldiers in the army, he was greatly influenced by Lilburne's pamphlets, and he often visited Lilburne in the

Tower in 1646 and 1647. He was almost certainly responsible for smuggling Lilburne's pamphlets out of the prison and for arranging for them to be printed and distributed. He organized Leveller meetings among the soldiers, and created a Leveller organization in the army. When the dispute between Parliament and the army broke out in March 1647, Sexby succeeded in persuading the majority of the soldiers to accept the Leveller doctrine that the army, having fought for the freedom of the people against the tyranny of the King, should now fight for this freedom against the tyranny of Parliament.

He built on the resentment of the private soldiers at the refusal of Parliament to settle their arrears of pay, and on their reluctance to enlist for service in Ireland. Nearly all English Protestants, Cavaliers as well as Roundheads, hated the Catholic Irish and were determined to reconquer Ireland and avenge the real and alleged cruelties which the Irish Catholics had committed against the English and Scottish Protestant settlers during the insurrection of 1641. But Sexby and the Levellers believed that the army should be employed, not in robbing the Irish people of their freedom, but in winning freedom for the common people in England. Sexby organized soldiers' councils, very like the soldiers' soviets which the revolutionaries formed in the Russian army in 1917. He arranged for each regiment in the army in the south to elect a number of private soldiers to the Regimental Committee, and each Regimental Committee elected two delegates to the Army Council of Agitators. He himself became the leading spokesman on the Council of Agitators.

Having created the soldiers' committees in the army in the south, Sexby wrote to his contacts in the army in the north and urged them to create similar committees there. He was so successful that the soldiers in Yorkshire not only elected Regimental Committees and a Council of Agitators, but also arrested their Commander-in-Chief, the Presbyterian General Poyntz, accusing him of treason in seeking to provoke a new civil war between Parliament and the army. They sent Poyntz as a prisoner to Fairfax's headquarters at Uxbridge. Fairfax, who was shocked at this act of indiscipline, released Poyntz at once.

During the summer of 1647 it was Sexby who forced the reluctant Cromwell to stand firm against the efforts of the Presbyterians in Parliament to force the army to submit to

Parliamentary authority. It was probably Sexby and the Council of Agitators who ordered Cornet Joyce, with Cromwell's knowledge and consent, to seize the King at Holmby House and remove him from the control of Parliament to army headquarters at Newmarket. But having got the King into their hands, Cromwell and Ireton entered into secret negotiations with him, hoping to gain his support for the overthrow of Presbyterianism and the establishment of a constitutional monarchy with the Anglican Church of England as the state religion and religious toleration for the Independent sects. When Sexby heard of these negotiations, he denounced Cromwell and Ireton at a meeting of the Council of Agitators, and demanded an end to any attempt to compromise with the King. Sexby and the Agitators were chiefly responsible for the march on London and the expulsion of the eleven Presbyterian leaders from the House of Commons in August 1647.

At the end of October the debates between the army Grandees and the Levellers were held in the parish church at Putney. The Levellers demanded that the vote at Parliamentary elections should be granted to every man except servants and other wage-earners, which would have given the vote to the tenant-farmers and small independent craftsmen who formed the majority of the rank-and-file of the army. Ireton maintained that the vote should be limited, as it had always been in the past, to landowners who held land to the value of forty shillings a year. Most of the participants in the debates were very muddled, and did not show the clarity of thought and capacity for logical argument which are to be found in the theological disputations of the sixteenth century, in the arguments of barristers in the law courts, and in the political arguments of Liberal Parliamentarians and Marxist theoreticians in later ages. Many of the speakers were almost incomprehensible, with their vague appeals to the spirit of God for guidance.

The Levellers found one officer who championed their cause— Colonel Rainsborough, a former seaman who, after joining the Roundhead navy at the start of the Civil War, had transferred to the land forces and distinguished himself in all Cromwell's campaigns. They were also helped by John Wildman, a young barrister of twenty-four, who was a leading supporter of the Levellers and had drafted several of their manifestos; he came to

Putney to argue for them in the absence of Lilburne, who was still in prison in the Tower three months after the army had occupied London and Westminster.

Sexby opened the discussion for the Levellers, and throughout the thirteen days of the Putney debates put their case more simply and vigorously than any of his colleagues. Whereas Rainsborough argued on general principles—'I think that the poorest hee that is in England hath a life to live as the greatest hee'—Sexby maintained simply that the common soldiers had not fought for the Roundheads in order to win freedom for everyone except themselves, and demanded the right to participate in deciding the government of their country. 'Wee have engaged in this Kingdome and ventur'd our lives,' he said at Putney, 'and itt was all for this: to recover our birthrights and priviledges as Englishmen, and by the arguments urged [by Ireton and the Grandees] there is none. I wonder wee were soe much deceived.'

For some reason which is far from clear, Sexby did not go with his regiment to serve under Fairfax in Kent and Essex when the Second Civil War broke out in May 1648. He was in London in August when Lilburne was released by the Presbyterians, perhaps in the hope that he would support them against his former ally Cromwell, who had left him in the lurch to rot in the Tower for a year after taking over the control of affairs in London. Instead Lilburne wrote to Cromwell, who was campaigning against the Scots, and sent Sexby to carry the letter to him. Lilburne wrote that though he had good reason to resent the way in which Cromwell had treated him, he would not kick Cromwell when he was down, but would support him and the Independents against Presbyterian persecution. Sexby found Cromwell immediately after his great victory at Preston. Cromwell told Sexby that he was very grateful to Lilburne and sent Sexby back to London carrying Cromwell's report of his victory over the Scots to the Speaker of the House of Commons. On receiving the news, Parliament, as was customary in such cases, voted Sexby £100 as a reward for bringing the good news.

This mark of favour from Cromwell and the Presbyterian Parliament may have played its part in winning over Sexby, but there are other possible explanations of why he cooled towards the Levellers in the autumn of 1648. In the previous year the Levellers had demanded justice against the King and had urged the hesitant Grandees to break with him; but now it was the champion of the Grandees, Ireton, who was insisting on taking immediate steps to bring Charles Stuart to justice, while Lilburne and the Levellers were arguing about a future constitution and maintaining that the army had no right to proceed with the trial and execution of the King, as this could only properly be done by a people's Parliament. Lilburne's theoretical and principled attitude about the King's trial was not likely to appeal to an activist like Sexby, and as Ireton and Cromwell were now prepared to agree to the Levellers' original demand that all men except wage-earners should be entitled to vote at Parliamentary elections, Sexby may have become impatient with Lilburne's opposition to the Grandees.

He played no part in the Leveller agitation and in the army mutinies in the spring of 1649, but was entrusted with a duty which must have been congenial to a man of his vigorous temperament. When the Scottish Covenanters denounced the execution of Charles I and the proclamation of the English republic and proclaimed Charles II as King, the new republican Council of State sent Sexby to arrest the Scottish Commissioners in London. Next year when Cromwell, on his return from Ireland, led the army into Scotland against Charles II and the Covenanters, Sexby went with him, with the rank of Lieutenant-Colonel.

He fought at Dunbar, and in the spring of 1651 played a leading part in the siege and capture of Tantallon Castle near North Berwick. But his new career as a Grandee came to a sudden halt. While he was in Scotland, he was court-martialled on a charge of withholding his soldiers' pay. It was quite a common practice for army officers to embezzle the money that they had received for their men's pay. In Sexby's case, he had not intended to appropriate the money for his personal use, but he had refused to pay six of his soldiers the arrears that were due to them until they had agreed to re-enlist for a further period of service. This was an irregularity and an arbitrary act of injustice which Cromwell would not tolerate in his army, and though Sexby protested that he had not intended to benefit himself but only to further the public interest, he was sentenced to be cashiered.

Despite this disgrace, Cromwell decided to make use of his abilities and keep him busy by sending him on a mission to France, where the Wars of the Fronde were in progress. The English government, finding that all the Kings and governments of Europe were united against the regicide republic, hoped to make an alliance with the rebel Frondeurs which would embarrass the King of France and perhaps be the first step towards the unification of all the revolutionary movements throughout Europe. In the autumn of 1651 Cromwell sent Sexby to visit the Prince de Conti, the brother of the Prince de Condé, the leader of the Frondeurs. Sexby offered Conti an English alliance, and urged him to adopt a republican constitution for France based on Lilburne's *Agreement of the People*, which had contained the Levellers' proposals for a Parliament elected by popular suffrage. He would have had a better chance of a favourable reception a few years earlier, when the Fronde, in its early days, was led by middle-class bourgeois and popular leaders; by 1651 the 'Fronde of the Princes' had replaced the first Fronde, and the leadership of the revolt had passed to aristocrats like Condé, who had no intention of proclaiming a republic. Sexby went to the south of France to contact the Frondeurs there, but when he was in Bordeaux the authorities ordered him to be arrested. He was warned in time, and escaped by climbing over the wall of the town during the night.

By the time that Sexby returned to England in August 1653, Cromwell had dispersed the Rump, and in December, after he had dissolved the Barebones Parliament, he was proclaimed as Lord Protector. He had thus antagonized both the republicans of the Rump and the Puritan 'Saints' like Harrison who had helped him drive out the Rump. Sexby, too, was indignant at Cromwell's actions. Cromwell had ordered that Sexby's old colleague, Lilburne, should be detained in prison after the jury had acquitted him at his trial. His other Leveller colleague, Wildman, who was much closer to him than Lilburne, was also arrested. Sexby may also have been annoyed by the difficulties which he had encountered in getting Cromwell's Council to pay him his remuneration and expenses for his mission to France. In May 1654 he reminded the Council that though he had received £1,000 for his first year in France, he had still not received a further £1,411 13s 4d which was owing to him for the second year that he and his agents had spent there. He assured the Council that although the sum might seem very large, the cost of living in France was so high that no one could live there on less than £200 a year; but the Council insisted that he was entitled to £430 less than he claimed.

But the real reason why he turned against Cromwell was probably a combination of resentment at the setbacks to his personal career and his disapproval of Cromwell's persistent suppression of the Levellers. By the beginning of 1655 he was working to create a united front of Levellers and Cavaliers against Cromwell. A section of the Cavaliers, led by the Duke of Buckingham, had put forward such a proposal to Lilburne in 1652; but Buckingham's plan had a much better chance of success now that the opportunist Sexby, and not the high-principled Lilburne, was handling the negotiations, and at a time when opposition to Cromwell as Lord Protector was so widespread in England. Sexby travelled all over the south of England, distributing leaflets denouncing Cromwell and making secret contacts with Cavaliers, Presbyterians and Republicans of the Rump. He met Lord Grey at Coventry, Hazelrig at Wood-stock, and other sympathizers at Bristol, Alton, Deal and Rotherhithe.

Cromwell's men searched everywhere for Sexby. They finally tracked him to a house in the village of Hartley Row in Hamp-shire, but he was warned and left the house a few minutes before the officers came for him, though his servant was captured with a portmanteau containing Sexby's clothes and documents. Sexby made his way into Sussex, where he contacted some friends of the Cavalier exile, George Goring, Earl of Norwich. They smuggled him on to a ship which took him to Flanders.

In Brussels he got in touch with the Spanish Governor of the Netherlands, Count Fuensaldanha. Before he left England he had contrived to get hold of Cromwell's plans for a naval campaign in the West Indies against the Spanish colonies of San Domingo and Jamaica, and he revealed all the details of the plan to Fuen-saldanha. He suggested to Fuensaldanha that the Spanish govern-ment should finance the projects of the Cavaliers and Levellers for insurrections in England and the assassination of Cromwell. Fuensaldanha sent him on to Madrid, where he was well received by the Spanish government, who placed one of the royal coaches at his disposal during his six weeks' stay, but were cautious about committing themselves to helping him with either troops or money.

On returning to the Netherlands, he took up residence in Bruges, and made contact with many of the exiled Cavaliers who frequented Charles II's court there. He not only drank the King's health in their company, but offered to place the Leveller and republican movement in England at their disposal without telling the Levellers and the republicans what he was doing. He offered to start a revolution in England if the Spanish government would send him 1,500 horsemen, but explained: 'I do declare that I shall not be able to effect that which is desired, except that those of the King's party shall endeavour that no mention be made of the King, before such time Cromwell be destroyed, and till then the Royalists that shall take up arms must speak of nothing but of the liberty of the country.' Charles II's Lord Chancellor, Hyde, was very sceptical about accepting Sexby's offers. He doubted whether Sexby would be able to do what he claimed, and was opposed to making any political concessions to Sexby and the Levellers, as this would mean 'lessening the power of the Crown and devolving an absurd power to the people'. He warned the Cavaliers that Sexby and the Levellers wished to overthrow Cromwell only in order to establish a republic, not to restore the King to the throne.

In Brussels Sexby met Colonel Titus, who had fought for the Roundheads in the Civil War and had been sent to the Netherlands by Cromwell to spy on the Cavalier exiles there. Titus became a double-agent and betrayed Cromwell's plans to the Cavaliers. Sexby collaborated with Titus in writing a short book, *Killing No Murder*, in which they justified the assassination of Cromwell. The book was written under the pseudonym William Allen and smuggled into England.

It was an entertaining and impertinent piece of bravado. It was dedicated 'To his Highnesse, Oliver Cromwell', and began by inviting Cromwell to commit suicide. 'To your Highnes justly belongs the honour of dying for the people, and it cannot choose but be an unspeakable consolation to you in the last moments of your life, to consider, with how much benefit to the world you are like to leave it. 'Tis then onely (my Lord) the titles you now usurpe will be truly yours, you will then be indeed the deliverer of your Countrey, & free it from a Bondage little inferiour to that from which Moses delivered his . . . All this we hope from your Highnes happie extirpation, who are the true Father of your Countrie for while you live we can call nothing ours, and it is from your death that we hope for our inheritances . . . May it please your Highnesse, Your Highnesse present Slave and Vassall, W.A.'

The book argued, with references to Biblical examples and the arguments of the classical writers of antiquity, that tyrannicide was justified, and claimed that Cromwell had all the character-istics of a tyrant: he ruled by means of the army; he surrounded himself with armed guards and secret agents; and he involved his people in foreign wars in order to prevent them from making a revolution at home, because this was Sexby's only explanation of Cromwell's decision to wage war against Spain. Sexby rejected the view that it would be wrong to murder Cromwell sur-reptitiously. 'Some I find of a strange opinion, that it were a generous and a noble action to kill his Highnes in the field; but to doe it privately they think it unlawfull, but know not why. As if it were not generous to apprehend a thief till his sword were drawn and he in a posture to defend himself and kill me.'

Sexby, as a former Cromwellian soldier, called on Cromwell's army to play the leading part in assassinating him and over-throwing his government. 'To us particularly it belongs to bring this Monster to justice, whom he hath made the instruments of his Villany, and sharers in the Curse and Detestation that is due to himself from all good men. Others only have their Liberty to vindicate, we our Liberty and our honour.' Only by ridding England of Cromwell could they atone for having brought him to power. 'And if we doe not, all mankinde will repute us Approvers of all the Villanyes he hath done.'

Sexby's first plan to assassinate Cromwell was for a former soldier in the Roundhead army, the Leveller Miles Sindercombe, to shoot him from a window of a nearby house at the State Opening of Parliament in September 1656 as Cromwell walked from Westminster Abbey to the House of Commons after attending the preliminary sermon in the Abbey. But as the Lord Protector came out into the street, he was surrounded by the people, and Sindercombe could not get him in the sights of his musket; so Cromwell went on to open Parliament in a speech in which he denounced Sexby as a great enemy of the Commonwealth, 'a wretched creature, an apostate from religion and all honesty'.

Sexby organized another attempt in the following January. He paid another soldier, Toop, £1,500 to shoot Cromwell from the window of a house in Hammersmith adjoining the highway along which Cromwell would pass on his journey from Whitehall to Hampton Court. At the last moment Cromwell changed his plans and went to Hampton Court by barge. Toop then planned to shoot Cromwell when he was walking in Hyde Park; but this also failed. Toop's next plan was to set fire to Whitehall Palace during the night when Cromwell was sleeping there; but he was caught in the act and arrested, and Sindercombe and the other conspirators were also arrested. Sindercombe committed suicide in prison, and the others were executed.

In view of the failure of these attempts and the arrest of all his agents, Sexby travelled secretly to England in June 1657 in order to build up a new organization of assassins. He disguised himself in working men's clothes and allowed his beard to grow. After six weeks in England he decided to return to the Netherlands. On 24 July he went on board a ship in the port of London; but a few hours before he was due to sail the authorities searched the ship, and he was recognized and arrested. He was brought before Cromwell and the Council, but Cromwell hardly spoke a word to him before committing him to the Tower. When he was interrogated in prison, he admitted that he was the author of *Killing No Murder* and of the assassination plots against Cromwell, but refused to name any of his accomplices. He had not been brought to trial when he died a natural death, from some form of fever, on 13 January 1658. His hated enemy and intended victim, Cromwell, survived him by less than eight months.

9

Robert Blake

Robert Blake was one of the most versatile and remarkable of the Roundhead leaders. As a young man his ambition was to be an academic scholar; but circumstances turned him first into a successful business man, then into a dogged and heroic soldier, and finally, after he had gone to sea for the first time at the age of fifty, into the second greatest admiral in British naval history. During his lifetime he was a revolutionary republican, but in the three centuries after his death he came to be regarded as second only to the High Tory, Nelson, in the estimation of the officers of the Royal Navy.

He was born in Bridgwater in the late summer of 1599. His father had been a gentleman owning a little land at Bishop's Lydiard, near Taunton, but he had moved to Bridgwater and become a trader, shipping goods from Somerset to the Netherlands. He not only built up a prosperous shipping business, but also acquired much more land in the neighbouring Somerset countryside. Robert Blake, who was the eldest of his fifteen children, was brought up as a typical West Country Puritan, and at the age of sixteen went to St Alban's Hall at Oxford. In 1617 a new college, Wadham, was founded for the benefit of West Country students, and Blake transferred to Wadham.

He stayed at Oxford for ten years, much longer than the ordinary student. He obviously had a liking for academic life, and though he failed to gain a fellowship at Wadham, this is said to have been only because he was so short—no more than five feet six inches in height—whereas the Master of Wadham wished to have tall, impressive-looking fellows. Blake learned to be fluent in Latin. He developed strong Puritan principles, and during the last years of James I's reign expressed stronger opinions against the King than most of his contemporaries would have dared. Some of his acquaintances at Oxford described him as being truculent, and others as sullen and morose; but he could nevertheless be a convivial companion, and enjoyed taking part in sports.

In 1625 his father died, and he returned to Bridgwater to manage the family business. He did this successfully for the next fifteen years. Although it has often been said that the future admiral did not sail in a ship until he was aged fifty, this is on the whole unlikely, because it was not unusual for shipowners to travel in their ships on occasions, and there is reason to believe that he travelled to Holland and spent some years at Schiedam, perhaps running the Dutch end of the business; but he was a business man, not a sailor, and undoubtedly spent most of his time in his premises in Bridgwater.

In the spring of 1640 Blake was elected to the Short Parliament as MP for Bridgwater; but his Parliamentary career lasted only three weeks, and he was one of the few Puritans of the Country Party to lose his seat in the general election for the Long Parliament in the autumn. When the Civil War began, he immediately enlisted and raised a troop for the Roundheads. In the spring of 1643 the Cavaliers under Sir Ralph Hopton and Sir Bevill Grenville drove the Roundheads before them from Cornwall to Wiltshire, winning the whole of the south-west for the King. In July Waller was defeated at Roundway Down, and Prince Rupert, coming south from Oxford, linked up with the Cornish Cavaliers and besieged Bristol.

Blake commanded a company under the Parliamentary commander, Colonel Nathaniel Fiennes, at Bristol. Fiennes refused Rupert's first demand for surrender, but after the town had been heavily bombarded and the Cavaliers had captured part of it by storm, he agreed to capitulate. He could consider himself lucky that Rupert consented to treat, because it was accepted under the rules of war that if a demand for the surrender of a town was refused, and the besieging army had to lose men in taking it by storm, they were entitled to refuse quarter to the besieged garrison and to sack the town. Blake was defending one of the outlying forts at Bristol, and after Fiennes had surrendered he refused to yield his fort but continued fighting for another day, claiming that he had not been officially informed by Fiennes about the capitulation. Rupert is said to have ordered that Blake be hanged for breaking the terms of the surrender, but was persuaded to countermand the order, and Blake was allowed to go free with the other Roundhead soldiers under the terms of the capitulation.

On the south coast Lyme Regis held out for Parliament, and Blake was appointed to command the garrison there. In April 1644 Prince Rupert's brother, Prince Maurice, besieged Lyme Regis, occupying the cliffs which surround the town on three sides; but as the Roundhead navy had complete control of the seas, Maurice could not prevent the Parliament's admiral, the Earl of Warwick, from sending ships to revictual Lyme Regis by sea. Everyone assumed that the little town, with its population of 3,000 and the 500 soldiers of the garrison, would soon fall; but Blake thought otherwise.

Maurice's first attempt to take Lyme by storm was repulsed, and though Blake used up nearly all his ammunition in defeating the attack, Warwick's ships brought in new stores. By the middle of May, when the siege had lasted for a month, Maurice at last succeeded in bringing up a cannon to the top of the cliffs and began a heavy bombardment of the town which caused great destruction; but thanks chiefly to Blake's determination, the defenders held out, and when the Cavaliers captured parts of the town and even the harbour in several attacks, Blake's men drove them out again after hand-to-hand fighting. At the beginning of June the Earl of Essex marched from Oxfordshire into Dorset, and defying the orders of the Committee of Both Kingdoms to turn back and go to Waller's assistance in the Midlands, pressed on to relieve Lyme. On 14 June, when Lyme had only a few days' rations left, Maurice raised the siege and withdrew before Essex arrived. Blake had saved Lyme Regis.

After relieving Lyme, Essex marched on into Cornwall, pursued by the King's army, and in September surrendered his army to Charles at Lostwithiel. The south-west was once again in the hands of the Cavaliers. But Blake, who had remained at Lyme, carried out a daring stroke in July 1644. Hearing that the important communications centre of Taunton was held by a weak Cavalier garrison, he marched from Lyme and captured Taunton without difficulty. He then proceeded to hold the town for a year in the heart of Cavalier territory, surviving three sieges. His position at Taunton was much more precarious than at Lyme, because as Taunton was an inland town it could not be replenished by sea, and there was no immediate prospect of any Roundhead force being sent to relieve it. The greatest danger was during the second siege by a Cavalier force under Lord Hopton, which began in March 1645. Blake built strong defences and street barricades, and removed the thatch from the roofs of many houses in order to provide fodder for his horses.

At the beginning of May, Hopton heard that a Parliamentary army under Fairfax was heading for the west, and decided to take Taunton by storm. After three days of fierce street fighting, he drove Blake's men into a small area around the church and the castle, but here the defenders held out. Hopton summoned Blake to surrender, and said that if resistance continued he would give no quarter and would kill all except seven of the garrison. Blake replied that if Hopton would give him the names of the seven men whom he would spare, he would send out their corpses to Hopton immediately. Meanwhile Fairfax at Blandford had received orders from the Committee of Both Kingdoms to march at once to the Midlands; but before setting out on the campaign which led to the decisive victory at Naseby, he detached a small force to go to the relief of Taunton. Hopton, whose intelligence was completely faulty, at first ignored the approach of the relieving troops, and then beat a hasty retreat from Taunton, believing that the advancing Roundhead force was much stronger than it really was.

Blake's defence of Lyme and Taunton had made him a popular hero in the west, and in the by-elections that took place in 1646 he was elected as MP for Bridgwater. But he played no part in the political struggles of 1647 or in the Second Civil War, and seems to have adopted a neutral attitude in the contest between the Presbyterians and the Independents. In religion he was a Presbyterian, perhaps because, like Sir William Waller, his sense of military discipline made him suspicious of religious toleration; but he had always favoured the idea of republicanism and could have had no sympathy with the Presbyterians' policy of alliance with the King. He survived Pride's Purge in December 1648, and was one of the thirty Presbyterian and neutral MPs who were allowed to remain with the fifty Independents in the purged House of Commons; and he did not withdraw in protest like most of these other thirty MPs. He therefore remained as a member of the Rump, more because of the actions of others than because of his own decision.

A month after the execution of Charles I and the proclamation of the republic, Blake was given the task of reorganizing the navy with two colleagues, Popham and Richard Deane, who had been one of the judges who had condemned Charles I. Traditionally the navy was under the supreme command of the Lord High Admiral. Fortunately for the Parliament, the Lord High Admiral in 1642 had been the devout Puritan, the Earl of Warwick, who had brought the whole of the fleet into the service of Parliament; but Warwick was a Presbyterian, and after the army took control in 1647 he resigned. This was one of the factors which had caused the navy to mutiny during the Second Civil War. After the establishment of the Republic, the Council of State abolished the office of Lord High Admiral and placed the Admiralty in commission, with Popham, Deane and Blake as the Commissioners. The Commissioners improved the efficiency of the navy, and drafted a code of discipline which prescribed capital punishment and flogging for only a very few offences, and was far more humane than the discipline afterwards imposed under Charles II and throughout the eighteenth century.

In May 1649 Blake sailed with a fleet to Kinsale on the south coast of Ireland, where Prince Rupert had proclaimed King Charles II and had assembled a fleet with which he hoped to plunder the Republic's shipping and to help the land operations of the Cavaliers against Cromwell in Ireland. Blake blockaded Rupert's ships in Kinsale Harbour. He had five ships against Rupert's eight and did not risk sailing into the inlet and fighting Rupert when he could effectively prevent Rupert from doing any damage simply by maintaining the blockade until Cromwell's land army, which was marching south-west from Dublin, arrived to destroy Rupert from the land side. But Blake's ships were scattered by a storm in October 1649, and Rupert slipped out of Kinsale and sailed south. He reached Lisbon, and the King of Portugal welcomed him and granted shelter to his ships in the Tagus.

The execution of Charles I had aroused great indignation among foreign sovereigns, none of whom had granted diplomatic recognition to the English republic. The Tsar of Russia expelled all the English merchants from his empire. In Holland, where the Protestant Republic was in fact governed as a hereditary Kingdom by the Stadholder, William of Orange, Charles II was welcomed as King of England and the government expressed their horror at the execution of Charles I. In May 1649 Dr Dorislaus, a Dutch lawyer who had lived for many years in England and had drafted the indictment for Charles I's trial, was received at The Hague as an envoy from the English republic; but two days after his arrival he was assassinated at his dinner table by a band of English Cavalier exiles, and though the Dutch government sent an apology to the English government, they made no effort to catch and punish the murderers. In France Cardinal Mazarin's government authorized French privateers to attack English shipping. Spain and Portugal were equally hostile, and only some of the cantons of Switzerland were friendly to England.

During the next few years, it became the function of Blake and his sailors to show the monarchs of Europe that the regicide republic could hit back hard and that the foreigners would suffer if they supported Charles Stuart. Blake gave his first demonstration of power at Lisbon, where he anchored outside the harbour which Rupert's ships had entered. The King of Portugal refused Blake's demand that Rupert be expelled. When some of Blake's sailors, going ashore in Lisbon on a few hours' leave, were murdered by Rupert's men, the Portuguese authorities did not arrest the murderers. Rupert, who had always been interested in mechanical gadgets, made an explosive device very like a modern torpedo, and sent an agent to carry it on board Blake's ship, pretending that it was some kind of gift. The agent was arrested and the plot failed, but the King of Portugal refused Blake's demands for the punishment of the guilty men.

Blake retaliated by blockading Lisbon. He remained there all the summer, seizing Portuguese ships. In September 1650 the Portuguese treasure fleet returned to Lisbon from Brazil; Blake plundered it. Rupert then proposed to the indignant King of Portugal that he and his Cavaliers should lead a joint attack of the Portuguese and Cavalier fleets on Blake's ships. The King of Portugal agreed, but though Blake's ships were outnumbered, they did so much damage to their attackers that Rupert and his men sailed away to Gibraltar, and the King of Portugal hastened to enter into diplomatic negotiations with England and offer an alliance to the republic.

Blake followed Rupert into the Mediterranean. After he had destroyed six of Rupert's ships off Cartagena, Rupert took refuge in Toulon, where the authorities, complying with Mazarin's policy, gave him asylum. Blake then plundered French vessels in the Mediterranean. Soon afterwards Mazarin prohibited French privateers from attacking English shipping, and Rupert sailed out of Toulon and made for the Azores, eventually reaching the West Indies, after a voyage in which his flagship was sunk and his brother Maurice was drowned.

Blake had meanwhile returned to England to patrol the coast in order to prevent any foreign government from sending an army to help Charles II in the campaign which culminated at Worcester. He next destroyed the Cavalier bases in the Scilly Isles and the Channel Islands, from which the Cavaliers were operating as privateers against the Commonwealth shipping.

Relations between England and Holland had deteriorated since 1649. The English government, despite their resentment at the Dutch connivance at the murder of Dr Dorislaus and their support for Charles II, had made every effort to bring about a reconciliation between the two Protestant states; but when the Dutch rejected their advances, the Rump Parliament passed the Navigation Act which enacted that only goods which had been carried in English ships could be imported into England. This was a heavy blow to Dutch commerce. In May 1652 the Dutch sent their famous admiral, Tromp, to make a demonstration of strength with a powerful fleet off the English coast. Tromp was one of the greatest naval commanders of the age and he knew these waters well, for in 1639, during the Thirty Years War, he had destroyed the Spanish fleet in English territorial waters off Deal. His orders now were to protect Dutch merchant shipping in the Channel and to refuse to salute the English flag, a gesture of respect which had traditionally been paid by all foreign ships to English ships in the Channel.

After sailing up to the entrance of Dover harbour and refusing to salute the English flag there, Tromp encountered Blake's fleet in the Channel. When he refused the salute, Blake fired a musket shot across his bows, and Tromp replied by opening fire with his cannon on the English fleet. In the battle which followed, Blake was victorious, and Tromp retired with heavy losses. Two months later, war was officially declared between England and Holland.

Blake followed up his victory over his famous adversary by entering into a running battle with him which ended when Tromp's fleet was shattered by a gale between the Orkneys and the Shetlands. He then won a victory over another Dutch admiral, Cornelius de With, off the Kentish Knock near the North Foreland, on 28 September. Blake lost the next round. On 30 November he was lying off Dungeness when Tromp appeared with a large fleet and prepared to blockade him. Blake had some forty ships against Tromp's eighty, but though twenty of his captains turned tail and fled, leaving him outnumbered by four to one, he decided to break out and attack Tromp at once. This was undoubtedly the wisest course to pursue, but Blake lost five of his twenty-two ships in the battle, and was lucky to escape under cover of fog and darkness. He had his revenge within three months. On 18 February 1653 Tromp attacked the English fleet, commanded by Blake and Deane, off Portland; but though the English were greatly outnumbered, reinforcements under Admiral William Penn (the father of William Penn, the founder of Pennsylvania) arrived in the middle of the action. In a three-day battle which began at Portland and ended off Cape Gris-Nez, Blake and his colleagues destroyed the Dutch fleet, although Tromp, by a skilful manoeuvre, escaped with a few of his ships to the shelter of the Dutch ports.

On the first day of the battle Blake had been wounded by a musket ball which tore Deane's breeches before lodging in Blake's thigh. The wound proved to be serious, and as soon as the battle was over, Blake was put ashore at Portsmouth. He was still convalescing when Cromwell dispersed the Rump in April. Blake was critical of Cromwell's action. As a stalwart republican, he was a supporter of the Rump and suspicious of a dictator, and events had caused him to be deeply committed to the war with Holland, which Cromwell opposed because he deplored hostilities between two Protestant states.

A few days after the dissolution of the Rump, Blake's two fellow-Commissioners at the Admiralty, Deane and Monck, issued a declaration of support for Cromwell's assumption of power; but Blake preserved a conspicuous silence. Cromwell nevertheless retained Blake in his office. As Blake was still suffering from his wound he did not sail with Deane and Monck to the coast of Flanders; but on 2 June 1653, when he was inspecting the fleet in the Thames, news came from Deane and Monck that they were in action against the enemy ships and needed reinforcements. Blake could not resist the temptation of sailing himself with the relieving fleet, and arrived in time to take part in the final stages of the battle off Nieuport. Deane had been killed early in the battle, but Monck had taken command and had won a great victory.

After staying for a month with the fleet which was blockading Holland and starving the Dutch into surrender, Blake fell seriously ill, and returned to England before the final battle of the war on 31 July, in which Tromp was killed and the Dutch suffered yet another defeat. By the following spring, the Dutch had agreed to Cromwell's terms and made peace. In England, Blake reconciled himself to Cromwell's régime, though republicans of the Rump, like Ludlow, spread rumours that Cromwell was both jealous and suspicious of Blake. In Cromwell's first elected Parliament in 1654, Blake was elected as MP for Bridgwater; but in October 1654 he went to sea again, though he had not fully recovered from the effect of his wound and was in poor health for the rest of his life.

Blake spent a year in the Mediterranean and off the coasts of Spain. His presence off Leghorn was enough to persuade the Grand-Duke of Tuscany to request the English Cavalier exiles to leave his territories. Blake also kept a watchful eye on the Spanish fleet, as Cromwell was on the point of going to war with Spain and sending an expedition to the West Indies; but Blake was careful to avoid beginning hostilities against the Spanish ships.

His most important action in the Mediterranean was to take firm measures against the Turkish pirates of North Africa, who for many years had been raiding the shipping of the European powers and carrying off their crews as slaves. During the reign of Charles I, when the English navy fell into disrepute, they had sometimes ventured as far as the coast of Sussex. Blake believed that they should be taught a lesson. When the Bey of Tunis refused to release his Christian prisoners and to promise to stop his piracy, Blake bombarded the Tunisian forts at Porto Farina in April 1655. He had no difficulty, a few months later, in persuading the Dey of Algiers to accept the same demands.

Blake's successes at sea not only raised the prestige of Cromwell's government abroad, but also won the support of many Englishmen who, though they hated their government, had a national pride in Blake's victories over the foreigners. Stories were told about him which were designed to show that he was a patriotic Englishman rather than a Roundhead. He was said to have told a meeting of his officers that 'it is not for seamen to mind State affairs, but to keep foreigners from fooling us'. His proud declarations that he would not permit any foreign government to punish an Englishman under any circumstances, as only Englishmen could sit in judgment on Englishmen, delighted his compatriots; and even his bitter enemy, Charles II's Lord Chancellor, Clarendon, wrote afterwards that Blake's action against the pirates of North Africa had 'made the name of the English very terrible and formidable in those seas'. Yet Blake was always a republican as well as a nationalist; like Napoleon and Stalin in later times, he enlisted the forces of nationalism in the service of the Revolution. When he visited Cadiz in September 1650 he told a group of Spaniards in the main square of the town that 'with the example afforded by London all kingdoms will annihilate tyranny and become republics. England had done so already; France was following in her wake; and as the natural gravity of the Spaniards rendered them slower in their operations, he gave them ten years for the revolution in their country.'

By the time that Blake returned to England from the Mediterranean in October 1655, Spain had declared war and Blake's services were required against the enemy whom Cromwell, reviving the traditions of the great Queen Elizabeth, was fighting on behalf of England and Protestantism. On 28 March 1656 Blake sailed from Portsmouth in his great new flagship of 1,634 tons, *The Naseby*, with eighty guns, commanding a fleet of forty-eight ships. He spent a year cruising off the coast of Spain and in the Eastern Atlantic, capturing Spanish merchant ships, while the Spanish battle-fleet did not dare to venture out of Cadiz harbour. In April 1657 he learned that the Spanish treasure-ships returning from Cuba were at Santa Cruz in Teneriffe. On 20 April he sailed into the harbour at Santa Cruz and destroyed every one of the sixteen Spanish ships without losing any of his own ships, and sailed for home, having won the greatest victory of his career, having ensured the outcome of the war, and having destroyed

Spain as a great European power. But his health, which had been deteriorating for some years, was failing. His fleet was within sight of Plymouth, where a great welcome had been planned for him, when he died on 17 August 1657. He was buried in Westminster Abbey after a great state funeral which Cromwell and all the Council attended.

Blake's death was an event of historical importance. It is impossible to say how his patriotism and his republicanism would have responded, if he had lived, to the events of 1659–60, and how he would have regarded the decision of his friend Monck to restore Charles II to the throne; but if he had been in command of the fleet in the months before the Restoration, he could not have failed to exercise a decisive influence, one way or another, on the course of events.

In 1661 Charles II ordered that Blake's body, along with those of Cromwell's mother and daughter, Pym, and other eminent Roundheads, should be removed from Westminster Abbey and flung into a pit in St Margaret's churchyard nearby. In later times, when Blake was remembered only as a patriot and not as a Roundhead rebel, and when even an ardent Royalist like Nelson could humbly declare that he did not consider himself to be Blake's equal as a sailor, men were indignant that Charles II could thus outrage the body of a great English admiral; but Blake himself would not have been surprised. He would have expected nothing less from those enemies of God, young Charles Stuart and his Cavaliers.

10

John Lambert

Some of the Roundheads who played a leading part in the Civil War, like Cromwell and Blake, who were born in 1599, did not become prominent until after they had reached the age of forty. Others, like Ireton and Lilburne, who were some fifteen years younger than Cromwell and Blake, were dead before they reached the same age. Major-General John Lambert hadachieved everything and lost everything by the time he was forty, and spent the rest of his life in prison.

It was his misfortune that he possessed the wrong mixture of personal ambition and devotion to principle. If he had been less ambitious, he might not have started the strife amongst the Roundheads in 1659 which let in Charles II and the Cavaliers; if he had been less principled, he might have won riches and honours, like his colleague Monck, by betraying his cause and his friends.

He was born in the autumn of 1619, the son of the squire of the village of Malhamdale near Skipton at the foot of the Pennines in the West Riding of Yorkshire. It was a very different district from the Puritan country of south-east and south-west England, but in this remote country area, which had been solidly Roman Catholic as recently as fifty years earlier, John Lambert was brought up as a Protestant and an opponent of the High Church ritualism of Archbishop Laud, although he was not reared in the fervently Puritan atmosphere in which most of his Roundhead colleagues spent their youth. There was always something of the adventurer, as well as the loyal Roundhead and Puritan, in this product of the gentry of the wild Yorkshire dales.

He was not quite twenty years old when, in September 1639, he married Frances Lister, the daughter of Sir William Lister of the neighbouring village of Thornton. She was beautiful, vivacious, haughty and daring, and a devoted wife and helper to her husband. The young couple had far to go and far to fall.

Lambert was twenty-two in the summer of 1642 when King Charles came to York from the south and prepared to raise an army of loyal north-countrymen to fight for his rights against the rebel Parliament in London. Most of the gentlemen of Yorkshire were prepared to join him. Lambert was one of the minority who were ready to fight for Parliament. His father-in-law, Sir William Lister, favoured a scheme by which the Yorkshire gentry would all agree to remain neutral and keep the war out of Yorkshire; but he had very little support for his impractical project.

Lambert joined the forces which Ferdinando, Lord Fairfax, was raising for Parliament in Yorkshire, and in view of the comparative shortage of local gentlemen in Fairfax's army he rose quickly to the rank of colonel. The Roundheads in the north had difficulty in holding their own against the Cavaliers under the Earl of Newcastle, but they succeeded in preventing the enemy from capturing the port of Hull. Lambert distinguished himself in the fighting at Hull. By the beginning of 1644 the situation had begun to improve for the Roundheads. Lambert served under Sir Thomas Fairfax in Cheshire when Fairfax marched against the force of Cavaliers which the Marquis of Ormonde had enlisted among the army in Ireland and sent back to England to fight for the King. In January 1644 Fairfax defeated these Anglo-Irish Cavaliers at Nantwich. Among the Cavalier prisoners captured at Nantwich was Colonel George Monck, who for the first but not the last time faced Lambert as an enemy in January 1644.

The intervention of the Scottish Covenanters changed the situation in the north. Lambert took an active part in the campaign in the spring and summer of 1644. In March he relieved the Roundhead garrison in Bradford after defeating a Cavalier force which was commanded by Colonel Bellasis, who was related to Lambert's wife. In July he fought gallantly at Marston Moor. Next year, when Sir Thomas Fairfax was appointed Lord General of the Parliamentary forces after Essex and the other generals had been forced to resign by the Self-Denying Ordinance, Lambert was appointed to succeed Fairfax as commander of the Roundhead forces in the north. But the fighting in the north was over, and Lambert remained inactive while Fairfax and Cromwell won the war at Naseby and in the west. Lambert did not go south till the last winter of the war, when he helped Fairfax and Cromwell to mop up the resistance of the Cavaliers in Devon and Cornwall, and in the summer of 1646 he was present at the siege and surrender of Oxford.

Lambert remained at army headquarters in the south and played a leading part in the political controversies of 1647. He became a friend of Ireton and worked closely with him, supporting the Independents against the Presbyterians and the Grandees against the Levellers. In July 1647 Sexby's agents in the north incited the soldiers of the northern army to arrest their commander, the Presbyterian General Poyntz, and send him as a prisoner to Fairfax at Uxbridge. Fairfax released Poyntz, but sent Lambert to replace him as commander of the army in the north with the rank of Major-General. His task was to reassure the soldiers that they were not being led by Presbyterian traitors to the cause, and to suppress any Leveller mutinies. Lambert succeeded in re-establishing discipline in the north by his combination of tact, charm and severity.

He was still in the north when the Second Civil War broke out in May 1648. The army was greatly outnumbered by its Cavalier, Presbyterian and Scottish enemies, and Fairfax and Cromwell could not afford to send any reinforcements to the north until they had crushed the rebels at Colchester and Pembroke. Lambert had therefore to hold the position in the north as best he could against the Scottish invaders and the Cavaliers who rose in revolt in Cumberland and Westmorland under Sir Marmaduke Langdale. He marched at once against Langdale and defeated him, capturing Carlisle and Appleby and taking Langdale prisoner before the Scots arrived; but when the Duke of Hamilton and the Scots crossed the Border with an army of 24,000 men, Lambert could do very little to hamper them, especially as fresh Cavalier revolts broke out in his rear at Pontefract and Scarborough. He was trying desperately to hold his own when Cromwell joined him at Knaresborough after the surrender of the Cavaliers at Pembroke. Together they marched their 9,000 men across the Pennines and attacked the Scots in Lancashire, where Lambert played a valiant part as Cromwell's second-in-command in the victory at Preston.

By October only Pontefract still held out for the King, but Pontefract had not yet fallen when Cromwell hurried to London in December after Ireton and the army had occupied London and purged Parliament of the Presbyterians with the object of putting the King to death and proclaiming the republic. Cromwell left Lambert in command at Pontefract, and as the town did not surrender until March 1649, Lambert played no part in the King's trial—a coincidence which turned out to his advantage twelve years later.

He remained in England with Fairfax during Cromwell's campaign in Ireland, but in the summer of 1650 he served with Cromwell in the campaign against the Scottish Covenanters. As Fairfax refused to lead the army against the Scots, Cromwell replaced him as Lord General and Lambert was appointed as second-in-command. As he rode out of London with Cromwell at the head of the army on the road to the north, the crowds cheered them enthusiastically. Cromwell remarked to Lambert that they would cheer just as loudly if he and Lambert were going to be hanged.

Lambert fought at Dunbar. Some commentators afterwards claimed that it was he who suggested to Cromwell the tactic of attacking the advancing Covenanters at their weakest point, which enabled Cromwell to defeat an army twice as large as his own. Other commentators gave the credit for the idea to Lambert's future rival, Monck. In any case, Lambert certainly played a leading part in carrying out the tactic, for he led the cavalry charge that routed the enemy. When Charles II and the Scots marched into England and Cromwell pursued them, Cromwell sent Lambert on ahead with part of the cavalry to link up with Harrison and harry the enemy; and Lambert took part in the victory at Worcester.

Lambert was now aged thirty-two. He was handsome and charming, and had a beautiful wife who shocked Lucy Hutchinson and other Puritans by her grandeur of style and her arrogance. Rumourmongers said that she was Cromwell's mistress. Probably the only germ of truth in the story is that Cromwell enjoyed her company, and did not regard her with the stern disapproval which many of his Puritan colleagues, and more especially their wives, showed towards her. He was as tolerant of her frivolities as he was of those of his daughter, Elizabeth Claypole. In conversation with Lambert, he would refer to Frances Lambert as Lambert's 'jewel'.

The Levellers had called the group of anti-Leveller army officers 'the Grandees', and it was a good description of the attitude of Lambert and his supporters. After the death of his friend Ireton in 1651, Lambert became the most prominent of the Grandees, and his easy-going charm aroused more resentment among the Levellers and sectaries than Ireton's taciturn Puritan determination.

By the beginning of 1653 Cromwell and most other people in public life had realized the urgency of establishing a new constitution and system of government for the republic. The supreme power was vested in the Rump Parliament, which consisted of about one-eighth of the MPs who had been elected more than twelve years before. This was not a satisfactory situation in the eyes of men who had been brought up to believe ardently in the importance of constitutional law. But what was to replace the Rump? None of the Roundheads favoured new elections which might well result in the election of a Parliament with a Cavalier or Presbyterian majority. The Levellers had proposed the election of a Parliament on a wide popular franchise from which men who had fought for the Cavaliers were to be excluded. Vane and the leaders of the Rump believed that the Rump should continue as a Parliament in perpetuity, co-opting new MPs to fill vacancies caused by death. Harrison and the sectaries wished to see the Rump replaced by a Parliament of Puritan sectaries appointed by Cromwell. Lambert favoured the abolition of Parliament and the establishment of a military dictatorship under which the country would be governed by a small junta of army officers. He saw no reason why the army who had defeated the King and the Scots should be governed by fifty MPs elected more than twelve years before. He is also said to have been angered by the fact that although he had been appointed to succeed Ireton as Lord Deputy of Ireland, the appointment was mysteriously rescinded before he could take up his duties, and Major-General Fleetwood, who married Ireton's widow, Cromwell's daughter Bridget, was appointed in his place.

It was widely believed that Lambert was chiefly responsible for persuading Cromwell to dissolve the Rump by force in April 1653, though Harrison played a more active part in driving out the MPs at the sword-point. Lambert accompanied Cromwell when he dismissed the Council of State on the same afternoon.

The Council of State was temporarily replaced as the supreme executive body of the state by a Council of Army Officers. When Harrison suggested that a new legislative body should be established consisting, like the old Jewish Sanhedrin, of seventy members, Lambert proposed instead that the only legislative body should be a committee of twelve army officers. Cromwell at first inclined to Harrison's view, but after he had become dissatisfied with the 140 sectaries of Barebones' Parliament he dissolved it and accepted the office of Lord Protector in December 1653. Lambert had urged Cromwell to adopt this course, and it was Lambert who drafted the Instrument of Government which proclaimed him as Lord Protector. The Cavaliers commented coarsely, as Heath wrote afterwards, that the Lord Protector's Instrument was to be found under my Lady Lambert's petticoat.

Though Lambert's Instrument of Government provided for the elected Parliament which sat during the year 1654, he encouraged Cromwell to dissolve it when it proved truculent; and when the Cavalier and Leveller conspiracies culminated in Penruddock's insurrection in March 1655, Lambert was the first to propose the establishment of the system of government by the Major-Generals. By the autumn the organization had been set up, and the eleven Major-Generals governed their parts of England by military law, being responsible only to the Lord Protector. Lambert himself was made governor of Northumberland, Cumberland, Westmorland, Durham and Yorkshire, with his seat of government at York; but he spent most of his time in London on the Protector's Council and near the centre of power, leaving the government of his district to his deputy, Colonel Robert Lilburne, John Lilburne's brother. The 'rule of the Major-Generals', though it lasted less than eighteen months, has been remembered for three centuries as a dreadful example of arbitrary tyranny, as a period when stern men in soldiers' breastplates, with close-cropped hair and unsmiling faces, suppressed all the people's sports and pleasures, asked little Cavalier boys 'When did you last see your father?', and forced the nation to submit to the authority of ranting Puritan preachers. In fact it was devised as a useful security measure by the handsome, debonair Major-General Lambert, with his long-flowing hair and his elegant wife.

In January 1657 Cromwell's second elected Parliament refused to renew the grants which were necessary to finance the government of the Major-Generals. Cromwell needed the support of the gentry in order to raise the money which he required for the war with Spain, and he agreed to end the system of government by the Major-Generals. Lambert, who had never liked the war with Spain, was strongly opposed to ending the rule of the Major-Generals, and urged Cromwell to dispense with Parliament and authorize the Major-Generals to raise the taxes by force. When Cromwell, instead, thought of pleasing the traditionalists and the constitutional lawyers by taking the title of King, Lambert opposed this. He is said to have been the first person to suggest this course to Cromwell, having put the idea forward when the Instrument of Government was under discussion in 1653; but he now organized opposition to the proposal among the army Grandees. Lambert and the Grandees did not welcome a step which would raise Cromwell's standing in the eyes of the lawyers and gentlemen, but would tend to make him less dependent on the support of the army officers. Some observers thought that Lambert's main reason for opposing the offer of the crown was that His Majesty King Oliver would be succeeded as King by his eldest son Richard, whereas His Highness the Lord Protector might well be succeeded by his greatest lieutenant, His Highness the Lord Protector John Lambert.

It was chiefly because of Lambert's efforts that Cromwell refused the offer of the crown, and this led to the first rupture between Cromwell and Lambert. Lambert was dismissed from the army and withdrew to the house at Wimbledon which he had been granted when Queen Henrietta Maria's property was confiscated. It was an imposing mansion, standing in 400 acres of woodland stretching from the top of Putney Hill down to the river.

Cromwell died in September 1658, having appointed his son Richard to succeed him as Lord Protector. At first everyone appeared to accept the situation, and the Cavaliers, who had always hoped that Cromwell's death would lead to a collapse of the republic and the restoration of Charles II, despaired of success. But by November the first signs of a rift had appeared between the new Lord Protector and the army Grandees, who were led by the Protector's brother-in-law, Lieutenant-General Fleetwood, and by his aunt's husband, Major-General Desborough. Lambert was still living in retirement at Wimbledon; but in January 1659 Richard Cromwell summoned a Parliament, hoping to rely on the support of the gentry against the army Grandees. Lambert was elected as MP for Pontefract. Several of the former leaders of the Rump, like Vane and Ludlow, who had been in prison or in retirement under Cromwell's rule, were also elected, and they criticized the Protectorate and called for a return to the Commonwealth of the years 1649–53. Three parties now formed—the Protector's party, the army leaders under Fleetwood and Desborough, and the republicans of the old Rump. Lambert spoke in Parliament in favour of the Protector, and declared that 'monarchy is the worst form of government'.

In April Fleetwood and Desborough carried out a military *coup* which compelled Richard Cromwell to dissolve Parliament. A month later they forced him to resign as Lord Protector. But other army officers had become suspicious of Fleetwood and Desborough. A number of them united with Ludlow and the Republicans in a plot in which Colonel Robert Lilburne was the chief actor. They forced the reluctant Fleetwood and Desborough to recall the MPs of the Rump of 1653, which was again set up as the supreme governing body of the republic. They also agreed that Lambert, who had kept discreetly in touch with Lilburne and Ludlow, should be reappointed to his command in the army.

The Cavaliers had taken heart from the quarrels between the Roundheads, but their hopes were again dashed in the summer of 1659. In August Sir George Booth, who had fought for the Roundheads in the Civil War but had been one of the Presbyterian MPs who were expelled in Pride's Purge, rose in revolt in Cheshire and proclaimed King Charles II. He was joined by the Earl of Derby and many other Cavaliers. Lambert was sent against them. He recaptured Chester, defeated the rebels, and returned to London with Booth as his prisoner.

Lambert has been held responsible for the downfall of the Commonwealth and the Restoration of Charles II; but a greater share of the blame falls on the quarrelsome, rigid Republican, Sir Arthur Hazelrig, one of the Five Members of 1642, Cromwell's colleague until the dissolution of the Rump, and a champion of the Independents against the Presbyterians. In September 1659 some of the junior officers who had served under Lambert against Booth, met at Derby and presented a petition to the Rump, protesting against their failure to obtain promotion and other rewards for their services against Booth. Hazelrig promptly suspected, quite wrongly, that Lambert was behind the petition, and was preparing a *coup* against the Rump. He demanded that Lambert be impeached and sent to the Tower. Lambert thereupon surrounded Parliament with his troops, and after tactfully avoiding a clash with other army units whom the Rump had summoned to protect them, dissolved the Rump at the swordpoint as Cromwell had done in 1653. Hazelrig appealed to other army generals to support the Rump against Lambert. General George Monck, the Commander-in-Chief in Scotland, declared that he was ready to uphold the lawful authority of the Rump.

The stage seemed set for a new civil war of Lambert and the army in England against Monck and the army in Scotland. Monck had several advantages over Lambert. He had at his disposal the £70,000 in the Scottish treasury, and would have had no difficulty in persuading the Scots to pay taxes to finance a campaign against Lambert and military government. Lambert had no money with which to pay his soldiers, and had no legal authority to raise taxes in England. The English tax-paying classes, knowing the tradition of John Hampden and remembering with disgust the rule of the Major-Generals, would not provide Lambert with money and welcomed the attitude of a general like Monck, who declared that he was ready to uphold the civil power against military dictatorship. Suddenly the people, disillusioned by the succession of government changes and *coups*, began on all sides to demand the restoration of King Charles II, though Monck repeatedly proclaimed that he had no intention of restoring the King.

Lambert, and more especially Frances Lambert, were being approached by Cavaliers who offered Lambert favours and wealth if he would agree to restore Charles II. The Cavalier agent, Lord Hatton, suggested to Charles II's Lord Chancellor in exile, Edward Hyde, that the only bait big enough to catch Lambert, and the only security which would convince him of Cavalier good faith, would be for Charles II to marry Lambert's daughter Mary. Hatton pointed out to Hyde that Lambert came from 'a very good gentleman's family', and added: 'The lady is pretty, of an extra-ordinary sweetness of disposition, and very virtuously and ingenuously disposed; the father is a person, set aside his un-happy engagement, of very great parts, and very noble inclina-tions.' But Lambert rejected all offers from the Cavaliers.

Lambert marched against Monck, and reached Newcastle, but he was anxious to avoid civil war, and agreed with Monck that he would not advance beyond Newcastle if Monck did not move his army south of Berwick. He sent Colonel Cobbet to Scotland to visit Monck and to win the support of Monck's officers; but Monck arrested Cobbet on a charge of subverting discipline in his army, and took steps to purge the army in Scotland of all sectaries and Anabaptists. When Lambert heard about Cobbet's arrest, he sent Colonel Zanchy to demand his release; but Monck arrested Zanchy too, on the excuse that Lambert had broken the terms of his undertaking not to advance beyond Newcastle.

This should have been enough to warn Lambert that Monck was his enemy, and that he ought to follow the advice that Sir Bulstrode Whitelocke had given him: 'Fight Monck.' But Lambert still wished to avoid civil war, and Monck, knowing that he could pay his troops and that Lambert could not, believed that time was on his side. He tricked Lambert into inaction by sending commissioners to Newcastle to negotiate a peaceful settlement of the dispute. Monck's commissioners, after some delay, reached an agreement with Lambert which Monck later refused to ratify. By this time the winter had begun. Cold winters were more common in the seventeenth century than today, and the winter of 1659–60 was exceptionally severe. By the end of November the roads between Newcastle and the Border were blocked with snow and ice, and this prevented Lambert from marching against Monck even if he had wished to do so.

Perhaps he could have accomplished the seemingly impossible march if he had been sufficiently determined, because the snow and ice still covered the ground a month later when Monck began his march south from Coldstream on 1 January. Lambert's forces were deserting. The Yorkshire gentlemen were refusing to fight for him, and expressed their support for Monck. Fairfax seized York, surrendered the city to Monck, and urged Monck to bring back Charles II. Lambert's army disintegrated, and Lambert himself returned to London to find that the Rump had reassembled and were awaiting the arrival of their deliverer, Monck. Lambert submitted to the authority of the Rump, and obtained a pardon for his recent actions. He decided to leave England and enter the army of King Charles X of Sweden.

But on 3 February Monck and his army entered London, and within a few weeks he had repudiated the authority of the Rump and announced his intention of calling a new Parliament which everyone knew would vote for the restoration of Charles II. On 5 March Lambert was arrested and sent to the Tower. He decided to make a last desperate attempt to prevent the return of Charles Stuart, the 'Common Enemy'. On the evening of 10 April he escaped from the Tower, climbing down from his window by a silk ladder which had been smuggled in to him, and escaping in a boat which was waiting for him in the river, while his maid-servant lay under the bedclothes in his bed in order to delude the jailer into thinking that he was still in his prison. After hiding for some days in London, Lambert made his way to the Midlands and issued a proclamation calling on all his supporters to rally to defend the 'Good Old Cause' and meet him on the battlefield of Edgehill; but before he could reach Edgehill he and his followers were surprised at Daventry on Easter Sunday, 22 April, by a troop which Monck had sent against him.

Monck's men were commanded by Colonel Ingoldsby, who had signed Charles I's death warrant and was therefore officially classified as a regicide by the Cavaliers, and was likely to be exempted from the pardon which Charles II was promising to the other Roundheads. Ingoldsby was determined to earn his pardon by capturing Lambert. When they met at Daventry, he and Lambert had about 700 men each. Lambert was anxious to avoid fighting, and sent some of his men to fraternize with Ingoldsby's soldiers. Ingoldsby refused to allow any of his men to speak with Lambert's emissaries, but he spoke with them himself and persuaded them that they were fighting for a lost cause. Several of them joined Ingoldsby, who rode up to Lambert and parleyed with him until most of Lambert's men had deserted. Ingoldsby then told Lambert that he was his prisoner. Lambert's officers were loyal to him to the last; they all offered to surrender if Ingoldsby would allow Lambert to escape abroad. Ingoldsby refused, and when Lambert galloped away, Ingoldsby pursued him and threatened to shoot him down if he did not surrender.

Lambert then surrendered. Monck's chaplain Gumble was surprised that so gallant a soldier as Lambert should have surrendered without a fight, and thought that it was because Lambert knew that God had deserted him.

Lambert offered money to Ingoldsby if he would allow him to escape abroad; but Ingoldsby valued his pardon from Charles II more than Lambert's gold and brought him as a prisoner to London. As they rode past Tyburn a crowd assembled and howled for Lambert's death. Lambert told Ingoldsby of how Cromwell had said in 1650 that the crowds who cheered them on their march to Scotland would cheer just as loudly if they were on their way to be hanged, and added that Cromwell's prophecy seemed likely to be fulfilled.

The only thing in Lambert's favour was that he was not classed as a regicide, having been absent in Yorkshire at the time of Charles I's trial. Charles II's first Parliament passed an Act of Indemnity which declared that all the Roundheads would be pardoned except those who were exempted by name in the Act. During the debates on the bill in the summer of 1660, the most sordid intrigues and bribery took place to decide who should be exempted. The House of Commons began by fixing an arbitrary number of seven victims, and then proceeded to argue as to who these seven should be. Having selected seven of the regicides to suffer death, the House of Commons were content; but the House of Lords demanded a far larger number of executions, and the King and his Lord Chancellor, the Earl of Clarendon (the former Edward Hyde, who was ennobled soon after the Restoration), adopted a midway position between the two Houses. Eventually the House of Commons agreed to provide twenty victims, and chose another thirteen regicides for death; but Clarendon then demanded that four more should also suffer death—Lambert, Vane and Hazelrig, who were not regicides, and Colonel Axtell, who had commanded the guards at Charles I's trial. The House of Commons decided to save Hazelrig from the death sentence, but agreed to the deaths of Lambert, Vane and Axtell, with the proviso in Vane and Lambert's case that if they petitioned for mercy after sentence of death had been passed, the King would consider their petition favourably. In the debate in the Commons, one of the most earnest advocates for Lambert was Sir George Booth, whose revolt in the previous year had been suppressed by Lambert, but who had been mercifully treated by his captor.

When the regicides were tried and executed in October 1660, Lambert was not put on trial, and in May 1661 he was transferred from the Tower to Guernsey, where Frances was allowed to live with him in a cottage on the island. But the government became alarmed by a number of Roundhead plots and attempted insurrections in London and elsewhere, and though Lambert himself was not connected with them, the plotters had referred to him in their intercepted correspondence. In June 1662 he was brought back to London, and he and Vane were put on trial for high treason, being accused of waging war against the King. They were both sentenced to death. Vane, who defiantly proclaimed his republican beliefs at the trial, was executed; Lambert, who pleaded guilty and adopted a submissive attitude, was pardoned by the King, the death sentence being commuted to imprisonment during the King's pleasure. All his property was confiscated, but the King granted it to Frances's Cavalier relative, Lord Bellasis, who held it in trust for her.

Lambert was sent to Castle Cornet in Guernsey, but now, as a convicted traitor, he was treated more harshly than before. Frances was not allowed to be with him, and the conditions of his imprisonment varied considerably from one time to another. Sometimes he was allowed to indulge in his hobby of gardening, while at other times he was confined all day in his cell and only allowed a short period of exercise walking on the parapet of the prison. According to Lucy Hutchinson, who disliked Frances Lambert, Frances was responsible for part of his troubles. One of the jailers approached Frances and offered to carry secret communications between her and Lambert. Frances thought that the man was an *agent provocateur* who had been employed by the government to trap her, and to safeguard herself and her husband she reported him to the authorities. He was not an *agent provocateur* but merely wished to do the prisoners a kindness, and he was sentenced to a term of imprisonment. After this, none of the jailers would do anything to help any of the Roundhead prisoners, and in their resentment at Frances Lambert's action they treated the prisoners more harshly.

As the years passed the authorities became more lenient. Frances was not allowed to live with him, but permission to do this was granted to his daughter, Frances. Another daughter, Mary, was allowed to visit him when he fell ill; but she was a further cause of friction between him and the prison governor, Lord Hatton, who in 1659 had suggested to Hyde that Mary might marry Charles II. She fell in love with Hatton's son, and to Hatton's fury she married him secretly. Hatton did not wish his son to be linked with the daughter of a traitor, though he had once recommended her as a suitable consort for the King of England. He drove his son out of his house and disinherited him.

In September 1670 Lambert was transferred from Guernsey to Drake's Island in Plymouth Sound, and soon afterwards permission was given to his wife to live there with him. They had a few happy years together before Frances died in 1676. This blow seems to have affected Lambert's sanity, and he began to lapse into senility at an early age. He was well enough to meet Charles II and his brother the Duke of York (the future King James II) when they visited Drake's Island in 1679 and expressed a wish to see him. He treated the King and the Prince with proper respect, and they treated him with courtesy. During the bitter winter of 1683-4, when fairs were held on the ice on the Thames in London and snowdrifts stood sixty feet high on Dartmoor, he caught a chill, and died in February 1684, at the age of sixty-four, having spent the last twenty-four years of his life in prison.

11

Thomas, Third Lord Fairfax

Thomas, third Lord Fairfax, was a very lucky man. He had no outstanding abilities as a general, but was appointed Commander-in-Chief of the Roundhead armies for reasons quite unconnected with his own merits. He was opposed to Cromwell's policy, but lived in retirement on a large pension during the Protectorate when many of Cromwell's other opponents were in prison. He only narrowly escaped being classified as a regicide, but remained at liberty under Charles II as he had done under Cromwell.

He was born on 17 January 1612 on his grandfather's estates at Denton, near Ilkley, in the West Riding of Yorkshire. His grandfather, Sir Thomas Fairfax, had served Elizabeth I as a soldier and diplomat, and was a member of the Council of the North which governed the north of England from York. His father Ferdinando performed the duties of a JP and a country gentleman at Denton, and sat as MP for Boroughbridge in the Parliaments of James I and Charles I. His mother was the daughter of Lord Sheffield, the President of the Council of the North. When young Thomas Fairfax was aged fourteen he went to St John's College, Cambridge. Next year, in 1627, his grandfather was rewarded for his many years of service by being created a Scottish peer with the title of Baron Fairfax of Cameron.

When Fairfax was seventeen he entered the Dutch service and fought in the Thirty Years War in the force commanded by Sir Horace Vere, one of the leading English generals of the time. After his return to England he married Vere's daughter Anne when he was twenty-five. He joined Charles I's army in the First Scots War, and marched with the King to Berwick; and though Charles signed a truce before any fighting took place, he knighted Fairfax in January 1640 for his services in the campaign. Four months later Lord Fairfax died, and Sir Thomas Fairfax's father

Ferdinando succeeded to the peerage. When Ferdinando died in March 1648, he himself became the third Lord Fairfax.

In the summer of 1642 the gentlemen of Yorkshire prepared to fight for the King against Parliament; but Fairfax and his father came down firmly on the side of Parliament. When King Charles was greeted by the Yorkshire gentlemen on Heyworth Moor on 3 June, Sir Thomas Fairfax presented a petition to him signed by the Roundhead gentlemen of Yorkshire. The King refused to receive it, and when Fairfax tried to lay it on Charles's saddle, Charles nearly rode him down.

Ferdinando, Lord Fairfax, was appointed to command the Parliamentary forces in Yorkshire, and Sir Thomas joined his father's army. During the first two years of the Civil War he fought in many engagements in Yorkshire, including the disastrous defeat at Adwalton Moor in June 1643. On one occasion he had the painful experience of witnessing the capture of his wife by the Cavaliers under the Earl of Newcastle, while he was unable to do anything to help her; but Newcastle sent Lady Fairfax back to her husband in his coach with an escort of horsemen for her protection.

Sir Thomas Fairfax had all the qualities required to make him a gallant officer, if not a great general. He was very tall, being well over six feet in height, and his hair and complexion were so dark that he was nicknamed 'Black Tom', as Strafford had been called before him. He was charming, and his gentle manners and humility endeared him to his enemies as well as to his friends. He always tried to spare the feelings of his defeated adversaries. It was said that anyone observing the modest way in which he spoke to his prisoners would think that it was he, and not they, who had been captured; and when he escorted King Charles I as a prisoner into Nottingham in 1647, the King was touched by his courtesy and consideration, and commented that he was a man of honour.

He was brave, and could take quick decisions in matters within his compass. When he was campaigning in Yorkshire in 1643, he was riding along a lane with two Cavalier officer prisoners in his charge when he suddenly met fifteen or sixteen armed Cavaliers. The sergeant commanding them came up to the officers whom Fairfax had captured, not realizing that they had been taken prisoner, and asked what they should do, as 'the round-heads (as they called them) came so fast upon them'. As the Cavalier officers had given their parole to Fairfax to be his true prisoners, they did not reply to the sergeant; but Fairfax, realizing his situation, immediately spurred his horse, and leaping over a high rampart escaped and rejoined the Roundhead forces. He showed less ability for taking quick and daring decisions as a political leader.

He fought at Winceby, at Nantwich and at Marston Moor, and in the spring of 1645 was appointed Lord General of all the Parliamentary forces, being almost the only Roundhead general who was not disqualified from serving in the army by the Self-Denying Ordinance. He commanded the army at Naseby, and in the campaign which culminated in the capture of Oxford and the end of the war, with Lieutenant-General Cromwell acting as his second-in-command. He held the post of Lord General throughout the political crisis of 1647-8. Prompted at every step by Cromwell and Ireton, he ordered the army to support the Independents against the Presbyterians, and stood for the Grandees against the Levellers.

The army acted in his name alone. Lilburne's appeals to the army to save the liberties of the people, and Prynne's protests against the army's defiance of Parliament, were all addressed to 'His Excellency the Lord General Sir Thomas Fairfax and the officers and soldiers of the Army', and all the army's manifestos were similarly issued in the name of Fairfax, the officers and the soldiers. After the Restoration, Fairfax claimed that he had never drafted or even read any of the manifestos which were signed in his name: thus, he wrote, 'hath a General's power been broken and crumbled into a levelling faction'. He certainly feared the Agitators and the Levellers. He later claimed that when Cornet Joyce removed the King from Holmby House to army headquarters at the orders of the Council of Agitators, he tried to compel the army to send the King back; and when the Agitators of the northern army arrested their Presbyterian commander, General Poyntz, on the grounds that he was a traitor, and sent him to Fairfax's headquarters, Fairfax released Poyntz at once. But though Lilburne and most political observers realized that Cromwell, not Fairfax, was the real leader of the army Grandees, many people, particularly foreigners abroad, thought that Fairfax was the great leader of the English revolution.

In the Second Civil War he acted with great determination in crushing the Cavalier rising at Maidstone and in driving the Essex rebels into Colchester, which he besieged. When Colchester at last surrendered at mercy, he ordered two of the Cavalier leaders to be shot—an action which was justified by the laws of war, and one for which he was prepared to accept responsibility even after the Restoration. He was much less happy when Ireton set the events in motion which led to the King's trial and execution and the proclamation of the Republic, though the army's Remonstrance of 20 November 1648, Pride's Purge, and the manifesto announcing the plan to suppress the House of Lords and bring the King to trial, were all issued in his name. After the purged House of Commons assumed sole legislative authority and set up the High Court of Justice to try the King, Fairfax received a large number of protests from Englishmen and foreign governments, and many pamphlets were published in London denouncing the action of His Excellency the Lord General Fairfax and the officers of the army as being an act of treason. These protests disquieted Fairfax, and his doubts were increased by the attitude of his wife, who was an ardent Presbyterian and was strongly opposed to the King's trial.

The Rump Parliament appointed 152 Commissioners to make the arrangements for the King's trial. The first Commissioner named in the commission was Fairfax. When the Commissioners met for the first time on 8 January 1649, only fifty-three of them came, but Fairfax was one of these. The Commissioners chose a rather obscure lawyer, John Bradshaw, to preside at the trial, and the opening of the trial was fixed for 20 January. Fairfax did not attend on the twentieth, but his wife came to the trial as a spectator, wearing a mask, as was the usual practice when ladies of rank appeared in public. When the roll-call of the Commissioners began with the clerk calling out Fairfax's name, Lady Fairfax called out from the gallery, 'He has more wit than to be there.' Later, when the indictment was read out to the King and he was charged in the name of 'the people of England', Lady Fairfax called out: 'It is a lie. Not one half, not one quarter of the people of England. Oliver Cromwell is a traitor.' Colonel Axtell, who was in command of the troops guarding the royal prisoner, levelled his pistol at the masked interrupter and she was hustled out by her friends. Her identity was not known to the general public, and it was widely believed that the masked lady was the well-known Cavalier activist, Lady Newburgh. The authorities undoubtedly knew that she was Lady Fairfax, but took no measures against her, not wishing it to become known that the protest had come from the Lord General's wife.

The King was sentenced to death on Saturday 27 January. Next day two envoys from the Dutch government arrived in London to urge the English government to show mercy to the King, and they made contact with the Commissioners of the Scottish Covenanters in London, who were strongly opposed to the King's trial and execution. They demanded to be permitted to make representations immediately to the House of Commons, because it was known that the King's execution had been fixed for Tuesday 30 January; but they were told that it was impossible for the House to sit on a Sunday, the Lord's Day. The House did not hear them until the Monday afternoon, and then gave them no answer.

The Dutch and the Scots made one last effort to save the King on the Tuesday morning, when they visited Fairfax at his house in King Street near Whitehall. He looked very tired, because he had spent the night in discussion with his friends, who had urged him to make a military *coup d'état* to save the King's life; but he had refused, on the grounds that it would lead to bloodshed and a new civil war. No one knew what hour had been fixed for the King's execution, and throughout the morning, while the House of Commons passed an Act which proclaimed the republic and made it an act of high treason to proclaim Charles II as King, the Dutch and the Scots urged the unhappy and evasive Fairfax to intervene to stop the execution. When they left him at noon, they found the street in Whitehall full of soldiers.

Fairfax made his way through the soldiers to Whitehall Palace, resolved to make an effort to save the King. He met Cromwell and Harrison, who took him into a room where they held a prayer-meeting for two hours. When Fairfax emerged from the prayer-meeting soon after 2 p.m. he met Sir Thomas Herbert in the passage, and asked him how the King was. Herbert told him that Charles had been beheaded a few minutes earlier. Herbert noticed that Fairfax looked surprised, and thought that Cromwell and Harrison had deliberately detained Fairfax at the prayer-meeting until after the execution had taken place. Fairfax went home, and consoled himself by writing a poem about the King's execution which ended with the lines:

> But if the Power Divine permitted this,
> His Will's the law and ours must acquiesce.

A week later, Fairfax had recovered sufficiently from the shock to attend a meeting of the Council of State. He did not break with the republican government, and in May, with Cromwell as his second-in-command, he led the army which suppressed the Leveller mutiny at Burford. This was a task which Fairfax could perform with a clear conscience, because he was strongly opposed to the Levellers: but he was increasingly perturbed at the course which events were taking. He was left in command of the army in England during Cromwell's campaign in Ireland, and in the summer of 1650 was invited to lead the invasion of Scotland against Charles II and the Covenanters. He said that if Charles and the Scots invaded England he would be willing to command the army against them, but refused to lead an invasion of Scotland. He resisted Cromwell's attempts to persuade him to change his mind, and resigned his office as Lord General. The Rump Parliament voted him a large pension of £5,000 a year and he withdrew to his estates in Yorkshire.

He lived quietly in retirement at Denton during the Commonwealth and the Protectorate, and though he occasionally took part in politics, it was in the capacity of a country gentleman rather than as a former Lord General and political leader. He was elected as MP for his father's old constituency of Boroughbridge in Cromwell's Parliament of 1654. As his peerage was a Scottish one, he had never been entitled to sit in the English House of Lords but only in the Scottish Parliament, and as the English House of Lords had been abolished in 1649, and Cromwell's Parliament consisted of only one Chamber with MPs from Scotland and Ireland as well as from England, he was entitled to sit in it as an elected MP. He did not play an active part in the debates, either as a supporter or critic of Cromwell's government.

In 1657 the Duke of Buckingham, who had been a close friend of Charles II in childhood, during the campaign in Scotland and in exile, returned to England and ostensibly made his peace with Cromwell. He fell in love with Fairfax's daughter Mary, who was on the point of marrying the Earl of Chesterfield. Although the banns for Mary's marriage to Chesterfield had twice been read out in church, she broke off the engagement and married Buckingham in Yorkshire in September 1657. Cromwell did not trust Buckingham, who was in fact in secret communication with Charles II, and a month after his wedding Buckingham had to go into hiding. In April 1658 he was arrested, and though he was allowed to live in London under house arrest, he escaped, and on being recaptured in August was sent to the Tower. Fairfax travelled to London to intercede for Buckingham, and had a stormy interview with Cromwell a few days before Cromwell's death; but six months later, Richard Cromwell released Buckingham after Fairfax had stood bail for £20,000 for his good behaviour.

When Richard Cromwell summoned his first Parliament as Lord Protector in January 1659, Fairfax again sat as MP for Boroughbridge but again played no leading part, standing aloof from the quarrels between the new Protector, the army and the Republicans. Under the influence of Buckingham, of his wife and daughter and of the neighbouring Yorkshire gentry, he had come to favour a restoration of the monarchy. When Monck marched against Lambert under the pretence of upholding the authority of the Rump, Fairfax raised the gentlemen of Yorkshire in his support. On 1 January 1660, the day on which Monck began his march south from Coldstream, Fairfax and his supporters seized the city of York, ignoring the protests of Colonel Robert Lilburne, who had been left in command there by Lambert. This rising in his rear disconcerted Lambert; and as Lambert's army disintegrated and Monck advanced, Fairfax was able to hand over York to Monck on 11 January. When he met Monck in York, he urged him to declare openly in favour of the restoration of Charles II. Monck refused to commit himself; he told Fairfax to go home and wait until he heard from him.

When Monck decided in London a few weeks later to invite Charles II to return, he was too busy to bother to tell Fairfax, and Fairfax played no further part in politics. His position at the Restoration might have been precarious if it had not been for his connection with Buckingham. The government's policy was to

pardon nearly all the Roundheads except the regicides. As the regicides were defined as the seventy-eight Commissioners who had sat
as judges at some session of the King's trial, along with four other
men who had played an active part in the trial and the execution,
Faifax just escaped coming within the definition, despite the fact
that his name stood first in the list of the King's judges and that
he had attended the preliminary meeting of the Commissioners
on 8 January 1649. His services to Monck in January 1660 might
not in itself have been sufficient to save him, because Thomas
Scot, who had also supported Monck against Lambert, was
executed as a regicide a few months later. Fairfax's relationship
with Buckingham was certainly a more important factor.

Fairfax lived on for eleven years under Charles II in retirement
at Denton, while his son-in-law and his daughter lived at court,
where Buckingham became a leading member of the government
after Clarendon's fall from power, and the letter B in the word
CABAL. Fairfax was left in peace in Yorkshire, though he
suffered much from ill-health and from the death of his wife in
1665. He died on 12 November 1671 at the age of fifty-nine.

12

Thomas Harrison

Thomas Harrison was the most extreme of all the Roundhead leaders. He carried Puritanism to its ultimate and most violent lengths. But he was far removed from the modern idea of a seventeenth-century Puritan. He was not a sombre, unsmiling, black-coated killjoy, but a strikingly handsome army officer, tempestuous and ebullient, who tended to overdress in rich clothes of the brightest colours and wore his hair as long as any Cavalier.

Unlike most of the other prominent Roundheads, he was not a gentleman by birth, but the son of a butcher of Newcastle-under-Lyme in Staffordshire, where he was born in 1606. His father realized his abilities, and although his low birth and poverty made it difficult for him to be admitted to the Inns of Court, he was articled as an attorney, or solicitor, at Serjeant's Inn in London.

He was thirty-six when the Civil War broke out, and immediately joined the lawyers' regiment in the Roundhead armies. He served in Manchester's army in East Anglia, and became one of the most enthusiastic of the officers whom Cromwell praised as 'godfearing' and whom Manchester's Presbyterian commanders denounced as Anabaptists and sectaries. He was undoubtedly one of the soldiers who, to the indignation of the Anglicans and Presbyterians, would go into the pulpit in the churches, although they had not been ordained, and preach extempore sermons with great moral fervour. He was as passionate in private life as in the pulpit. The Presbyterian Richard Baxter, who served as a chaplain in the Roundhead army, said that Harrison when sober behaved in as excited a manner as most men did when they were drunk.

Harrison fought under Cromwell at Marston Moor, at Newbury, and at Naseby, and rose to the rank of major. He strongly supported Cromwell in the quarrel with Manchester. After Marston Moor he hurried to London, and, to the indignation of the Presbyterians, played a prominent part in disseminating the Independent propaganda that Cromwell was solely responsible for the victory at Marston Moor. In July 1645 he fought in the battle of Langport, when Fairfax and Cromwell marched against the Cavaliers in Somerset. In the middle of the battle, when the Cavaliers began to give ground, Harrison surprised his comrades by suddenly breaking out into song, singing a thanksgiving psalm with unbelievable exultation, 'as if he had been in a rapture'.

In October 1645 he was in Cromwell's force which besieged Basing House, the well-fortified residence of the Roman Catholic Marquis of Winchester near Basingstoke. Basing House had held out for three years against several Roundhead sieges and had caused a great deal of trouble to the Parliamentary forces in several campaigns. Cromwell laid siege to it on 8 October, and took it by storm eight days later. As the defenders had refused his call to surrender they were not entitled to quarter by the laws of war, and as they were most of them Papists Cromwell showed them no more mercy than he was afterwards to show in similar circumstances in Ireland. His friend Hugh Peters, the Puritan preacher, reported to Parliament that seventy-four people had been killed in the house, including one woman, 'who by her railing provoked our soldiers (then in heat) into a further passion. There lay dead upon the ground Major Cuffle (a man of great account amongst them, and a notorious Papist), slain by the hands of Major Harrison (that godly and gallant gentleman) and Robinson the player, who, a little before the storm, was known to be mocking and scorning the Parliament and our army.' This man killed by Harrison, 'Robinson the player', was a professional actor who played comedy parts on the London stage. Some observers reported that Harrison cried out, as he killed him, that the Lord would not forgive those who were half-hearted in killing His enemies. Several of the inmates of Basing House, including the Marquis of Winchester and the architect Inigo Jones, escaped with their lives. The conquerors then proceeded to remove all the Popish ornaments in the house in order to take them to London to be publicly burned.

In the by-elections of 1646, Harrison was elected to the Long Parliament as MP for Wendover, a constituency which had formerly been represented by a very different type of Roundhead, John Hampden. After serving for a few months with the army in Ireland, he returned to play an active part in the events of 1647, urging the army to take action against the Presbyterians in Parliament and joining in the discussions with the Levellers at Putney. In the Putney debates in November 1647 he called the King a 'man of blood'. It was the first time that the phrase had been used, but it soon became a common expression in the army and among the Independents. Although Harrison's rank as a major placed him among the Grandees, his social origin and his determination to bring the King to justice put him closer to the Levellers. He was much more sympathetic to them than were Grandees like Cromwell, Ireton, Fairfax or Lambert, but he was too concerned with the religious aspect to take much interest in social questions or the issue of the Parliamentary franchise.

At the outbreak of the Second Civil War, Harrison, after attending the meeting of the army at Windsor where it was decided to bring 'Charles Stuart, that man of blood' to justice, was sent to join Lambert's army in the north. He showed great daring in the fight at Appleby, where he was seriously wounded, but he had recovered sufficiently to return to the south in time to play an active part in the events which led to the King's trial and execution. When Ireton was trying to gain the support of the Levellers in establishing the Republic and bringing the King to justice, he used Harrison as a go-between with Lilburne. Harrison succeeded in persuading Lilburne to attend the talks with Ireton and the army Grandees at Windsor, but could not prevent the breakdown of the talks at Whitehall after the army had marched on London and expelled the Presbyterian MPs in Pride's Purge.

On 30 November 1648 Ireton sent Colonel Ewer to bring the King from Newport in the Isle of Wight to Hurst Castle on the mainland, and on 15 December Cromwell ordered Harrison to bring him to Windsor. Harrison met Charles and his escort at Alresford in Hampshire, and was in charge of the soldiers who guarded the King on the journey. The Cavaliers were indignant that this duty had been entrusted to Harrison, whose fanatical hatred of the King was well known, and when Charles heard that

Harrison would be in charge of him he thought that the intention was to assassinate him. But he was surprised to find that Harrison was courteous and correct in his behaviour, and that he rode a gallant horse and wore a velvet cap on his head 'and a new buff coat on his back, with a crimson silk scarf about his waist, richly fringed'. The King commented that he was a fine-looking soldier, and that to judge by his face he was not the kind of man that he was made out to be.

On the first evening, at Farnham, where they lodged in a gentleman's house, the King took Harrison by the arm and led him to an alcove where they talked for half an hour. He told Harrison that he had heard that Harrison intended to kill him. Harrison assured the King that he had no such intention, that the steps to be taken against him 'would be open to the eyes of the world', and that 'the law was equally obliging to great and small, and that justice had no respect of persons'. Charles did not like this answer. He abruptly broke off the conversation and went to his supper.

Harrison allowed Charles to spend the following night at the house of the ardent Cavaliers, Lord and Lady Newburgh, at Bagshot. He made no attempt to stop the Newburghs from expressing their loyalty and sympathy to the King, and from providing him with the best food and wine at their disposal, but he placed guards at every door and foiled the plot for Charles to escape on Newburgh's fastest racehorse.

During the weeks before the King's trial and execution, Harrison was at the centre of affairs in Whitehall Palace, being in constant touch with Cromwell and Ireton, and often sharing a bed with Ireton in the palace. He sat as a judge at every session of the King's trial, and signed the death warrant. The cry of the common soldiers who lined Westminster Hall during the trial and escorted the King as he walked through the streets—'Justice! Justice!'—summed up Harrison's view of the trial and execution.

Harrison did not go with Cromwell to Ireland, but remained in England, suppressing a Cavalier rising in the Midlands and achieving a reputation for great severity in his military government of South Wales. When Cromwell and Lambert invaded Scotland, Harrison, who had been promoted to the rank of Major-General, was appointed as Commander-in-Chief of the

army in England, and when Charles II and the Scottish Covenanters invaded England, Harrison marched against them, heading
them off from London while Cromwell pursued them from the
rear. Harrison linked up with Lambert's vanguard at Preston and
with Cromwell's main army at Warwick, and fought in the
victory at Worcester.

Harrison supported Cromwell's dissolution of the Rump
Parliament in April 1653, and played an active part in it. None of
the political leaders of the Rump—not Vane, with his cool
political expertise, or Marten, with his philosophical republicanism and his love affairs—qualified, in Harrison's eyes, for the
leadership of God's Saints. He was filled with godly wrath
against them. On the morning of 20 April he took his seat in the
House, as Cromwell did, and when Cromwell sent in his troopers
with their muskets and drawn swords, Harrison himself pulled
the Speaker, Lenthall, out of the Chair and pushed him out of the
Chamber. That afternoon Cromwell dissolved the Council of
State and replaced it with a committee of thirteen army officers.
Harrison was for a time the chairman of the committee, and thus
in effect the head of the English state. It was at his suggestion
that Cromwell summoned the Barebones Parliament, consisting
of 140 nominated Puritan zealots, in July 1653; but Lambert, the
Grandees, the gentry and the lawyers were working against him.
When the Barebones Parliament attacked the administration of
justice and demanded the abolition of tithes, Cromwell dissolved
it in December and assumed the office of Lord Protector.

Harrison protested strongly against Cromwell's action. He and
twenty-seven other members of the Barebones Parliament
refused to leave the House, and were driven out by the soldiers,
just as Harrison himself had driven out the MPs of the Rump
eight months before. A few days later Harrison was dismissed
from the army.

Cromwell, Lambert and Thurloe, the Secretary of State, believed
that Harrison was one of their most dangerous opponents. He
had always been regarded as an Anabaptist by his critics, and he
now came under the influence of the Fifth Monarchy Men. They
believed that the four monarchies referred to in the Book of
Revelation would be followed by the Fifth Monarchy, the reign

of King Jesus. They were therefore not prepared to submit to the reign of Oliver Cromwell.

In February 1654 Cromwell ordered Harrison to go to his house in his native Staffordshire and to stay there under house arrest. He complied with the order, but in September he was arrested and brought before Cromwell, who tried unsuccessfully to win his support for the government. After a short imprisonment he was released, but in February 1655, at the time of the Cavalier and Leveller plots which culminated in Penruddock's rising, he was rearrested and imprisoned in Carisbrooke Castle in the Isle of Wight, where Charles I had been held prisoner seven years before. One of the other Fifth Monarchy Men at Carisbrooke, who refused to obey the orders of the jailers and tried to preach to them, was beaten up by the soldiers of the garrison; but Harrison himself, who was always referred to as 'the Major-General' by his comrades and the jailers, suffered no physical ill-treatment, and seems to have been less uncooperative than some of his fellow-prisoners.

After thirteen months' imprisonment he was released in March 1656 because his father was very ill and his wife was also in poor health. In 1648 he had married Katherine, the daughter of his namesake Ralph Harrison, a merchant of Highgate; all their children died in infancy. After his release from Carisbrooke, Harrison was allowed to stay under house arrest in his house at Highgate.

The republican leader, General Edmund Ludlow, who had been a leading member of the Rump and strongly objected to its dissolution, had also been imprisoned by Cromwell's government, and then released. Ludlow visited Harrison at Highgate and asked him why he had helped Cromwell to dissolve the Rump. Harrison's answer showed that if he lacked dialectical skill, he was very clear in his mind as to what he was about. He said that he had supported the dissolution of the Rump 'because he was fully persuaded that they had not a heart to do any more good for the Lord and his people'. When Ludlow asked him whether he now regretted having done it, he said: 'Upon their heads be the guilt, who have made a wrong use of it; for my own part, my heart was upright and sincere in the thing.' He added that there were more important things than civil liberty, and cited a text from Daniel, 'that the saints shall take the kingdom and possess

it.' But when Ludlow began to point out the flaw in this argument, Harrison said that he could not argue any more.

In the spring of 1657, when Cromwell thought of accepting
the crown, the Fifth Monarchy man, Venner, who would
acknowledge neither King Charles nor King Oliver but only
King Jesus, made plans for an insurrection. The government
became alarmed, and Harrison was arrested, although he was not
involved in Venner's plot. He was soon released, but was
arrested for the fourth time by Cromwell's government at the
time of the conspiracies of February 1658 and sent to the Tower,
though once again he was soon freed. After Cromwell's death he
lived quietly in Staffordshire. Neither Richard Cromwell, the
army Grandees, nor the republicans of the Rump could command
his allegiance, and he did not respond to Lambert's call to rally to
defend the Good Old Cause from the 'Common Enemy', Charles
Stuart.

But the Cavaliers and Presbyterians had not forgotten his
activities in December 1648 and January 1649. Since the deaths of
Cromwell, Ireton and Bradshaw, he was the most prominent of
the surviving regicides. He had not only sat as one of the King's
judges and signed the death warrant, but had brought Charles
from Hurst Castle to London for his trial and execution; and
because of his extremist views and his low social origin, he had
neither important political allies nor influential Cavalier relatives
to intercede for him. When the House of Commons, in its first and
more merciful mood, decided to limit the number of regicides to
be capitally punished to seven, they agreed at once that Harrison
should be one of the seven, and he was arrested in Staffordshire
and brought to the Tower in May 1660 before Charles II had
landed at Dover.

When the trial of twenty-nine of the regicides began at Hicks
Hall in London in October 1660, Harrison was the chief
defendant. He was the first to be charged with high treason for
having compassed the death of the King. He was treated with
courtesy by the court, being always addressed by his rank of
Major-General, but he cannot be said to have had a fair trial in
the atmosphere of near-hysteria which prevailed on the subject of
the murder of King Charles the Martyr. He was not allowed to be
represented by counsel, because this right was never granted to
defendants in cases of high treason.

When he was called upon to plead Guilty or Not Guilty, he tried to challenge the jurisdiction of the court, arguing that as the execution of the King had been ordered by the High Court of Parliament in 1649, it could not be punished now by the present court, which was inferior to the High Court of Parliament; but after he had been called on to plead twelve times, and had eleven times been interrupted when he tried to challenge the jurisdiction, he pleaded Not Guilty. He made no attempt to placate the court or excuse himself. He proudly declared that the execution of Charles I 'was not a Thing done in a Corner. I believe the Sound of it hath been in most Nations. I believe the Hearts of some have felt the Terrors of that Presence of God that was with his Servants in those Days (however it seemeth good to him to suffer this Turn to come on us).'

His judges consisted not only of old Cavaliers like the president, Sir Orlando Bridgman, and Chief Justice Finch, who had sat in judgment more than twenty years before on Prynne and Hampden and had returned to England after many years in exile: among them were Harrison's old comrade-in-arms, Monck, his old commander Manchester, and Denzil Holles, one of the Five Members of 1642. But he was not allowed to comment on this injustice and on the arbitrariness of singling-out him and his fellow-regicides for punishment. When he began to say: 'Divers of those that sit upon the Bench were formerly as Active——' he was interrupted and told that it was not for him to cast reflections on the court. He caused more indignant interruptions when he tried to argue that he had acted under the lawful authority of the established government in 1649. When he declared that the execution of Charles I 'was done rather in the Fear of the Lord', Bridgman stopped him and declared 'Christians must not hear this'; and old Finch, prejudging the issue, said: 'This must not be suffered, that you should run into these damnable Excursions, to make God the Author of this damnable Treason committed.'

Harrison's argument that the execution of Charles I had been carried out under the authority of Parliament was particularly exasperating to the Presbyterians who had fought in the Civil War for the privileges of Parliament, but strongly condemned the Independents for the death of the King and for Pride's Purge. Denzil Holles intervened from his place on the bench to declare that the murder of King Charles the Martyr had not been authorized by Parliament—which consisted of the King himself, the House of Lords and the House of Commons—but only by one-eighth of the House of Commons. He added that Harrison had no right to claim that he had acted by the authority of a Parliament which he himself had afterwards helped to dissolve in 1653 when he pulled the Speaker out of the Chair.

The Cavaliers did not give the regicides the clean, painless death that the regicides had given to Charles I. Harrison was sentenced to be hanged, drawn and quartered—to be drawn on a hurdle, face downwards, through the streets to Charing Cross, and there to be hanged, cut down while still alive, to be castrated and disembowelled and his privy parts and entrails burned before his eyes, before he was to be killed by having his head cut off, after which his legs and arms were to be cut off and his head and limbs displayed in some public place. He showed great courage and resolution as he prepared for death. On the morning of his execution he said his last good-bye to his wife, telling her that he had nothing to leave her except his Bible. He made a short speech to the other prisoners at Newgate, where he had been confined, and went up to the roof of the prison to look for the last time over London. He then went down to the hurdle and helped fasten the cords which bound him to it.

When he arrived at Charing Cross, he encountered a howling, jeering crowd of spectators, for there was no sympathy for the regicides among the majority of the population of London in October 1660. One of the spectators mocked him, calling out: 'Where is your Good Old Cause?' Harrison put his hand on his breast, and replied: 'Here it is, and I am going to seal it with my blood.' In his speech from the scaffold he said that if he appeared to tremble, it was not through fear, but from the effects of a debilitation in his health which he had suffered ever since he was wounded at Appleby in 1648. He said that God 'hath covered my head many times in the day of Battel. By God I have leaped over a Wall, by God I have runned through a Troop, and by my God I will go through this death.'

He was hanged, cut down alive, castrated and disembowelled. Some onlookers said that as the hangman was burning his genitals and entrails before his eyes, Harrison rose up and struck him in the face. Others said that he was already dead, and that it was merely that his arm twitched convulsively after death and moved in the direction of the hangman. But his wife and friends were sure that they would see him again very soon, when he returned with King Jesus, as Jesus's chief lieutenant, to establish the Fifth Monarchy.

13

William Prynne

If Major-General Lambert, the originator of the dictatorship of the Major-Generals, and Major-General Harrison, the extremist Fifth Monarchy man, were far removed from the popular idea of the gloomy Puritan, William Prynne the moderate politician, the conscientious lawyer, the ardent supporter of the Restoration, comes very close to the traditional picture. He never married, and it is very unlikely that he ever had a mistress. He was very abstemious in food and drink. He lived only for his work. He never showed any sign of affection for any human being, and though he denounced bishops, Jesuits, Catholics, Independents, Levellers, Jews and Quakers with great bitterness, there is something almost frighteningly unemotional about his cold, conscientious hatred. He had only one form of self-indulgence. As he sat, hour after hour in his study, writing his books and pamphlets, wearing a long quilt cap to protect his eyes, he ordered his servant to bring him a pot of ale every three hours, which he would drink while he paused for a moment from his work.

He was born in 1600 in the village of Swainswick in Somerset. His father was a prosperous tenant farmer who farmed the lands of Oriel College, Oxford, at Swainswick; his mother was the daughter of a Bath merchant who had been Mayor of Bath some years before. Prynne was brought up from childhood in the atmosphere of West Country Puritanism. He was educated at Bath Grammar School, and at the age of sixteen went to Oriel College, Oxford, and five years later to Lincoln's Inn. In 1628 he was called to the bar. If he had lived in the previous century, he would have taken holy orders; but though in many ways—in his dogmatic method of arguing on the basis of texts, his respect for the royal supremacy, and his hatred of Roman Catholics—he resembled the religious controversialists of an earlier period, he also shared to the full the seventeenth-century Puritan's devotion to the English common law.

In 1627 he published the first of his pamphlets attacking the High Church followers of Laud and the 'Arminians' in the Church of England hierarchy for bowing at the name of Jesus and for adopting other ritualistic practices, and above all for their thinly-veiled criticism of the Calvinist doctrine of predestination. Prynne was never a champion of liberty for its own sake. It is typical of him that whereas other Roundheads, such as Hampden and Lilburne, first clashed with authority when they upheld the cause of freedom from arbitrary taxation and freedom of publication, Prynne first fell foul of the King and the government when he demanded that Parliament should introduce legislation making it a criminal offence to question the doctrine of predestination.

In 1628 he published his book *The Unloveliness of Love-Lockes*. It was an attack on the wickedness of the vain courtiers and gentlemen who wore their hair long and curled it. He believed that it was sinful for a man to have long hair. On the other hand, women ought to wear their hair long, as a sign of their subjection to men; and the fashionable ladies who cut their hair short and and 'frizled' it into pretty curls were nearly as wicked as the Popish nuns who cut off all their hair and shaved their heads in flagrant disobedience to the law of Moses.

In November 1632 he published an immensely long book on which he had been working for many years—*Histrio-Mastix, The Players Scovrge, or Actors Tragedie*, in which he denounced the theatre. After listing a number of 'sinfull, wicked, unchristian pastimes', such as 'effeminate mixt Dancing, Dicing, Stage-playes, lascivious Pictures, wanton Fashions, Face-painting, Health-drinking, Long haire, Love-lockes, Periwigs, women's curling, pouldring and cutting of their haire, Bone-fires, New-yeares-gifts, May-games, amorous Pastoralls, lascivious effeminate Musicke, excessive laughter, luxurious disorderly Christmas-keeping, Mummeries', he proceeded to concentrate, for the remaining eleven hundred pages of his book, on the evil of stage-plays, actors and actresses.

It is sometimes said, in extenuation of Prynne's denunciation of the theatre, that actors and actresses in his time were low and

immoral people. In fact the stage was less immoral in 1632 than
it was in the years after the Restoration of 1660, when Prynne was
enthusiastically praising the virtues of King Charles II and taking
care to make no reference at all to the immorality of the King's
friends on the London stage; and it shows a misunderstanding
of Prynne's character to think that he objected to the theatre
because of the immoral conduct of actors and actresses in his
time. He attacked the theatre because he found many texts in the
writings of the early Christian Fathers which condemned the
theatre, though he casually conceded, in one passing sentence
in his book, that he could find no passage in the Bible which
expressly did so. There is comparatively little in *Histrio-Mastix*
about the immorality of actors and actresses in Charles I's
England, but a vast amount about what St Cyprian and other
writers had written about the immorality of actors and actresses
in Rome and Constantinople more than a thousand years before,
all confirmed by lengthy quotations, often in the original Latin,
from the early Fathers. There are also references to theatres
collapsing and killing members of the audience in London in
1583, in Magdeburg in 1380, and in Bavaria in 1200, and to an
actor who had been turned into an ass by two witches when
travelling to Rome in 1012. As in all Prynne's writings, there is
an almost unbroken succession of references to texts in the
margin of the pages, which led his opponents to call him sarcastically 'Marginal Prynne'.

Though Prynne, with his precise reasoning and his references
to patristic texts, is closer to a Tudor theologian than to a Stuart
pamphleteer, he did not write with the passion of a Luther or a
Knox, but with the cool detachment of a lawyer and in the most
formal terms of a medieval disputation. 'If Stage-Playes bee those
Workes of Satan, those Pompes, and Vanities of this wicked
World, which every Christian hath seriously renounced, and
solemnly vowed against in his very Baptisme; they must of
necessitie be pernicious, abominable, vnseemly, and vnlawfull
vnto Christians. But Stage-Playes are those workes of Satan,
those Pompes, and vanities of this wicked world, which every
Christian hath seriously renounced, and solemnly vowed against
in his very Baptisme. Therefore they must of necessitie bee
pernicious, abominable, vnseemly, and vnlawfull vnto Christians.'
And thus, on and on, until he reached his twenty-sixth and last

John Lambert

Thomas, Lord Fairfax, by Faithorne after Walker

Thomas Harrison, engraving by M. van der Gucht

Hugh Peters, by Dobson

Archibald Johnston, Lord Warriston

Mrs. Hutchinson,
by Walker

Colonel Hutchinson,
by Walker

(*Left*) John Milton

George Monck, Duke of Albemarle, by Lely

accusation against the theatre: 'The last unlawfull Concomitant of Stage-playes, is, profuse lascivious laughter, accompanied with an immoderate applause of those scurrilous Playes and Actors, which Christians should rather abominate than admire.'

This long and very boring book, with its many Latin passages, could never have become a popular incendiary publication; but it gave Laud and the bishops, who had resented Prynne's earlier attacks on High Church ritual and Arminianism, an excuse to strike at him. Two months after Prynne had published *Histrio-Mastix*, a masque had been presented at court in which Queen Henrietta Maria had acted one of the parts, and King Charles had proudly watched as a member of the audience. Prynne had stated, in *Histrio-Mastix*, that amateur actors were less wicked than professionals, but he had nevertheless denounced them as sinful, along with anyone who went to see a play performed. He was therefore arrested on a charge of seditious libel and accused of having vilified the King and Queen in *Histrio-Mastix*, although he had published the book before the Queen had taken part in the play. After a year in prison he was brought before the Court of Star Chamber, and sentenced to stand twice in the pillory, to have part of each ear cut off, to be imprisoned during the King's pleasure, and to be fined £5,000. In order to increase the severity of the punishment, his ears were cut on different occasions, one being cropped in Palace Yard on 7 May 1634, and the other in Cheapside three days later. He had the further mortification of being deprived of his Oxford degree and disgraced by the Inn to which he was so proud to belong. He had dedicated *Histrio-Mastix* 'to the Right Christian, Generous Young Gentlemen Students of the 4 famous Innes of Court, and especially those of Lincolnes Inne'; but the benchers of Lincoln's Inn not only disbarred him and expelled him from the Inn, but also joined with the other Inns of Court to present Shirley's theatrical masque, *The Triumph of Peace*, at very great expense before the King and Queen at Whitehall.

A month after his ears had been cropped, Prynne wrote a protest against his punishment and sent it to Laud. The Archbishop handed it to the Attorney-General and instructed him to take fresh proceedings against Prynne so that he could be sentenced to further punishment for this new seditious libel. When the Attorney-General asked Prynne whether he admitted writing the protest to Laud, Prynne said that he must first see the document; and when the Attorney-General showed it to him, he snatched it up, tore it into little pieces, and threw it out of the window, so that there was no evidence on which he could be convicted of the new offence.

Prynne spent the next three years in the Tower, secretly writing pamphlets which he managed to smuggle out to his sympathizers. In 1637 he wrote a nine-page pamphlet, *Newes from Ipswich*. It had nothing to do with Ipswich apart from the fact that Ipswich was falsely given as the place of publication. It was an attack on the bishops for having by implication challenged the doctrine of predestination by illegally cutting out of the collect for the royal family in the Book of Common Prayer the reference to God as 'the father of thine elect and of their seed'. By a far-fetched interpretation, Prynne argued that the bishops had thereby asserted that the King and the royal family were not members of the Elect, but were Reprobates, and he called on 'our most pious King Charles' to 'hang up such Archtraytors to our faith, Church, Religion, and such true-born sons to the Romane Antichrist'.

The authorities discovered that Prynne was the author of *Newes from Ipswich*, and his 'most pious King Charles', instead of hanging up the bishops, permitted them to proceed against Prynne on a charge of seditious libel for having published it. Prynne was brought from prison before the Court of Star Chamber. Archbishop Laud proposed that the remaining parts of his ears should be cut off. Chief Justice Finch thought that this punishment was too lenient, and that he should in addition be branded in the face with the letters 'SL' for 'seditious libeller'. He was sentenced to undergo both punishments, to stand for two hours in the pillory, to be fined another £5,000—which was more than the total value of his property—and to be imprisoned for life. Dr Burton and Henry Bastwick, who had preached and distributed pamphlets against bishops, were sentenced to lose their ears at the same time. The sentence was carried out on a warm summer day on 30 June 1637 in Palace Yard in Westminster. When Prynne's ears had been cropped in 1634 there had not been much public sympathy for him; but on this occasion great crowds gathered around the pillory, cheering the victims, and rushed forward to dip their handkerchiefs in the martyrs' blood as the ears were cut off. Prynne, whose ears were cut in a particularly cruel fashion because he had given the executioner only half-a-crown as a tip, made a speech as he stood in the pillory, and proudly declared that the letters 'SL' with which he had been branded stood not for 'seditious libeller' but for 'Stigmata Laudis', the 'stigma of Laud'.

Immediately after his ordeal, Prynne was taken to Caernarvon Castle, which had been chosen as his place of imprisonment on account of its remoteness and the difficulties which he would have in making contact there with supporters who might smuggle out his writings. On the way to Caernarvon he and his guards stopped at Chester, where he was entertained at a banquet by the Mayor and city corporation, who hailed him as a martyr for English freedom and the Protestant religion. After some months in Caernarvon Castle he was transferred to a prison that was even more remote, the castle of Mont Orgueil in Jersey.

In November 1640, after Prynne had spent nearly eight years in prison, the Long Parliament ordered the arrest of Archbishop Laud and the release of all his victims. Prynne returned in triumph from Mont Orgueil, and was greeted at Temple Bar by a crowd which included 2,000 horsemen and 100 coaches. His conviction was annulled by Act of Parliament, and compensation was voted to him, though in fact he never received the money. Although he was not an MP, the House of Commons appointed him to serve on the committee which was preparing the impeachment of Laud for high treason, and he was one of the most energetic members of the committee. The spiteful, arrogant and universally-hated Archbishop was nearly seventy years of age and broken in health and spirit, and as he was no danger to the Parliamentary cause, the proceedings against him were allowed to drag on for four years. He was not beheaded until January 1645.

Prynne had therefore time to build up the case against Laud with patient and painstaking thoroughness. He examined Laud, searched his cell in the Tower, and once searched his person. During one of these searches he found and confiscated Laud's private diary, which the Archbishop had kept for many years and in which he had expressed many superstitious fears about astrological and other portents which Prynne and the House of Commons could now use to discredit him.

Prynne's participation in the prosecution of Laud must have been a sweet revenge for him, but in the books which he published about the case he refers only briefly to the sufferings which he himself had undergone at Laud's hands. There is none of the self-pitying propaganda in which Lilburne always indulged in his writings. In one section of his lengthy book *A Breviate of the Life of William Laud* he denounces Laud for his attempt to force the English Prayer Book on the Scottish Covenanters; but by far the greater part of the work is an attack on Laud for being a secret Papist sympathizer and for his laxity in enforcing the penal laws against Roman Catholics. Prynne condemned Laud much more for his failure to persecute Papists than for his persecution of Presbyterians and Protestant Nonconformists.

At the outbreak of the Civil War—when he had the satisfaction of seeing Parliament close all the London theatres 'while these sad causes and set-times of humiliation do continue'—Prynne supported the Roundhead cause enthusiastically. He had stoutly upheld the principle of royal Absolutism in its Protestant Elizabethan form even when he was suffering at the hands of Laud, arguing that he was a victim of the tyranny of the bishops, not of the King. He now justified the armed resistance to Charles I on the grounds which were being put forward by Parliament in its official statements—that the Roundheads were defending themselves and fighting to rescue the King from his evil counsellors.

In two very long books, *The Soveraigne Power of Parliaments and Kingdomes*, and *Hidden Workes of Darkenes brought to Publike Light*, which dealt with Laud's trial, he put forward his interpretation of the causes of the Civil War: it was all the fault of the Jesuits. The English Protestants had feared and hated the Jesuits ever since the government propaganda campaign which had been launched against them in Elizabeth I's reign; but Prynne was partly responsible for the increasing hysteria about Jesuits which gripped England in the seventeenth century and did not disappear altogether for more than two hundred years. He blamed the Jesuits for all the political disasters which had occurred in Europe in the past fifty years, not only for the conspiracies against Elizabeth I, the Gunpowder Plot of 1605 and the assassination of Henry IV of France, but for the Portuguese national rising against Spain in 1640, a peasant revolt in Sweden and the murder of the boy-Prince Dimitry by Boris Godunov in Russia.

But he believed that the chief target of the Jesuits' machinations was England. Having failed to overthrow the Protestant religion in England, and to re-establish Popery, by their assassination plots against Queen Elizabeth and King James, they had resorted to more subtle methods: they had induced Laud to introduce Popish practices into the Church of England in the hopes that this would provoke the King's loyal Protestant subjects to justifiable resistance, which would give the King's secret Papist advisers the excuse to start a civil war; then, when England was occupied and exhausted with civil war, a foreign Papist power, such as Spain or France, could invade and conquer England, enslave freeborn Englishmen and reintroduce Popery.

By 1644 Prynne was fighting another enemy. He ardently championed the Presbyterians against the Independents. He strongly opposed the demand for religious toleration, and attacked writers like Milton and Lilburne, though Lilburne had suffered martyrdom for protesting against Prynne's own martyrdom at Laud's hands. Prynne objected not only to Lilburne's plea for religious toleration, but also to his social doctrines. Prynne attacked the Levellers in his pamphlet *The Levellers Levelled to the very ground*, quoting the Epistle of St Peter on the duties of servants to obey their masters.

The clash between Parliament and the army in 1647 brought Prynne into action with a series of pamphlets in which he denounced the army and the Independents for advocating religious toleration and for challenging the privileges of Parliament for which they had all taken up arms against the King. As always, he took his stand first and foremost on the rule of law, quoting countless medieval precedents in support of the privileges and sovereignty of Parliament. He denounced the expulsion of the eleven Presbyterian MPs by the army in August 1647. It was a consolation for him that next year the ban on stage-plays, which had been imposed in London for the duration of the Civil War, was made permanent throughout England when a statute was passed making it a criminal offence to act in or watch any theatrical performance.

On 7 November 1648 Prynne was elected at a by-election as

MP for Newport in Cornwall, but he sat in the House of Commons for less than a month. After he had spoken in favour of the negotiations with the King in the debate of 5 December, he was one of the forty-one MPs who were arrested next day in Pride's Purge, and confined in 'Hell' and the tavern in the Strand. This caused him to write an indignant pamphlet. He had placed very little emphasis, in his writings, on the sufferings that he had experienced when Laud's men had cut off his ears and branded him and imprisoned him for eight years; but he wrote now in the most passionate way about the hardships which he had undergone at the hands of his former allies—these more radical Puritans, these believers in freedom of conscience—who had illegally confined him for twenty-four hours in a cold room with nothing to eat or drink except biscuits and wine.

He also wrote indignantly against the King's trial and execution, the abolition of the House of Lords and the proclamation of the Republic. When the House of Commons in January 1649 assumed sole legislative power and set up the court to try the King, he published a seven-page pamphlet, *Articles of Impeachment of High-Treason exhibited by the Commons of England in a Free Parliament against Lieutenant-General Oliver Cromwell Esquire, Commissary-General Henry Ireton Esquire, Sir Hardresse Waller Knight and Colonel, Colonel Pride,* and nine others, including Cornet Joyce, Hugh Peters and Marten. He demanded 'that the said Traitors and every of them may be forthwith apprehended, secured and brought to Trial, before they ruine King, Parliament, and the Kingdoms of England and Ireland and enslave them to their Tyrannie.'

He followed this with another pamphlet a few days later, *A Breife Memento to the Present Vnparliamentary Ivnto Touching their present Intentions and Proceedings to Depose and Execute Charles Steward, their lawfull King.* He considered that to put the King on trial and execute him betrayed the principles for which Parliament had fought the war and their repeated declarations that they meant no harm to the King's person; the project of establishing the Republic violated the fundamental laws and liberties of the realm of England. He believed that Cromwell and the army leaders were secret agents of the Jesuits. In 1605, at the time of the Gunpowder Plot, the Jesuits had tried unsuccessfully to commit regicide; this time they were going to succeed. It was obvious that the Independents were Jesuits, because they not only had the same objective—regicide—but used the same means to win the support of gullible dupes, by demanding religious toleration.

After the King's execution, Prynne withdrew to his Somersetshire home at Swainswick. The Republican government, acting with a tolerance which Charles I and Laud would not have shown him and which he would not have shown to the Independents, allowed him to remain at liberty for eighteen months, despite the fact that he refused to pay his taxes on the grounds that they could not lawfully be levied by an illegal government. But on the evening of Sunday 30 June 1650 a body of soldiers arrived at the house, armed with a warrant from Prynne's old friend and fellow-barrister, John Bradshaw, who had presided at Charles I's trial and was now the President of the Council of State. They searched the house, removed Prynne's papers and arrested Prynne, and after marching him through the streets of Bristol imprisoned him in Dunster Castle near Minehead.

During his imprisonment he wrote a series of indignant letters to Bradshaw, who was the only signatory of the warrant for his arrest, protesting against the illegality of his detention. He did not impugn Bradshaw's authority by challenging the legality of the republic and the Council of State, but claimed that the search of his house and his arrest were illegal under the English common law, because they had been carried out on a Sunday, after sunset, and by officers and soldiers of the army, not by a local JP and the village constable. He reminded Bradshaw that he was a former friend, 'and one of mine own robe (much contemning the Kings Star-Chamber Lords and Prelates illegall Warrants and Proceedings in this kind against me) from whom I expected no such unjust exorbitant Warrants or Military violence as this; yet Stranger, in regard of my self the Sufferer, who having been such an Eminent Martyr, both in body and Estate, suffering near 8 years Imprisonments, close restraints, exile, 3 Pillories, Stigmatizing, a double losse of eares, & excessive Fines, for the defence of our religion, Laws, Publick Wealth, & Liberty of the Nation, without receiving one penny recompence for all my losses, and suffrings, though promised, voted, many Thousands . ... If you pretend necessity of State, or the publick Peace and Safety, for these Illegal Proceedings; it is but the very same

Plea the Prelates pretended for my close Imprisonment, and banishment heretofore; the King, for the Loans, Excise, Ship-money; and the Army for my last restraint, violence to both Houses, and their secured secluded Members.' He afterwards wrote that, although he could not prove it, he had little doubt that his arrest had been the result of a Jesuit plot.

Bradshaw did not make Prynne's letter an excuse for bringing new proceedings against him, as Laud had tried to do in a similar situation sixteen years earlier. He even replied to Prynne's protest; but Prynne remained in Dunster Castle for a year without being brought to trial or charged with any offence. In June 1651, after a fortnight in Taunton Castle, he was transferred to Pendennis Castle on the south coast of Cornwall near St Mawes. Here he wrote a pamphlet, *Pendennis and all other standing Forts Dismantled,* arguing that all military forts and castles like Pendennis should be demolished because they were a financial burden to the English taxpayer, a threat to his freedom, and useless as a defence of the realm against foreign invasion and against the real menace which threatened it, the infiltration of foreign Jesuits.

In the autumn of 1652 the government offered him his freedom if he would give an undertaking, and enter into recognizances for £1,000, not to agitate against the government. He refused, but was nevertheless released unconditionally in February 1653.

For the next six years he lived quietly under Cromwell's government at his house at Swainswick, and though he continued to write and publish pamphlets, these did not directly attack the government. He wrote a pamphlet on the Lord's Day Sabbath, to prove that it ran from dusk to dusk, and not from midnight to midnight or from dawn to dawn. He also wrote a pamphlet, *The Quakers unmasked, And clearly detected to be but the Spawn of Romish Frogs, Jesuites, and Franciscan Freers; sent from Rome to seduce the intoxicated Giddy-headed English Nation.* It was provoked by one of many instances in which a wandering Quaker preacher had been prosecuted before the JPs at Bristol, because throughout the country the Quakers were being persecuted by local Justices and mobs, despite the attempts of Cromwell and Lambert to prevent the persecution. Prynne argued that these travelling Quakers were Jesuits who had secretly entered England from abroad: as the Jesuit emissaries who had been coming to England since the reign of Elizabeth I had failed in their attempts to convert the English to Popery, the Pope had ordered them to adopt more subtle tactics and pretend to be Quakers and other kinds of Nonconformists in order to split the unity of the Protestant Church. He denounced 'those in present power'—he did not venture to name Cromwell—for conniving at the Quakers' activities by their lenient punishments.

In 1655 Cromwell summoned a conference of divines and other leading personalities to consider the petition of the Jewish leader, Menasseh ben Israel of Amsterdam, that the Jews should be readmitted to England for the first time since their explusion by Edward I in 1290. Both financial and religious issues were involved. Cromwell was not blind to the economic benefits which England would derive from the presence of Jewish merchants in the City of London, but the religious question was uppermost in the minds of the leaders at the conference in Whitehall. Interest in Judaism and a sense of affinity with it had developed among many Puritans as a result of their reading of the Old Testament. Prynne published a pamphlet violently denouncing the decision to readmit the Jews. He argued partly on the legalistic grounds which always appealed to him, claiming that the statutes passed by lawful Parliaments in 1290 and on subsequent occasions, by which the expulsion of the Jews was ordered and confirmed, could only be repealed by an Act of another lawful Parliament and not by order of Cromwell's government; but he also opposed the readmission of the Jews on grounds of general principle, because they were not Christian Protestants and should be granted no more toleration than anyone else who was not a Presbyterian. He surveyed the history of Jewish residence in England for the two hundred years before 1290, making all the traditional accusations against the Jews of murdering Christian children, like St Hugh of Lincoln, in order to use their blood for the Passover cakes, and described with unconcealed relish the many massacres of Jews during this period 'by Gods just curse and vengeance on them for their sins'. Surprisingly, he did not accuse the Jews of being secret agents of the Jesuits.

When the coalition between Lambert and the republicans brought back the Rump after the fall of Richard Cromwell in May 1659, Prynne emerged from retirement. He thought that if the MPs of the Rump, who had been driven out by Cromwell's troopers in 1653, were now to return to a revived Long Parliament, so might the 'excluded members'—the Presbyterians who had been similarly kept out by armed force in Pride's Purge in 1648. He therefore arrived at the House for the first meeting of the Rump Parliament on 8 May 1659, but was not allowed to enter the chamber. He was again excluded when he tried to take his seat next day. On 10 May he managed to slip into the chamber with two other excluded members without being noticed; but when his presence was spotted, the Speaker adjourned the House for dinner, and when the sitting was resumed after dinner, Prynne was prevented from re-entering the chamber. He withdrew to Swainswick, but during the growing crisis of the summer and autumn of 1659, as the popular feeling in favour of the restoration of Charles II was rising throughout the country, he published a succession of pamphlets in which he violently attacked the republicans of the Rump and the rule of the army.

In October Lambert dispersed the Rump, but by Christmas his army in Yorkshire had begun to disintegrate, and Monck was on the point of marching south from Coldstream with the ostensible object of restoring the Rump. Hazelrig and the republicans in London, defying Lambert and his supporters, reconvened the Rump. When the Rump met on 27 December, Prynne and Waller and other Presbyterians who had been excluded by Pride's Purge again tried to take their seats, and were again excluded; but they had not long to wait for victory. On 3 February 1660 Monck entered London with his army; by 11 February he had defied the authority of the Rump, and had summoned a meeting of Parliament in which both the Rumpers and the excluded Presbyterian members were invited to sit. On 21 February Prynne and all the survivors of Pride's Purge took their seats in the House, and as they constituted a majority over the Rumpers they carried a resolution for the dissolution of the Long Parliament and for a new general election. Everyone knew that the new Parliament would recall Charles II to the throne.

On 25 May Charles II landed at Dover; his first action on setting foot on English soil was to kiss a Presbyterian Bible. Three days later he reached London, and spent his first night in Whitehall Palace in bed with Barbara Villiers, then Mrs Palmer and later

Countess of Castlemaine and Duchess of Cleveland. Prynne noticed the kissing of the Bible, but unlike Pepys and other commentators he ignored the adultery with Barbara Palmer. He had been so obsessed for the last twelve years with his hatred for the republicans and the Independents that he welcomed the Restoration without qualification, and was ready to overlook all the faults of Charles II and the Cavaliers. He believed that he himself had largely contributed to bringing about the Restoration by his pamphlets during the previous year, and he was highly gratified when the King received him at Whitehall and thanked him for his loyalty.

In the first Parliament of Charles II's reign, which sat throughout the summer of 1660, the chief question to be settled was the punishment of the regicides and which of them should be exempted from the provisions of the Act of Indemnity and reserved for death or some lesser punishment. Prynne, who was elected as MP for Bath, was pitiless. While the House of Commons, the House of Lords and Clarendon argued about the number of victims and which of the Roundheads should be selected to fill up the prescribed quota, Prynne adopted the most logical position: he demanded that all who were guilty of high treason, either because of their part in the death of King Charles I or for having waged war against King Charles II, should be executed. He did not apply this argument to the Roundheads like himself who had fought in, or supported, the First Civil War against Charles I, because he relied on the old fiction—which to him was certainly a reality—that they had been fighting to rescue the King from the Jesuits.

In the debates in Parliament, Prynne demanded the death penalty not only for his old enemies like Milton and Hugh Peters, but also for such harmless persons as Richard Cromwell and Mr Justice Thorp, who had been dismissed from the judicial bench by Oliver Cromwell in 1655 for his leniency towards the Cavalier rebels in the north, but had on one occasion made a speech justifying the execution of Charles I. Prynne also demanded that every official who had served the Commonwealth government should be compelled to repay to the state all the salary that he had received while in office. This proposal, and the demand for the death penalty for Milton, Richard Cromwell and Thorp, were rejected, and though Prynne succeeded in getting Fleetwood exempted from the Act of Indemnity, Fleetwood eventually escaped with nothing worse than disqualification for life from holding any public position. In every case where a petition for mercy was under consideration, or some corrupt bargain was being concluded to save a Roundhead from death or life imprisonment, one of the relevant factors was that Prynne would use his influence in the House of Commons in favour of the most severe penalty and would vilify anyone who recommended leniency. In October 1660 his enemy Hugh Peters and Sir Hardress Waller, who had made him spend a night on the bare boards with only biscuits and wine to eat and drink at the time of Pride's Purge, were brought to trial as regicides. One of the judges of the court was Chief Justice Finch, who in 1637 had insisted that Prynne be branded in the face because merely to cut off his ears was too lenient a punishment.

The alliance between the Cavaliers and the Presbyterians did not survive for very long after the Restoration. The Marquis of Argyll, who had crowned Charles II King of Scots at Scone in 1651, was executed in 1661, and several other leading Scottish Presbyterians who had supported the King against Cromwell at the time of Dunbar and Worcester were put to death soon afterwards. In England, to Prynne's distress, bishops were reintroduced into the Church of England, though some of the ritualistic practices which Laud had initiated were not revived. At the communion service which preceded the opening of Parliament in May 1661, Prynne refused to kneel to receive communion; it was therefore refused to him.

In July the first bill in the series of legislation which became known as the Clarendon Code was introduced in the House of Commons. It provided that all members of city and other corporations were ineligible for office unless they took two oaths, the first repudiating the Solemn League and Covenant of the Presbyterians, and the second accepting the doctrine that to take up arms against the King in any circumstances whatever was an act of high treason. Prynne denounced the bill in the House of Commons and in a pamphlet, and defended the Covenant, pointing out that the Presbyterian Covenanters had fought and worked to restore King Charles II.

But now at last the significance of the Restoration, which he had worked for and welcomed, was brought home to Prynne. He was violently denounced in the House as a seditious rebel, and ordered to retract and submit. The sufferings which he had undergone under Charles I, which for twenty years had been regarded both by his Presbyterian friends and by his Independent enemies as an honourable badge of martyrdom, were now cited against him to his discredit. The Speaker addressed him, reminded him that he had once been rightly condemned to the degrading punishments of the pillory, branding in the face, and the loss of his ears, and warned him that he deserved to be subjected to these punishments once again for his present offence, but that in view of his services to the King at the time of the Restoration he would be shown mercy if he recanted. Prynne thereupon humbly asked the House for pardon, not on account of his own merits, but as a mere mercy, and stated, with tears in his eyes, that his conscience had told him that he had done wrong. The Cavaliers were jubilant at his humiliation; the intrepid martyr who had defied Laud and Cromwell had abjectly succumbed.

Prynne offered no more opposition to the Clarendon Code, but acquiesced in the Acts which ejected both Independent and Presbyterian ministers from their livings and prevented them from teaching in the universities or in any school, and from coming within five miles of any town. He dedicated his books and pamphlets to Clarendon, for whom he expressed the greatest admiration both as a lawyer and as the chief pillar of Charles II's royal authority. When Clarendon fell from power in 1667 after the disasters of the Dutch War, and the House of Commons tried to impeach him, Prynne once again risked the disfavour of the House by opposing the bill and speaking in Clarendon's defence. At the King's suggestion, Clarendon escaped to France. Clarendon had never reciprocated Prynne's admiration for him; he thought that Prynne was a troublesome rebel.

Prynne's submission to the Anglican government earned him peace and quiet in his old age. He was appointed Keeper of the Public Records at the Tower of London, and was regarded as a leading expert on questions of constitutional law and history, being sometimes consulted by the King himself when constitutional difficulties arose. In outward appearances, at least, he became a courteous Cavalier gentleman of the older school. When the Oxford historian, Anthony Wood, visited the Tower in 1667 in order to consult the records for his historical researches, he was charmed with Prynne's manners, and commented that Prynne had received him 'with old-fashioned compliments, such as were used in the reign of King James I'.

Prynne spent the last years of his life writing *An Exact History of the Popes intollerable Usurpations Upon the Liberties of the Kings, and Subjects, of England & Ireland*, in which he intended to reveal all the attempts of the Popes throughout history, up to the seventeenth century, to subvert the King's power in England. He died before he could complete the work. By the time of his death he had written three volumes which together contained nearly two million words—or three times the length of Tolstoy's *War and Peace*—and he had only covered the period up to the death of Edward I in 1307. In his dedication to Charles II, he summed up the reasons why he supported the royal supremacy. All wise nations throughout history, whether pagan or Christian, had always entrusted matters of religion to the care and management of their sovereigns, because otherwise the people would 'be inevitably subjected either to a foreign Papal, or domestick Prelatical, Classical, Anabaptistical, or Independent usurped dangerous authority', which would always be able to enlist the support of the King's subjects against him 'under specious pretexts, of preserving the Churches, or their own Consciences liberties', and would forcibly deprive the King of his crown, and even of his life. 'Whoever stears the helm of Subjects consciences, though but a Bishop, or Rooke, will easily give checkmate to his King, if he cunningly play his game.'

Prynne died in his chambers in Lincoln's Inn on 24 October 1669, at the age of sixty-nine.

14

Hugh Peters

There must have been something hateful about Hugh Peters because so many people hated him, but it is not easy for us today to discover what it was. To judge from his portrait, he may well have been a surly, overbearing man, but neither his actions nor his writings provide any explanation for the vicious hatred with which he was regarded by such different types of persons as Prynne, Lilburne, the Cavalier ballad-mongers, and the London mob.

He was born in the little fishing port of Fowey in Cornwall in the summer of 1598. His father's surname was Peter, and Hugh Peter himself used the surname 'Peter' for most of his life; but his contemporaries usually called him 'Hugh Peters', and he eventually adopted 'Peters' as his surname and published his books under that name. His father was a merchant of Fowey, where the tradition of Protestant anti-Spanish piracy was well-established at the end of the reign of Elizabeth I.

When Hugh Peters was fifteen he went to Trinity College, Cambridge. In later years his Cavalier enemies told many scandalous stories about his university days—how he was publicly flogged for drunkenness and other acts of misconduct, and was eventually expelled for stealing the King's deer from Woodstock Park; but he was certainly not expelled from the University, because he was awarded his BA degree in 1618 and his MA degree in 1622.

He left Cambridge after taking the BA degree, and spent some years in Essex and in London. According to the Cavalier pamphleteers, he became an actor in Shakespeare's company of players—Shakespeare himself had died a few years before—and often acted the part of the Fool in Shakespeare's plays; but it seems more likely that he was employed as a schoolmaster.

About the year 1623 he experienced one of those great spiritual conversions which affected so many of his Puritan friends, and as a result was ordained as a priest. He became vicar of Rayleigh in Essex, and soon afterwards moved to London as vicar of St Sepulchre's in Farringdon Without, which today stands on Holborn Viaduct. He soon became one of the most forceful and popular preachers in London.

In 1625, before he left Essex, he married Elizabeth Reade, a wealthy widow. He was aged twenty-seven and she was at least fifty. She had married her first husband four years before Peters was born, and at the time of her marriage to Peters she had eight children and four grandchildren. The Cavalier pamphleteers afterwards wrote that Peters forced her to marry him by a trick; he and a friend broke into Mrs Reade's room during the night and raped her, and then threatened to expose her and ruin her reputation if she did not consent to marry Peters. There is no reason to believe the story, but Peters's marriage to a wealthy widow twice his age was bound to be interpreted adversely.

Peters's Puritan sermons brought him into conflict with the Bishop of London. He also angered the Bishop by his activities in helping to raise money for the Protestant ministers in the Rhineland who had been ejected by the Catholics during the Thirty Years War. The Bishop objected to this, because the collection for the ministers was organized by English Protestants who condemned King Charles's policy of neutrality in the Thirty Years War, and was interpreted as a gesture of opposition to the King. The Bishop was particularly angry at Peters's frequent references, in his sermons, to the fact that Queen Henrietta Maria was a Catholic; in his prayers for the Queen, Peters prayed that she should be led to renounce the idols that she had been taught to worship in her father's house. He was summoned several times before the Bishop, and compelled to subscribe to various articles in which he accepted the Bishop's High Church doctrines. (Many years later when Prynne was conducting the impeachment of Laud, he found the document that Peters had signed among Laud's papers, and denounced Peters for having submitted to the Bishop of London instead of suffering martyrdom.) But Peters continued to put forward Puritan doctrines in his sermons, and eventually he was forbidden to preach. He therefore decided to leave England, and in 1629 was appointed preacher to the congregation of English merchants in Rotterdam.

Peters held the position of minister in Rotterdam for six years, though on two occasions he temporarily abandoned his flock. The first occasion was in September 1631, when he joined the Dutch army in response to an appeal for volunteers to defend Bergen op Zoom from the attack launched from Antwerp by the Spanish Catholic armies. The second occasion was when he visited the camp of the great hero of the Protestant Cause, Gustavus Adolphus, King of Sweden, at Nuremberg in the summer of 1632, where he met the King a few months before Gustavus was killed winning his victory at Lützen. As a preacher in Rotterdam, Peters was as successful as he had been in London, though in later years the Cavaliers told stories about his drunkenness and lascivious conduct with women in Rotterdam.

During his years in Rotterdam he was continually troubled by the English ambassador, who had been ordered by Laud to inquire into the orthodoxy of the English congregations in Holland. Eventually the English government put pressure on the Dutch authorities to prevent Peters from preaching, by threatening to take reprisals against Dutchmen in London and even to withhold the supply of arms to the Dutch in their war with Spain. Peters therefore decided to emigrate to the English settlement in Massachusetts Bay in America. The Cavaliers later wrote that he had left Rotterdam to escape the vengeance of a husband whose wife he had seduced.

He arrived at Boston in October 1635. The first immigrants had arrived there from England five years before, though at Plymouth, thirty miles to the south, there had been a Puritan settlement since the arrival of the first colonists in *The Mayflower* in 1620. The territory was part of King Charles's realm, but under the terms of their charter the inhabitants were building up a small Puritan community which was governed by an elected Governor and Council, and was largely dominated by its Church. The Church was governed by its elected pastor and elders, like the Presbyterian Church in Scotland, but as the community was small and virtually out of contact with the other English Puritan settlements in America, there was no General Assembly or other form of national organization imposing discipline on the congregations. Heretical deviations from Calvinism, though treated more leniently than heresy had ever been treated in England, were punished in the last resort by excommunication from the Church, and this sentence was often followed by banishment from the colony. A number of immigrants arrived at Boston in 1635 about the same time as Peters, among them young Henry Vane, the son of King Charles's Secretary of State, who soon after his arrival was elected Governor in the place of his defeated opponent, John Winthrop.

On his arrival, Peters was elected minister of the church of Salem, near Boston, and during the six years that he remained in Massachusetts he played an active part in all aspects of the life of the settlement. He persuaded them to build a fishing fleet instead of relying on the fishermen of Newfoundland for their supply of fish. He was zealous in exhorting the inhabitants, including the women and children, to spend their time in useful work for the development of the colony instead of in idle pastimes. He was chiefly responsible for the opening of an educational establishment at Cambridge, just outside Boston, which was called Harvard College in honour of a young immigrant from London, John Harvard, who died soon after he arrived in Massachusetts and bequeathed money in his will for educational purposes. In the political disputes in the colony, Peters supported Winthrop's party against the Governor, Vane, who was afterwards to be his ally in England.

During Peters's years in Massachusetts the colony was shaken by the activities of Mrs Anne Hutchinson, who had arrived from Lincolnshire in 1634. She preached and taught to the people of Boston that although the leading divine in the community, John Cotton, and one or two other ministers taught the proper Calvinist doctrine of predestination, the rest of the ministers were guilty of the heresy of believing in salvation by works. The majority of the ministers, including Peters, denied her accusations and denounced her for having made them. Cotton, after at first encouraging her support, repudiated her and stood firm with his fellow-ministers; but some of the other ministers supported her, as did Henry Vane, the Governor.

In December 1636 Peters and some of the other ministers invited Mrs Hutchinson to take part in a private discussion about her opinions. She agreed to do so after they had promised her that nothing that she said would be used against her in any legal proceedings. Six months later, the elections for the Governor and Council were fought on the issue of Mrs Hutchinson's accusations. Vane and her other supporters were heavily defeated, and Winthrop, the new Governor, and his followers on the Council ordered that all Mrs Hutchinson's supporters should be disarmed and disfranchised. Mrs Hutchinson was then put on trial for heresy, and to her indignation the statements which she had made in the discussion in December with Peters and the other ministers were cited against her.

Peters was one of the leading advocates for the prosecution at the trial. He told Mrs Hutchinson: 'I would commend this to your Consideration that you have stept out of your place, you have rather bine a Husband than a Wife, & a preacher than a Hearer; & a Magistrate than a Subject, & soe yow have thought to carry all Thinges in Church & Commonwealth, as yow would, & have not bine humbled for this.' The court held that Mrs Hutchinson was 'a dangerous Instrument of the Divell raysed up by Sathan amongst us to rayse up Divisions & Contentions & to take away hartes & affections one from another'. She was excommunicated and banished from Massachusetts. She settled in Dutch territory in the modern state of New York, where she was murdered by Indians in 1643.

Soon after the banishment of Mrs Hutchinson, Roger Williams and his supporters were denounced by the church in Massachusetts for having taught that religious toleration should be extended to all persons, including Catholics, Jews and Turks, and that the church should renounce the power to punish dissidents for doctrinal heresies. Peters played an active part against Williams, who was banished with his supporters in 1638 and founded a new colony in Rhode Island.

During his residence in Massachusetts, Peters was again involved in some slightly unsavoury matrimonial difficulties. When he came from Rotterdam to Massachusetts in 1635 his wife, who had lived with him in Rotterdam, went to England, but next year she returned to Rotterdam. In the summer of 1637 she arrived in Boston. During the controversy with Roger Williams's supporters, one of them embarrassed Peters by pointing out that the aged Mrs Peters had not been granted a certificate of good conduct by the minister and elders of the English church at Rotterdam which would entitle her to be admitted as a member of the congregation in Massachusetts. Soon afterwards Mrs Peters died. Within a few months one of the citizens of Massachusetts was threatening to expose Peters for breach of promise of marriage to his daughter, who had broken off an engagement to a wealthy young man because Peters had asked her to marry him; but Peters instead married Mrs Deliverance Sheffield, a widow whose husband had died soon after they had arrived in Massachusetts from England in 1637. Some of the people who had travelled to Boston in the same ship as Mrs Sheffield warned Peters not to marry her, because she had shown signs of insanity on the journey; but Peters seems to have been fascinated by her, and told a friend that he was too deeply involved with her for it to be possible for him to withdraw from the marriage without causing a scandal.

The disadvantages of being married to an insane wife had been brought home to Peters by the tragic case of Dorothy Talbye. In December 1638 Peters preached an edifying sermon at her execution. She was a mad woman who had been excommunicated by the Church of Salem, as mad persons always were, on the grounds that they were possessed of the devil. As the sentence of excommunication meant that no one outside her family was allowed to speak to her, it is perhaps not surprising that, as Peters censoriously stated at her execution, excommunication only made her worse. She had a delusion that God had commanded her to kill her husband and children and herself, and after trying to starve herself to death, she killed her three-year-old daughter in order to save the child from future misery. She was sentenced to be hanged. She asked to be beheaded on the grounds that it was a less shameful and painful death, but her plea was refused, and as she swung on the rope, clutching desperately for the ladder, Hugh Peters told the people that this was her just punishment for defying the sentence of excommunication that the church had passed on her.

A few months before he left Massachusetts, Peters had a narrow escape from death. In April 1641 he was sent, with another minister from Boston, to visit the scattered communities along the Piscataqua River some seventy miles to the north, at the southern point of the modern state of Maine, which came within the area of Massachusetts Bay as defined in the King's charter and was therefore within the jurisdiction of the authorities at Boston. The inhabitants of this territory had taken their personal quarrels almost to the point of civil war, and were excommunicating each other as heretics. Peters and his colleague were sent to the Piscataqua to try to reconcile the quarrelling inhabitants. On one of his journeys in the district, Peters and his companions lost their way in the great forests, and wandered through the snow, without food, for two days and one night, uncertain as to whether they would ever find their way back to civilization. Eventually they reached the coast, and were able to follow it until they arrived at their destination.

In the summer of 1641 Peters was sent to England by the authorities in Boston in order to negotiate an extension of their charter and to act as the colonists' agent in London. As there was no ship which was sailing direct to England from Boston, he travelled by way of Newfoundland; leaving Boston on 3 August, he reached Newfoundland on 17 August, and landed at Bristol on 27 September. Strafford had been executed five months earlier, Laud had been imprisoned in the Tower for nearly a year, and the conflict between King and Parliament was coming to a head. Peters spent the next few years representing the interests of the Massachusetts Bay colony in London, but he did this only as a sideline, having decided to stay in England permanently and assist the Roundhead cause in the Civil War.

His first intervention in English politics was in connection with Ireland. The greatest indignation had been aroused in England over the real and alleged sufferings of the English Protestant settlers at the hands of the Catholic Irish rebels during the rising of November 1641. King Charles had announced his intention of suppressing the revolt, and he had put an end to all hopes of compromise by complying with Parliament's request that he issue a declaration in which he promised that he would never grant religious toleration to Roman Catholics in Ireland and confiscated the land of all Irishmen who had taken any part in the rebellion. But Parliament, while on the one hand suggesting that Charles was in secret contact with the Irish rebels, refused to vote him arms and supplies to suppress the rebellion because they feared that, having obtained them, he would use them, not against the Irish rebels, but against the English Parliament.

Charles's forces in Ireland were therefore reduced to holding Dublin and other defensive positions. In the summer of 1642 Parliament sent its own expeditionary force, under the command of Lord Forbes, to suppress the rebellion. There were thus three sides in Ireland—the Catholic rebels, the King's army, and the Parliamentary force under Lord Forbes.

Hugh Peters accompanied Lord Forbes's expedition. It was the first of many occasions on which he served in the combined capacity of army chaplain and official war correspondent whose duty was to report to the House of Commons on the progress of the campaign. He marched with Forbes against the Irish rebels in the south and pursued them into Galway. When Forbes passed a castle on the line of march which was held by the King's troops, he called on it to surrender, and as it did not, he burned the surrounding town. When Peters returned to London he presented his report to Parliament. Both in his report and in his other writings and sermons, he emphasized that the King was in league with the Irish Papists. 'An Irish Rebel and an English Cavalier', he wrote sarcastically, 'in words and actions we found as unlike as an egge is to an egge.'

During the winter of 1642–3 he was one of the Puritan preachers who stirred up the people of London and the neighbourhood to resist the Cavalier army at Turnham Green and to reject the agitation in favour of ending the war by a negotiated peace. His forceful style of speaking and his robust humour attracted a great deal of attention, and many stories, some scandalous, were told about him and published in *Mercurius Aulicus*, the Cavalier newspaper at Oxford. In the year of his death a little book was published, *The Tales and Jests of Mr Hugh Peters*, which contained fifty-nine stories about Peters, many of them in the style of the *Heptameron*, with Peters in the place of the lascivious friars. Some of these stories were new versions of almost identical tales which had been published about other persons in various books in the reigns of James I and Elizabeth I.

In some of the stories, the reader's sympathies are with Peters, as in the one in which Peters, when staying the night at an inn, tricks the miserly innkeeper into producing a capon for Peters's supper, after the innkeeper had pretended that he had no food in the house. In others the laugh is against Peters. One of the stories, which was already in wide circulation by 1643, tells how

Peters, having decided to seduce a butcher's wife, went to her bedroom in the middle of the night, but found the door locked. She called out to him, from within the room, that if he put his hand under the door he would find the key there; but when Peters did this, his hand was caught in a rat-trap, and he was unable to free himself until he had aroused the whole household and his lechery and discomfiture had been revealed for all to see.

One of the stories is based on an incident which did in fact take place when Peters was preaching in the village of West Ham in 1643. Some gentlemen in the congregation walked out, apparently in protest against the Roundhead propaganda which Peters was putting forward. As they were leaving the church, Peters called out to one of them: 'Sir . . . I pray you hear me speak a few words to you before you be gone. I'll tell you a tale that shall be worth your hearing and yet not so long as to hinder you from any business.' At this the gentleman paused, and stood leaning on the font near the church door while Peters continued: 'There was a gentleman that kept an ape, a cock, a dog and a rod. The ape would show his master tricks; the dog would fetch; the cock would eat up crumbs; but, you will ask, what served the rod for? To whip such fools that when they are going away from hearing a sermon, will come in again to hear a tale.'

In the summer of 1643 Peters was sent into Sussex to rouse the support of the people. Parliament relied on the district for supplies of Wealden iron for cannon and ammunition, but although Sussex had been captured for Parliament by Sir William Waller early in the war, it was not entirely loyal to the Roundhead cause. At Lewes, Peters preached a sermon in which he appealed to the women of Sussex; according to the Cavalier newspaper, he called on the wives 'to hug their Husbands into this rebellion'. He spent the next winter in Holland, travelling among his old congregation at Rotterdam and elsewhere, collecting money for the relief of the Protestant refugees who had fled from the Papist rebels in Ireland, and also making sure that the English traders in Holland would not contribute to the King's cause or give any other help to the Cavaliers.

By the summer of 1644 he was back in England, sailing with Warwick's ships to relieve the garrison which was holding out under Blake in Lyme Regis, and praising the heroism of the defenders in a stirring report to Parliament. He accompanied

Essex's army on the march into Cornwall, and was with Essex when the army was trapped and surrounded by King Charles's forces in the Fowey peninsula. When Essex himself escaped by sea, the cavalry cut their way through to the east, and Skippon and the infantry capitulated to Charles at Lostwithiel. Peters quietly slipped away and stayed in his relatives' houses in his native town of Fowey until the Cavalier army had left the district.

By the time that he returned to London, the war of sermons and pamphlets between the Presbyterians and the Independents was in full swing. In this conflict, in which the Presbyterians called for the supremacy of a national Presbyterian Church and the suppression of doctrinal heresy, and the Independents demanded freedom for the Independent congregations and religious toleration, Peters's original position was ambiguous. In 1643 he wrote a long book, *Church-Government*, in which he described the system of organization of the church in Massachusetts. This was hailed by the Independents as a method of organization in which independent congregations had complete self-government and were not subjected to the discipline of a national church. On the other hand, neither Peters nor the other ministers of the Church of Massachusetts had believed in religious toleration. Peters now found himself the ally of Lilburne, Milton and his old opponent in Massachusetts, Roger Williams, and became a champion of religious toleration in the struggle against Presbyterian intolerance. The Presbyterians hastened to point out the contradiction between Peters's attitude to religious toleration in Massachusetts and in England, and used it as an argument to prove that the Independents only favoured religious toleration as long as they were in opposition, and would not adhere to it when they came to power. But Peters became one of the Independents' leading champions, and was given the nickname of the Archbishop of Canterbury of Independency.

He was again vexed with family troubles. When he left Boston in August 1641 he had not intended to remain permanently in England, and he left behind his wife Deliverance and their four-month-old daughter Elizabeth. Soon afterwards Mrs Peters went mad, and was duly excommunicated and deprived of the custody of the child. In 1643 she was banished from Massachusetts and put on a ship for England. Peters sent her back to Boston in 1646, telling the congregation in Massachusetts that she was now cured; but she had another relapse, and was again excommunicated in 1648 and banished to England, where she arrived with their daughter, now seven years old. The Presbyterians had by now found out about her, and referred to her madness in their pamphlets as a proof that God had punished Hugh Peters by making her insane.

As the First Civil War drew to a close, Peters seemed to be ubiquitous, always there to serve the Roundhead cause in some place and in some capacity. In January 1645 he was on the scaffold at Laud's execution, urging the old Archbishop to repent and renounce his Arminian and High Church errors in the last minutes of his life. In April he was sent to the Isle of Wight to interrogate the Duchesse de Chevreuse, the famous French conspirator and confidante of the Queen Regent of France, Anne of Austria; Madame de Chevreuse had been detained by the Roundhead authorities because they suspected that she had been sent on a secret mission by Cardinal Mazarin to the Cavaliers in Ireland. In June Peters was at Naseby, riding along the Roundhead lines shortly before the start of the battle, with a Bible in one hand and a pistol in the other, calling on the troops to smite the enemies of the Lord. In July he was with the army at the storming of Bridgwater and in August at the siege of Bristol, but to the indignation of the Presbyterians he was given leave of absence and sent to south-eastern England to work for the return of Independent candidates in the by-elections for the Long Parliament. In September he was preaching electioneering sermons at Reading and East Grinstead. By October he had rejoined the army and was with Cromwell at the storming of the Papists' stronghold at Basing House, cheerfully reporting to Parliament how '8 or 9 Gentlewomen of ranke running forth together were entertained by the common souldiers somewhat coarsely, yet not uncivilly, they left with some clothes upon them'. In February and March 1646 he was with Fairfax in Devon and Cornwall, and played an important part in negotiating the surrender of the last Cavalier forces at Bodmin. On 2 April he was in London preaching to both Houses of Parliament at St. Margaret's Westminster on the great victory that had been won.

Peters played a leading part in the events of 1647. When

Cromwell hurriedly left London on 4 June, the day after Cornet Joyce seized the King at Holmby House, Peters rode beside him on the journey to the army headquarters at Newmarket. He was at Cromwell's side, giving spiritual advice to him and to Ireton and preaching to the soldiers, throughout the weeks that led up to the march on London in August. He stood with Cromwell and Ireton and the Grandees in the controversy with the Levellers, and took part in the Putney debates in November. When the Second Civil War broke out, he went with Cromwell to the siege of Pembroke, where he played an important part by bringing naval guns from the ships in the Bristol Channel, which enabled Cromwell to bombard the town into surrender instead of waiting to starve it out, thus gaining valuable time in which to march against the Scots in the north. During the siege, Peters fell ill; he had for some years been suffering from periodical outbreaks of fever, which sometimes produced bouts of melancholia and nervous depression which occasionally amounted almost to insanity. He consulted the local physician at Milford Haven during his illness. It was not his last encounter with Dr William Yonge of Milford Haven.

When Cromwell marched north against the Scots, he left Peters at Leicester to conduct a preaching tour throughout the South Midland counties. Peters's propaganda, together with the presence of some army units, prevented any rising in the area in support of the Cavaliers and Presbyterians. After Cromwell's victory at Preston, the defeated Scottish leader, the Duke of Hamilton, fled to the south but was captured at Uttoxeter. Peters was sent to interrogate him. The Duke afterwards stated, before his execution, that if he could have spoken to Peters a few months earlier he would not have led a Scottish army into England in support of Charles I.

Peters was in London at the time of Pride's Purge. At 3 pm on 6 December, the day of the purge, he visited the forty-one imprisoned MPs in Queen's Court in Westminster, wearing a long sword at his side, and took a list of the names of the MPs who were confined there. When Prynne and his companions angrily asked him by what law they were being held prisoner, Peters answered that it was by the law of the sword. It was the first of several occasions on which he was accused by his opponents of showing his contempt for the law.

A fortnight later, after King Charles had been brought from Hurst Castle to Windsor and there were already rumours in the air that he was to be brought to trial, Peters preached for three hours to the Lords, MPs and soldiers in Palace Yard at Westminster on Friday 22 December 1648, which had been appointed as a fast day by Parliament. 'It was a very sad Thing', he said, 'that this should be a Question amongst us, as among the Old Jews whether our Saviour Jesus Christ must be crucified, or that Barabbas should be released, the Oppressor of the People: O Jesus, where are we, that that should be a Question amongst us? . . . I have been in the City, which may very well be compared to Hierusalem in this Conjuncture of Time, and I profess those foolish Citizens for a little Trading and Profit they will have Christ [and he pointed to the Redcoats on the steps of the pulpit] crucified, and that great Barabbas at Windsor released.' Then, turning to the peers and MPs, he continued: 'My Lords and you Noble Gentlemen of the House of Commons, you are the Sanhedrin, and the great Council of the Nation, therefore you must be sure to do Justice, and it is from you that we expect it; you must not only be Inheritors of your Ancestors, but you must do as they did, they have opposed Tyrannical Kings, they have destroyed them . . . Do not prefer the great Barabbas, Murderer, Tyrant, and Traytor, before these poor Hearts [pointing to the Redcoats] and the Army, who are our saviours.'

At the private meetings of the officers, Peters strongly urged that the King should be brought to trial and execution, and his great influence with Cromwell—he was Cromwell's favourite chaplain—was decisive in overcoming Cromwell's last hesitations. After the House of Commons' resolution for the trial was passed on 1 January, Peters was active on Cromwell's behalf overcoming the reluctance of the Commissioners to sit as judges and to sign the death warrant.

The King's trial began on Saturday 20 January 1649. On Sunday the twenty-first Peters preached at Whitehall, with Cromwell and Bradshaw, who was presiding at the King's trial, among his audience. He took as his text 'Bind their Kings with Chains, and their Nobles with Fetters of Iron', and in his sermon he told one of his typical stories, about a major, a bishop and the bishop's man. 'The Bishop's man being Drunk, the Major laid him by the Heels; the Bishop sends to the Major to know by what Authority he imprisoned his Servant; the Major's Answer was, there is an Act of Parliament for it, and neither the Bishop nor his Man are excepted out of it . . . Here is a great Discourse and Talk in the World, what? Will ye cut off the King's Head, the Head of a Protestant Prince and King? Turn to your Bibles, and you shall find it there. Whosoever sheds Man's Blood, by Man shall his Blood be shed . . . I will even answer them as the Major did the Bishop, here is an Act of God, Whosoever sheds Man's Blood, by Man shall his Blood be shed; and I see neither King Charles, nor Prince Charles, nor Prince Rupert, nor Prince Maurice, nor any of that Rabble excepted out of it . . . This is the Day that I and many Saints of God besides have been praying for these many Years.'

Peters was present as a spectator at the trial, and apparently acted as a cheer-leader among the soldiers when they demanded 'Justice! Justice!' as the King passed in and out of the hall; and on the last day of the trial, on Saturday 27 January, after sentence of death had been passed, he led the cry of 'Execution! Execution!' Next day, on Sunday the twenty-eighth, he preached again, in St James's Chapel, on the text from the 149th Psalm, 'Bind their Kings with Chains, and their Nobles with Fetters of Iron'. He referred to the fact that the King had refused his offer to preach to him: 'I did intend to insist and preach upon before the poor Wretch, and the poor Wretch would not hear me.' He was ill in bed two days later with one of his attacks of fever, and could not attend the King's execution.

Peters had now become one of the most unpopular men in London. One day in the spring of 1649 he went to the Customs House of the Port of London with his physician, Dr Massey, apparently to examine some pamphlets which were being brought into England from abroad. The porters and labourers in the Customs House demonstrated against him and threatened to attack him. Peters thereupon went with Dr Massey to the Tower to complain to the Lieutenant and to request him to send soldiers to arrest the demonstrators; but by the time that the soldiers arrived, the culprits had escaped. John Lilburne was imprisoned in the Tower by order of the Council of State, awaiting his trial for high treason for having incited the Leveller mutinies in the army. At Peters's suggestion, he and Dr Massey and the Lieutenant had dinner with Lilburne at the Lieutenant's table.

Like most of Peters's political opponents, Lilburne had taken a strong personal dislike to Peters, whom he had described, after the abortive negotiations between the Grandees and the Levellers in December 1648, as 'the grand Journey- or Hackney-man of the Army'. He afterwards published a pamphlet in which he gave his version of his talk with Peters at dinner in the Tower, to which Dr Massey replied in another pamphlet, giving Peters's side of the story. The two accounts are hardly contradictory. Lilburne asked Peters by what law he was imprisoned, and Peters replied, as he had replied to Prynne on the day of Pride's Purge, that it was by the law of the sword. He proceeded to point out to the indignant Lilburne the many absurdities of the English common law, and urged him to believe rather in the law of God as laid down in the Ten Commandments. This was the hub of the matter, and showed the difference between Peters and the constitutional lawyers who venerated the English common law. The only law that really mattered for Peters was the Ten Commandments, and he believed that if God placed the power of the sword in the hands of His Saints, they need not trouble about the law of England provided that they fulfilled the law of God.

In September 1649 Peters joined Cromwell in Ireland, and was present at the capture of Wexford when the garrison was massacred at Cromwell's orders. In October Cromwell sent Peters to England to arrange for reinforcements to be sent to Ireland. Peters fell seriously ill with one of his fevers on the journey, and when his ship reached Milford Haven he was lying exhausted on the deck. His friends got in touch with Dr William Yonge, the physician at Milford Haven who had cared for Peters in the previous year, and Peters was carried to Yonge's pleasant house on the river. He recovered from his illness within five days, but remained in Yonge's house, as an uninvited guest for another ten weeks. He sat up, night after night, talking to Yonge, often until midnight or 1 a.m., having no idea of the depths of the hatred which his host felt towards him.

Eleven years later, after the Restoration, Dr Yonge was the chief witness against Peters at his trial, and not content with the part that he played in bringing about Peters's arrest, trial and execution, he proceeded soon afterwards to publish a book full of the most libellous and untrue allegations against Peters. He told the court in 1660 that during those ten weeks eleven years before when Peters had stayed in his house, Peters had boasted to him of his intimacy with Cromwell and his influence in affairs of state, and in particular of how he, Hugh Peters, had been responsible for persuading Cromwell to send Cornet Joyce to seize the King in June 1647 and to bring the King to trial and cut off his head. Yonge claimed that as he listened to Peters with mounting horror, he pretended friendship in order to lead Peters on to incriminate himself, so that he could one day bring the regicide to justice. Peters denied Yonge's allegations. He said that Yonge was a zealous supporter of the republic in 1649, and had offered to serve the Republican government as an informer, but had afterwards turned violently against Peters when Peters refused to use his influence to obtain the restitution of Yonge's property which had been confiscated by the republican government.

Peters did not go to Scotland with Cromwell, but remained at Milford Haven, making himself universally unpopular by the rigour with which he enforced obedience to the orders of the Council of State. In November 1650 he returned to London, and next year published a book, *Good Work for a Good Magistrate*, in which he put forward his ideas for the government of England. The ideas did not differ greatly from the projects of social and economic reform which Lilburne and the Levellers and other thinkers had put forward; profiteers must be prevented from overcharging the poor for the price of food and other essentials, justice must be firmly administered, order must be enforced and the state protected by a people's militia, and the law must be reformed by simplifying the common law and abolishing absurd old legal precedents. This last proposal infuriated Prynne and the lawyers. Prynne accused Peters of wishing to destroy historical legal documents and records.

In September 1651 Peters met Cromwell again for the first time for two years when Cromwell entered London in triumph after his victory over Charles II at Worcester. Peters preached to the victorious troops at the thanksgiving service. Thinking back to the first skirmish at Worcester in September 1642, he told the troops: 'When your wives and children shall ask where you have been, and what news, say you have been at Worcester, where England's sorrows began, and where they are happily ended.'

Peters, like Cromwell, was saddened by the outbreak of the war with Holland, because he had always hoped that the republic would use its armed forces to liberate the oppressed Protestants of France and Germany, not to fight wars for commercial advantage against other Protestant states. Apart from this general sense of religious solidarity with Protestant Holland, he remembered the hospitality which he had received in Holland twenty years before. After the first battle between Tromp and Blake in the Channel in the summer of 1652, he and Cromwell tried to patch up an agreement with the Dutch envoy, but both the Rump and the Dutch government were resolved on war. His opposition to the Dutch War, as well as his close friendship with Cromwell and his old faith in the army, was one of the reasons which led him to support Cromwell's dispersal of the Rump. He was less happy when Cromwell dissolved the Barebones Parliament and became Lord Protector, because, though he was not a supporter of Harrison and the extreme sectaries, he sympathized with them and with the efforts of the Barebones Parliament to reform the law, which had aroused the anger of the lawyers.

A month after Cromwell became Lord Protector, Peters was appointed in January 1654 to the Commission which was set up to draft a religious settlement for the nation; but the Commission never completed its labours. Next year he was one of the Commissioners who met at Whitehall to consider whether the Jews should be permitted to return to England. He had enraged Prynne by writing a book in which he favoured the return of the Jews, but during the conference he wavered in this opinion, because of his uncertainty as to whether the Sephardic Jews of Amsterdam, who had applied for readmission to England, were the Jews of the Old Testament.

By 1656 he had begun to have misgivings about some of Cromwell's actions. When his old friend, the republican Ludlow, was released from prison by Cromwell, Peters visited him at his house in Essex. Ludlow told him that Cromwell's policy, by splitting the unity of the Independents in the struggle against the common enemy, would result in 'the return of the family of the late King, who would not fail to do all that revenge could inspire them with'. Peters said that he agreed with Ludlow, but that there was no one in Cromwell's entourage who had the courage to tell him so, and added that ever since the battle of

Worcester he had feared that Cromwell would try to make himself King.

In the summer of 1658 Peters rendered his last service to Cromwell when, under the terms of Cromwell's alliance with Mazarin, English soldiers were sent to fight with the French against the Spaniards at Dunkirk, it being agreed that Dunkirk should become an English possession after it was captured from the Spaniards. Peters once again went with the English army in his dual capacity as chaplain and war correspondent. He had a somewhat frosty interview with Mazarin at Dunkirk, for Mazarin objected to Peters's sermons to the English garrison at Dunkirk, whom he had incited against the native Catholics in the town. The English commander at Dunkirk sent Peters home to England as soon as possible.

He played no part in the conflicts of 1659, being over sixty and in poor health; but when Monck marched to London in January 1660, Peters was one of a number of prominent republicans who tried to win the favour of the general who held the fate of England in his hands. Like Hazelrig and the regicide Thomas Scot, he hurried to greet Monck, and went out to meet him at St Albans. The Presbyterian and Cavalier pamphleteers and ballad-mongers were pouring out publications denouncing the Rump and the republicans and rumours of a restoration of Charles II were in the air; but Monck was still ostensibly acting on behalf of the Rump, and was periodically denouncing Charles Stuart. Peters preached a sermon at St Albans welcoming Monck, but Monck's chaplain, Price, who saw and heard him, said that he looked and sounded as if he were preaching his own funeral oration. He spoke with Monck several times at St Albans and after Monck entered London, and offered to be his chaplain; but Monck, ominously, appointed a Presbyterian to that position.

When Parliament, in the weeks before and after the arrival of Charles II, drew up the lists of the regicides who were to be executed, no one thought of including Peters in the list; but in June 1660 Charles II was informed that his father's library had been entrusted to Peters's charge after his execution in 1649. Peters was therefore summoned to appear before the House of Lords and reveal what had happened to the books. But Peters, seeing the mood of the Parliament and its desire for revenge on the regicides, had gone into hiding, taking refuge in Southwark among the Quaker, Anabaptist and Fifth Monarchy sects who frequented the district. Hearing of the warrant for his arrest, he wrote to the House of Lords, telling them that he had only held the late King's books for a short time, and had then handed them over intact to another official; but he remained in hiding.

Parliament had included among the regicides the Commissioners who had sat as judges at Charles I's trial, the counsel for the prosecution and the clerk of the court, and the commanders of the soldiers who had guarded the King at the trial and execution. But no one knew the identity of the man who had committed the ultimate act of regicide—the headsman who had cut off the King's head. He had taken the precaution of wearing a mask on that occasion, as had his assistant. It was generally thought, in view of the professional expertise with which he had beheaded the King, that the headsman was the public executioner, Brandon, who had since died, and that he had been helped by his regular assistant; but Parliament now added to the list of regicides who were to suffer death the two executioners 'who were upon the scaffold in a disguise' when the late King was put to death. The ridiculous rumour spread that Peters had been the executioner or his assistant. The people recited a rhyme:

The best man next to Jupiter
Was put to death by Hugh Peter.

The astrologer, William Lilly, went to Prynne and told him that many people believed that Peters might have been the executioner, though he himself thought that it was Cornet Joyce. This information about his old enemy was welcome news to Prynne, who raised the matter in the House of Commons. Meanwhile Dr Yonge of Milford Haven had come forward to denounce Peters as a traitor on the strength of the conversations which he had had with him when he was his patient and guest in 1649. Parliament added Peters's name to the list of those who were exempted from the provisions of the Act of Indemnity and liable to suffer death.

Peters had many sympathizers in Southwark, but the local constable was determined to catch him. Somebody denounced

Peters, and the constables came to the house where he was hiding. One of the women in the house, a Quaker, had given birth to a child a few days before and was still lying-in. She invited Peters to hide under the bedclothes in her bed with her—an incident which was afterwards distorted by the Cavalier propagandists—and this succeeded in fooling the constables, who left the house without finding Peters. But soon afterwards Peters decided to move for safety to another house. He was stopped in the street by the constables, who recognized him, and though he strongly denied that he was Peters and claimed that his name was Thompson, they took him to the Tower, where, after continuing for some time to insist that a mistake had been made, he at last admitted his identity.

In October he was tried with the other regicides at Hicks Hall in London, with Dr Yonge as the chief witness against him. After his former servant, who was now a Cavalier, had given evidence that Peters had been ill in bed all day on 30 January 1649, the court seemed ready to accept the fact that Peters had not been upon the scaffold on that day; but, apart from Dr Yonge's evidence that Peters had told him that it was he who had first suggested to Cromwell that they should put the King on trial and execute him, there was the evidence of several witnesses who had heard his sermons on 22 December 1648 and 21 January 1649. It was stretching a point to condemn a man for regicide merely because he had compared Charles I to Barabbas, or for anything else that he had said in those sermons, but he could not expect justice in the hysterical atmosphere of October 1660, when charged with the murder of the man whom the Solicitor-General at his trial called 'this blessed King, this Glorious Saint', and when Cavaliers were declaring that the beheading of King Charles the Martyr was a greater crime than the crucifixion of Christ.

He was found guilty, and sentenced to be hanged, drawn and quartered. He spent his last days writing to his daughter Elizabeth, who was now aged nineteen, and his letter was later published by his supporters under the title *A Dying Fathers Last Legacy to an Onely Child*. He told Elizabeth that, despite all the lies that had been told about him, he had never been unfaithful to her mother since the day that he married her. He told her that he had nothing to leave her except the advice to read good books, and that as all his property would be confiscated she would find it very difficult, without a dowry, to get a husband. Her only course would probably be to become a domestic servant. This would give her the opportunity to serve God by showing the virtues expected of a servant of submission and obedience to her employers.

His wife, Deliverance Peters, was quite mad again. She was still living in 1677 when a collection was organized in London to relieve her in her destitution and madness. Elizabeth Peters did succeed in finding a husband. She married in 1665 a tradesman in London, and had eight children, including three sons who served the Protestant Cause as soldiers in the armies of William III. After her husband's death she was left in extreme poverty, and in 1703 she petitioned to be granted part of her father's confiscated property. She was awarded £195, which was enough to bring her some comforts during her last years.

But for Hugh Peters there was no comfort in October 1660. The hated Puritan preacher was put to death with refinements of cruelty, and amid the exultation of a jeering crowd who disgusted even some of the Cavaliers. He was executed at Charing Cross at the same time as John Cook, who had been counsel for the prosecution at Charles I's trial and had afterwards been appointed a Judge of the High Court in Ireland. Cook suffered first, and Peters was made to watch his execution from within the ropes on the scaffold. As he was waiting for Cook to die, a man in the crowd came up to him and cursed him for his part in the King's death. Peters replied: 'Friend, you do not well to trample upon a Dying-man; you are greatly mistaken, I had nothing to do in the death of the King.'

One of the spectators described his last moments. 'When Mr Cook was cut down, and brought to be Quartered, one they called Col. Turner, called to the Sheriffs men, to bring Mr Peters near, that he might see it; And by and by the Hangman came to him all besmeered in Blood, and rubbing his bloody hands, together, he (tauntingly) asked, 'Come, how do you like this, Mr Peters, how do you like this work?' Peters replied: 'I am not (I thank God) terrified at it, you may do your worst.' As he stood on the ladder with the rope around his neck, he said to the Sheriff: 'Sir, you have here slain one of the Servants of God before mine eyes, and have made me to behold it on purpose to terrifie and discourage me; but God hath made it an Ordinance to me for my strengthening and encouragement.' But 'what Mr Peters said further at his Execution, either in his Speech or Prayer, it could not be taken, in regard to his voyce was low at that time, and the people uncivil.'

15

Archibald Johnston, Lord Warriston

The Civil War in Britain began in Scotland, and at every stage during the next twenty-three years events in Scotland had a decisive influence on the struggle in England. If the Highland chief, Archibald Campbell, Marquis of Argyll, was the most powerful leader of the Scottish Covenanters, Archibald Johnston, Lord Warriston, was the most representative, the most intelligent, and the most remarkable.

Archibald Johnston was born in Edinburgh on 28 March 1611, the son of a prosperous Edinburgh merchant. His mother's father was a well-known feudal lawyer. Presbyterian Calvinism had been established as the state religion and the only legal form of worship in Scotland for fifty years before Archibald Johnston's birth, and he was educated under the close surveillance of the Kirk. He grew up to become a combination of subtle lawyer and fanatical Presbyterian.

He was educated at Glasgow University, and called to the bar in Edinburgh in November 1633, when he was aged twenty-two. He was already keeping a diary in which he jotted down every day, sometimes at considerable length, his innermost feelings and his faith in God. The first entry begins with a sentence of 302 words, in which he prayed to God for guidance, 'as thou hast oft greaved my soule unto the verry death by presenting unto my memorie the doolful catalog of my abominable works, words, and thoughts, desyrs, desseigns, or resolutions since ever I kneu good or evil—quhilk [which] sight ever maid my knees to smite on against another, as Belschazzars at the sight of mene mene tekel, and rent my heart as Hezekiah his cloths at the hearing of Rabschakeths blaschemies . . .'

In July 1637 Archbishop Laud persuaded Charles I to order that the Church of England service as laid down in the Book of Common Prayer should be adopted in Scotland in place of the Presbyterian service which had been used there for seventy-eight years. On the first occasion that the service was used in St Giles's church in Edinburgh, a riot broke out. As the dean began the service, the congregation—who may well have been led, as they are traditionally supposed to have been, by the herb-woman, Jennie Geddes—howled him down with cries of 'A mass! a mass!', and threw their stools at him and at the Bishop of Edinburgh. The authorities were unable to quell the riot in the town, or the protest movement which rapidly spread throughout the Scottish Lowlands. Archibald Johnston played a leading part in the movement from the start. It was he who read out the protestation to the King's herald at the Mercat Cross of Edinburgh, declaring that the people of Scotland would not obey the King's proclamation which ordered them to submit to his authority; and it was Johnston who drafted the Covenant that was signed in 1638 by nearly the whole population of the Lowlands of Scotland.

At last, in the summer of 1639, King Charles gathered an army and marched against the Covenanters; but when he reached Berwick he found that the Scots across the Border were in such great strength that he was happy to negotiate a truce. Johnston was one of the Covenanters' representatives in the truce negotiations, and behaved with the outspoken bluntness which made him so many enemies during his lifetime. He harangued the King with such rudeness that Charles ordered him to hold his tongue, and as Johnston continued with his speech, Charles refused to hear him any further and declared that he would only negotiate with more reasonable men.

Next year Charles marched again against the Scots, with a larger army; but the Covenanters forestalled him and invaded England, and the English army mutinied. Johnston went with the Covenanter army, and played a leading part in the peace negotiations at Ripon in October 1640 in which the King agreed to all the Covenanters' demands. Johnston was particularly adamant during the negotiations on the question of the amnesty, refusing to agree to the King's demands that the few Scots who had supported the royal cause should be granted immunity from prosecution and punishment by the victorious Covenanters.

In the summer of 1641 Charles, after agreeing to the execution of Strafford and all the other demands of the Long Parliament in London, went to Scotland and tried to win the support of the Covenanters by a policy of appeasement and granting favours to the leaders. He made Argyll a Marquis, and Archibald Johnston a Judge of the Court of Session with the title of Lord Warriston, which was the name of the property near Edinburgh which Johnston had purchased five years before. The King also knighted him and gave him other benefits. It did not weaken Warriston's loyalty to the Presbyterian cause.

Warriston was the chief representative of the Covenanters in the negotiations with Pym and Sir Henry Vane the younger in London and Edinburgh in 1643, which resulted in the treaty by which the Church of England became a Presbyterian Church and the Scottish Covenanters agreed to enter the Civil War on the Roundhead side. After the Covenanters marched into England in January 1644, Warriston spent much time in London as one of the Scottish delegates on the Committee of Both Kingdoms, though he was also elected to the Scottish Parliament and attended to his Parliamentary duties in Edinburgh. In 1646 the King surrendered to the Scots at Newark. Warriston was with the King at the headquarters of the Covenanter army at Newcastle, and conducted the negotiations with the representatives of the English Parliament which culminated in the treaty by which Charles was handed over by the Scots to the English Parliament in January 1647 in return for the English Parliament paying the money needed for the wages of the Covenanter soldiers—a transaction which was represented by the Cavaliers as a shameful bargain by which the Scots sold their King for money, like Judas.

Warriston, as a zealous Presbyterian, strongly supported the English Presbyterians in their disputes with the Independents which began in 1644 and culminated in the conflict between Parliament and the army in 1647. Like all the Presbyterians, he was strongly opposed to religious toleration, and denounced the Independent and Anabaptist sects. But he distrusted Charles I, and opposed the Presbyterians' plan to join forces with the King against the army. When the Second Civil War broke out in May 1648, the Scottish Covenanters split. Some of them, under the leadership of the Duke of Hamilton, signed the 'Engagement' with the King, under which Charles agreed, in return for Scottish military aid, to make England a Presbyterian state for three years and at the end of that time to discuss the possibility of extending this period indefinitely; but as Charles would not become a Presbyterian himself, the majority of the Kirk of Scotland refused to be a party to the Engagement. Warriston, along with Argyll, refused to support the Engagers and Hamilton's invasion of England, and when Cromwell, after defeating Hamilton's army at Preston, marched to Edinburgh, Warriston welcomed him as an ally.

On 23 January 1649 Warriston moved the resolution in the Scottish Parliament by which all the Lords and MPs who had supported the Engagement with Charles I were expelled and deprived of the right to hold any public office in Scotland. But only a week later the army leaders in London beheaded Charles I, and when the news reached Edinburgh all the Covenanters united against the English regicides. The Covenanters had never contemplated the establishment of a republic, because there was nothing about a republic in the Old Testament. The Kirk, like Samuel and the Prophets, claimed the right to depose wicked kings; but when Samuel deposed Saul, he replaced him with another king, David, not with a republic. Warriston was present when Charles II was proclaimed King of Scots at the Mercat Cross in Edinburgh on 5 February 1649, and he negotiated the treaty of Breda with Charles II in Holland, under which the young King agreed to become a Presbyterian in return for the armed support of the Scottish Covenanters against the English Republic.

Before sailing to join the Covenanters in Scotland, Charles II tried to regain the throne without their assistance by a rising led by his loyal supporter, James Graham, Marquis of Montrose. Montrose had been one of the leaders of the Covenanters, and a close collaborator with Warriston, in the rising and wars of 1637–1640, but he objected to the Covenanters' decision to intervene in the English Civil War on the Roundhead side, and joined the Cavaliers. He raised an army of Highlanders on the King's behalf and attacked the Covenanters in the rear while they were fighting for the Roundheads in England, and won several brilliant victories before being finally defeated by the Covenanters and taking refuge abroad in 1646. His action in leading the wild Highlanders into the Lowlands had aroused great resentment among the Covenanters, who considered it to be their duty to exterminate Montrose's supporters with the same ferocity that Moses and Joshua had used against the original inhabitants of the Promised Land. Warriston and his colleagues, following in the footsteps of John Knox in the previous century, were careful to remind their followers that the sin for which God had punished Saul was his refusal to massacre all the inhabitants of Amalek.

In the spring of 1650 Montrose offered to invade Scotland and reconquer it for Charles II with the aid of loyal Cavaliers, thus freeing Charles from the necessity of relying on the Covenanters and becoming a Presbyterian in order to regain his thrones. Montrose landed in the far north, but was defeated by a Covenanter army, captured on the moors of Wester Ross and brought as a prisoner to Edinburgh. He had already been condemned as a traitor in his absence by the Scottish Parliament, and sentenced to be hanged at the Mercat Cross. He was not granted any further trial, but Warriston read out the sentence to him and behaved with his usual rudeness. Warriston also visited him on the morning of his execution, and found him combing his long hair and arranging his curls. Warriston upbraided him for his vanity, but Montrose replied that his head was still his own, and that after he was dead Warriston could do what he liked with it.

In view of Montrose's failure, Charles II had to rely on his second string and join Montrose's enemies. He landed in Scotland, and Cromwell's army crossed the Border. Warriston was one of the Commissioners appointed by the Kirk to represent them at their army headquarters. The Covenanter commander, General Leslie, manoeuvred Cromwell into a position where he was trapped at Dunbar, and Leslie, taking possession of the hills above Dunbar, hoped to starve Cromwell into surrender. By the end of August 1650 Cromwell's position was serious; but on 2 September Warriston persuaded the other Commissioners of the Kirk to order Leslie, against his better judgment, to descend from the hills and attack Cromwell. Warriston was sure that the God of Battles would give victory to the Kirk if Leslie attacked; but Cromwell, seeing the Covenanters advance, said 'God is delivering them into our hands', and next day completely defeated an army twice as large as his own. Warriston fled with the defeated Covenanters. For the rest of his life he never failed to note in his diary on 3 September that it was the anniversary of Dunbar.

After the defeat, Warriston joined Charles II at Perth and proceeded to give him a long lecture, telling him that the defeat at Dunbar was a punishment for the sinfulness of the King's private life. On several occasions he forced his presence on Charles and denounced him for his immorality; and Charles, who decided that Presbyterianism was no religion for gentlemen, developed a greater hatred of Warriston than of any of the other Covenanters with whom he came into contact.

After the defeat of Charles II and the Scots at Worcester, Cromwell and his Commander-in-Chief, General Monck, ruled Scotland at first like a conquered province; but after a few years they looked around for collaborators who would reconstitute a form of civil government in Scotland, though Monck, as Commander-in-Chief, remained the real power in the country. Again the Covenanters split, some being prepared to co-operate with Cromwell and others refusing. Argyll and Warriston were prepared to co-operate, and Warriston, going a good deal further than Argyll, intrigued successfully to obtain his re-appointment to his old office of Lord Clerk Register, which involved having the custody of the Scottish official records. He was also appointed a member of Cromwell's Upper House in the Parliament of the United Kingdom which was summoned in 1658.

This collaboration with Cromwell made Warriston unpopular in certain circles in Scotland. In May 1656, when he went to church in Calder, he was confronted by a woman who accused him of being a party to the deaths of Charles I and Montrose—though Warriston considered that 'God had His own honour' in Montrose's death. Warriston told her to be quiet, 'because the apostle forbids a woman to speak in the church'. When the officials tried to eject her, she clung to a pillar and prayed for Samson's strength to pull it down on them all. Warriston congratulated himself on his patience in the face of her insults, but was distressed to see that some of the people in the church laughed, and he wrote in his diary: 'The Lord punishes me in this sense as the congregation hath heard, and by it I will be for this week the song of the drunkard and subject of the laughter in the streets.'

Warriston was anxious when he heard of Cromwell's death on

3 September 1658, because he feared that it might lead to unrest and to dangerous developments in England and Scotland. 'It seemed remarkable his dying on 3 September', he wrote in his diary, 'the day of Dumbar 8 yeers, and Worcester 7 yeers, as 1638 and 1645, so 1658 is lyk to bring the juges.' But he consoled himself with the thought that God's providence had arranged for Cromwell to die at 'the tyme of Ch.St. [Charles Stuart's] lowest condition and incapacity to sturre'.

When Fleetwood and Desborough overthrew Richard Cromwell in May 1659, Warriston weighed up the arguments in favour of joining with them, or of supporting their opponents Ludlow and Vane and the republicans of the Rump. He decided to draw lots, thus leaving the decision to God. The lots told him to do nothing. He was nevertheless offered, a few days later, a seat on the Council of State which the republicans set up as the supreme executive body of the republic under the Rump Parliament. He accepted, and became one of the two Scottish representatives on the Council, and often acted as its President. The thought that he had been appointed to this exalted position without having intrigued for it moved him deeply, and on 25 May 1659 he noted in his diary: 'Now sitting at Counsel table in Whythal I wounder to see Charles Stewart and Oliver Cromwell their families secluded from it and poor Wariston, a stranger, brought into it without my hand.'

He soon fell out with his colleagues on the Council of State because he opposed their policy of religious toleration, and urged vigorous measures to suppress Quakers and Anabaptists. When Hazelrig denounced Lambert after the army officers had presented the Derby petition to the Rump in September 1659, Warriston's first reaction was to support Hazelrig on the grounds that it was the Anabaptists in the army who were behind the Derby petition; but after Lambert had dispersed the Rump and set up a Committee of Safety to govern on behalf of the army, Warriston accepted a place on the Committee of Safety. By the end of December, Lambert's army in Yorkshire had disintegrated, Monck was about to march from Coldstream to London, and the Rump reassembled. Warriston heard that Monck had denounced him in Scotland as an enemy of the state, and realized that he had backed the wrong side. On 26 December he noted in his diary that Lambert and the army 'had proven treacherous to God, to the Protector, to the Parliament, and now to Fleetwood: what a madnesse was it in me to trust them and hazard my all with them.'

But hope alternated with despair. Five days later, on 31 December—the day before Monck's army left Coldstream—Warriston thought that perhaps he would be able to change sides yet again and join Monck and his party. 'It would be, I thought, a strange and wonderful act if the Lord made thes men yet for al thats past and gon to call me to their counsels, and I will readily obey it and saye I followed Gods call of me.' But by 6 January he was writing in despair and remorse: 'And whereas I thought I was following the call of providence . . . the treuth is I followed the call of providence when it agreed with my humor and pleased my idol and seemed to tend to honor and advantage; but if that same providence had called me to quyte my better places and tak me to meaner places or non at all, I had not so hastily and contentedly followed it.' He considered whether it would be advisable to petition Parliament and the new Council of State which Hazelrig had established. 'I begged the Lords direction of me whither I shal now give in a paper to the House or Counsel to mitigate their rage and anger against me, and after prayer I cast the lott: it was No.'

When Monck arrived in London, Warriston and his wife hurried to Whitehall to try to gain his favour. Monck's body-guard would not let him approach Monck, and thrust him back and manhandled him. After trying for several days, he managed to speak to Monck on 24 March; but Monck rudely denounced him as an enemy of the state, and Lady Warriston had no more success with Mrs Monck.

Three days later, Warriston decided that he might be safer in Edinburgh than in London. He drew lots, and received the Divine command to return to Edinburgh; but when he arrived there, his friends could give him no comfort. Everyone told him that he and Argyll were the two most hated men in Scotland. On 14 May the people of Edinburgh lit bonfires to celebrate the return of Charles II, with old Jenny Geddes, who had started the revolution of 1637, throwing her herb-stall into the flames to show her loyalty to the King. Lady Warriston was forced by the people to light a bonfire too. 'At the tyme of the bonfyres', wrote Warriston, 'their was great ryot, excesse, extravagancy, superfluity, vanity, naughtinesse, profanetye, drinking of healths; the Lord be merciful to us.' Six days later, he heard that the House of Commons in London had selected seven of the regicides for execution, and that his name was not among them. His only comment was: 'Lord be blissed their is nothing as yet against me.'

But Charles II was determined to crush the Scottish Covenanters, and especially to show no mercy to Warriston, who had lectured him on his morals ten years before. He ordered that Warriston and two other leading Covenanters should be arrested. The two others were seized, but Warriston, who had ridden out of Edinburgh on that day to visit a friend, was warned as he was on the point of re-entering Edinburgh and, turning his horse's head, escaped into the country.

On 16 July 1660 a reward of £100 Scots was offered to anyone who brought him in, and anyone who harboured or helped him was to be prosecuted for high treason. Warriston found friends who were prepared to hide him, though whereabouts we do not know, as he was wise enough to leave the name of his hiding-place blank in his diary. On 10 September he wrote: 'I acknowledge the Lord had, be His ordinance of lotts thryse lately preserved my lyfe, in His bringing me from London (in which if I had remayned I had been taken and layd fast on suspicion of Lamberts rysing) . . . Then in sending me to, and keeping me in——, and now lately in bringing me out of —— befor the search, and preserving me as yet well heir.' He heard that two troops of soldiers were searching for him in the west, 'reeling and raging through honest folks houses for me. The Lord blindfold them never to find the right doore.'

Some time during the winter of 1660–1 he succeeded in getting on board a ship, disguised as a merchant, and escaping to Holland. But Charles II's agents were on the watch for regicides and other traitors in Holland, and Warriston went on to Hamburg. He was safer in Hamburg than in many places, but for some reason he left Hamburg in the spring of 1661 and went to Bolbec, near Le Havre in France. Perhaps someone recognized him in Hamburg, or perhaps the casting of lots on this occasion led him astray.

He lived at Bolbec in complete secrecy for nearly two years. Soon after he arrived, he wrote a long letter to his wife, who had remained in London, but he feared it would be too risky to send it: 'I cast the lott whither I should send it or not, and it was negative.' But in the spring of 1663, his wife joined him in Rouen. She was followed by an English government agent, who seized Warriston while he was at his prayers, and took him to the French authorities and demanded his extradition to England. The magistrates in Rouen imprisoned Warriston and referred the matter to the King's Council in Paris. The Council decided to refuse the request for extradition, but were overruled by Louis XIV, whose brother had married Charles II's sister Henrietta, and who was on excellent terms with his brother of England. He ordered that Warriston be handed over to the English government.

Warriston was taken to London and lodged in the Tower, and from there was sent by sea to Edinburgh, where he had already been attainted as a traitor in his absence by the Scottish Parliament at the time of Argyll's execution in 1661. He landed at Leith on 8 June, and by order of the Privy Council was forced to walk bareheaded amid a jeering crowd from the shore at Leith to the Tolbooth in Edinburgh. He was broken in health, both physically and mentally, and hardly recognized his children when they were brought to him. He was put on trial, charged with high treason against the King for having accepted office under Cromwell and sat in Cromwell's Upper House—the same offence which had been committed by many men who were at liberty in England. But Warriston, who saw now that God had turned against him, admitted that he had erred in collaborating with Cromwell. He was hanged at the Mercat Cross in Edinburgh on 22 July 1663, after he had confessed his guilt in his speech on the scaffold.

16

John Milton

The Puritan pamphleteer, John Milton, the champion of the Independents against the Presbyterians, the theoretical defender of regicide, the Secretary of the Republican government and of Cromwell as Lord Protector, did not think it wrong to write poetry in his spare time. His poetry, which was appreciated by his political enemies even in his own lifetime, has won him such a prominent place in the eyes of subsequent generations that his role as a Puritan propagandist has been largely forgotten. But Milton was, in his way, very typical of one kind of Puritan.

He was born in London on 9 December 1608. His father, who was a scrivener and an accomplished musician, had been brought up as a Roman Catholic but had become an ardent Puritan. John Milton was educated by tutors at his father's house in Bread Street, and at the age of sixteen, in February 1625, went to Christ's College, Cambridge. His father had intended him for the church; but though John Milton was a devout Puritan, and from the first was interested in theological and philosophical questions, he found literature a strong counter-attraction. In any case, the High Church policy which Laud and his supporters were beginning to impose on the Church of England made him reluctant to become a clergyman.

He remained at Cambridge, where his soft complexion won him the nickname of 'the lady' from his friends, though he was athletic and showed skill as a fencer. In 1632 he moved to Horton in Buckinghamshire, and lived there with his father. Some of his more famous poems—his sonnet to Shakespeare, *L'Allegro* and *Il Penseroso*, and his *Ode on the Morning of Christ's Nativity*—were written in his early twenties at Cambridge and Horton. His

Puritan beliefs did not prevent him from celebrating 25 December as the day of Christ's nativity, or from writing his masque, *Comus*, for a theatrical performance at Ludlow Castle in 1634, the year in which Prynne suffered for his denunciation of the theatre in *Histrio-Mastix*. Milton's Puritanism, though more extreme than Prynne's, was more tolerant and artistic.

In 1637 Milton's Cambridge friend, Edward King, was drowned while crossing the Irish Sea. Several of King's friends at Cambridge contributed poems in memory of King. Milton's contribution was *Lycidas*, and he took the opportunity to introduce a few famous lines—'The hungry sheep look up and are not fed'—which undoubtedly referred to Laud's persecution of the Puritans; it was the year in which Prynne, Bastwick and Burton underwent their ordeal and triumph in the pillory. Milton's lines

> But that two-handed engine at the door
> Stands ready to smite once, and smite no more

may well have been a prophecy that Laud would meet his just retribution at the hands of the headsman, though Milton certainly did not foresee in 1637 that a similar fate would befall King Charles himself.

In April 1638 Milton left England for a visit to France and Italy. He afterwards stated that he avoided all the temptations open to an unmarried man while he was in Italy, but he seems to have run some risk while he was there because of his cautious attempts to proselytize for Protestantism among the Papists. He was in Naples when he heard that the Scottish Covenanters had risen in revolt and that the King was preparing to march against them. He immediately set out for England, saying that he could not stay in Italy while freedom was being fought for in Britain.

He returned to the England of 1639-40, with the revolutionary uprising against the King, the victory of the Scots, and the summoning of the Long Parliament. He now made a great sacrifice for the cause, and virtually gave up writing poetry in order to devote himself to political propaganda, though he occasionally wrote a poem even at the most critical moments of political and military crises, like his sonnet *When the Assault was*

intended to the City, written when the Cavalier vanguard was at
Turnham Green in November 1642. As he had not taken holy
orders, he could not enter the pulpit like Goodwin and the
Puritan ministers; but in his pamphlets in 1641 and 1642 he
supported the 'Root and Branch' campaign for the abolition of
bishops.

By 1644 he was engaged in another struggle. In the war of
pulpit and pamphlets between the Presbyterians and the Independents, he became one of the leading pamphleteers for the
Independents. His first venture in this new contest may perhaps
have been influenced by personal factors. At the beginning of
the Civil War he married the sixteen-year-old daughter of an
Oxfordshire landowner whose family supported the Cavaliers.
His relations with his wife were unhappy from the first. She may
have refused to permit him to consummate the marriage, and
soon left him and returned to her family in Cavalier territory in
Oxfordshire, informing him that she would never live with him
again. After the battle of Naseby, when it was clear that the
Roundheads had won the Civil War, she returned to Milton in
London and next year, after the fall of Oxford, her Cavalier
parents and relatives also arrived and took refuge in Milton's
house. His wife bore him three surviving children, all daughters,
and died in 1652.

It was soon after his wife left him that Milton, in 1644, published his book *The Doctrine and Discipline of Divorce*, in which he
advocated that a husband should be entitled to put away his
wife for what we today would call incompatibility of temperament. Divorce was not permitted in England, as the Church of
England had not departed from the practice of the old Roman
Catholic Church as far as divorce was concerned; it had been
permitted in Scotland by the Presbyterian Kirk since the Reformation of 1560, but only for adultery and desertion. Prynne and
the Presbyterian ministers therefore attacked Milton's book on
divorce, and demanded that it be burned by the common hangman.

This led Milton to publish another and even more controversial pamphlet—his *Areopagitica*, in which he urged the
abolition of censorship and demanded freedom of the press. It
brought an outburst of denunciations from the Presbyterians,
and placed Milton firmly on the side of the Independents and

religious toleration. This naturally led him to support the army against Parliament in the struggle of 1647, and when the army in December 1648 decided to expel the Presbyterian MPs, to proclaim the republic and proceed to the trial and execution of the King, Milton supported them energetically. In February 1649—three weeks after the King's execution—he published a pamphlet, *The Tenure of Kings and Magistrates: Proving, That it is Lawfull, and hath been held so through all Ages, for any, who have the Power, to call to account a Tyrant, or wicked KING, and after due conviction, to depose, and put him to death; if the ordinary MAGISTRATE have neglected, or deny'd to doe it.* He justified this thesis by Old Testament texts, by the writings of sixteenth-century Protestant theologians, and by reason. But he refused an invitation from the Council of State to write a book against the Levellers.

Soon afterwards, Milton was appointed Latin Secretary to the Council of State, which involved drafting diplomatic documents from the English government to foreign powers. He also undertook an important propaganda duty—to write a learned book in Latin justifying the execution of the King. It was a reply to a book by the French Protestant theologian, Salmasius (Claude de Saumaise), who had quoted a mass of Scriptural and other authorities in order to denounce the English regicides. Salmasius's book had been circulated at the courts and universities of Europe. Milton's *Pro popolo anglicano defensio*, which was published in 1651 and was sent by the English government to Queen Christina of Sweden and to other foreign rulers and learned men, replied in the same spirit, and even if it failed to persuade the distinguished foreign readers of the justice of the English government's cause, at least it showed them, as they readily acknowledged, that the English republicans were not illiterate rebels, but could produce a propagandist whose scholarship and theology were as learned as those of Salmasius.

But the importance of Salmasius's book was minimal compared with the extraordinary effect produced by *Eikon Basilike*, which was supposed to have been written by Charles I but was really written by John Gauden, a clergyman who had originally been a Roundhead but had become a Cavalier by 1648, though it is possible that Gauden may have compiled the book from notes made by Charles himself. The book was a defence of the King's actions against the Roundheads. It did a great deal of harm to the republican cause, and played an important part in the Cavalier reaction and the cult of King Charles the Martyr which led to the Restoration and the persecution of the regicides eleven years later. The first edition was published in London on the day after the King was executed, and sixty editions had been printed before the end of the year, some published in The Hague and in Ireland and smuggled into England, and some printed in London. The book was sold more or less openly in England, because the republican government, with their dislike of censorship, made only half-hearted efforts to suppress it. There could not be a clearer example of the tolerance of Cromwell and the republicans than their failure to prevent the circulation of so damaging a piece of propaganda.

In October 1649 Milton published his book *Eikonoklastes*, in which he replied to *Eikon Basilike*. He clearly hinted that *Eikon Basilike* had not been written by Charles I, but he made the tactical error of replying to the arguments on the assumption that Charles was the author, instead of concentrating on exposing it as a forgery. After the Restoration Gauden told Clarendon and the Duke of York—the future James II—that he had written it. Clarendon wrote to Gauden, in reply, that he was very sorry that Gauden had told him, because the information would please no one except Mr Milton. Charles II appointed Gauden Bishop of Exeter, and later Bishop of Worcester, as a reward for the service which he had rendered and for keeping quiet about it.

Milton's eyesight was failing, for he was suffering from the disease which today is known to be glaucoma. He was warned that if he continued work on his book against Salmasius he would go blind, but he nevertheless went on working, convinced that he must make the sacrifice for the cause. Soon afterwards he became blind, to the great joy of the Cavaliers, who believed that it was a punishment of God for his sin in writing in support of the regicides. But he carried on his duties as Latin Secretary to the Council of State, and after Cromwell dissolved the Rump and became Lord Protector, Milton continued as Latin Secretary to Cromwell's government. He occasionally wrote a poem; the massacre of the Protestant Waldenses by the Duke of Savoy led him not only to draft an official diplomatic protest from the English government, but also to write his poem *On the late massacre in Piemont*.

After Cromwell's death, Milton at first watched impartially as the conflict developed between Richard Cromwell, the army, and the Rump; but as Monck marched on London and the rumours of a restoration spread throughout the country, Milton became alarmed. In March 1660, after Monck had recalled the Presbyterian MPs who had been expelled in Pride's Purge and was on the point of announcing his intention of restoring Charles II, Milton published a pamphlet, *The Ready and Easy Way to Establish a Free Commonwealth, and the Excellence thereof compared with the Inconveniences and Dangers of readmitting Kingship to this Nation*. In it, he proposed that the whole of the British Isles should be governed as one republic, with a considerable amount of devolution in government to provincial councils. He followed this pamphlet with two more, in March and April 1660, in which he strongly attacked Charles II and the House of Stuart. This was an action of almost quixotic courage, a splendid final gesture in defence of the republic at a time when public opinion was running strongly in the opposite direction. It made Milton very unpopular, and forced him to go into hiding to save his life from popular fury.

In view of Milton's recent activities, it was widely believed that he would be exempted from the Act of Indemnity and would suffer punishment as a regicide because of his books in favour of Charles I's execution. Prynne, who had regarded him as a menace ever since he had championed religious toleration and freedom of the press in 1644, urged that he should be made liable to suffer death; but Milton found supporters in the House of Commons, including his fellow-poet, Andrew Marvell, the MP for Hull. He was also helped by Sir William Davenant, the Cavalier poet and playwright, who had been protected by Milton when he was in difficulties under the Commonwealth. But as Marvell and Davenant were not very influential people, it is not easy to explain why Milton was able to escape, though it may have been due to the efforts of Arthur Annesley, afterwards Earl of Anglesey, and Monck's brother-in-law, Sir Thomas Clarges. His blindness seems to have helped him, because it could be argued that this punishment which God had inflicted on him made it unnecessary for further punishment to be imposed by man.

He was also fortunate that, either because of a cunning manoeuvre by his friends or more likely purely by chance, his critics concentrated on his famous book *Eikonoklastes*, and completely overlooked his earlier work, *The Tenure of Kings and Magistrates*, which had been published as early as February 1649. It must therefore have been written before the King's execution, which made it possible to argue that Milton was a party to the regicide before the act, and not merely a supporter of it after the act. But though Milton was arrested in August 1660, and his books were burned by the common hangman, he was released in December, having not been mentioned at all in the exemptions to the Act of Indemnity, and receiving therefore the whole benefit of the Act and escaping all punishment.

He spent the rest of his life in complete retirement, at his houses in London and at Chalfont St Giles in Buckinghamshire. He rose at 4 am in summer and 5 am in winter. During the morning his daughters read the Bible in Hebrew to him, and took down the writings which he dictated as he sat in his room, always neatly dressed in black. After a light dinner, at which he took very little wine, he listened to music in the afternoon and took exercise by walking, or swinging in wet weather. At 8 pm he ate a simple meal, usually of olives, and sat up, smoking a pipe and drinking a glass of water, before going to bed.

His family life was not altogether happy. After the death of his first wife he married a second wife in November 1656, but she died fifteen months later. In February 1663 he married for the third time. He was fifty-four, and his wife was twenty-four. She cared for him with much kindness, but her presence was resented by the three daughters of his first marriage. Of the three daughters, one was a cripple with a serious speech impediment, while a second resented his somewhat stern conception of parental authority and his doctrine about the purpose of living of men and women respectively—'Hee for God onely, shee for God in him'. But his greatest poetical works were produced in these last years of personal sorrows and political defeat—*Paradise Lost*, *Paradise Regained* and *Samson Agonistes*. They were published during his lifetime and were warmly praised by as enthusiastic a Cavalier as John Dryden, though it was not until twenty-five years after Milton's death, after the Revolution of 1688, that it was possible for him to gain widespread public recognition as a poet.

He died on 8 November 1674, a month before his sixty-sixth birthday. His wife survived him by fifty-three years, living on into the reign of George II.

17

Lucy Hutchinson

Women did not play a leading part in the Roundhead movement. The Puritan teaching was that man should serve God, and woman should serve God by serving man. The superiority of men over women, and the duty of wives to obey their husbands, were accepted by all religious groups and in all social classes in the seventeenth century. It was only at court and in the higher ranks of society that women, as the object of adoration by courtiers and poets, could more than hold their own with men. The veneration of women, in literature and in real life, was too closely associated with sexual license to be tolerated by the Puritans. On the other hand, the Puritan preachers emphasized the duty of the husband to love and respect his wife—an aspect of marital relationships which it was more difficult to persuade the ordinary husband to accept than his right of mastery over his wife. The Puritan teaching seems in many cases to have produced very happy marriages, and charming, cultivated wives who were deeply in love with their husbands.

Lucy Apsley, who became the wife of Colonel John Hutchinson, was the daughter of Sir Allen Apsley, the Lieutenant of the Tower of London, where she was born on 29 January 1620. Her father's family were gentlemen of Pulborough in Sussex. She was a precocious child. She could read English perfectly by the age of four, and already at that age was taken to hear sermons, which she could often memorize. At a time when women, even in the highest ranks of the aristocracy, were usually uneducated and sometimes illiterate, she had eight different tutors at the same time when she was aged seven; but though they taught her Latin and foreign languages, music, dancing, writing and needlework, it was only her books that really interested her.

Like many of her contemporaries, she was brought up with a

fervent belief in religion, but in her younger days she had her lighter side. 'It pleas'd God that thro' the good instructions of my mother, and the sermons she carried me to, I was convinc'd that the knowledge of God was the most excellent study, and accordingly applied myselfe to it, and to practise as I was taught; I us'd to exhort my mother's maides much, and to turne their idle discourses to good subjects; but I thought, when I had done this on the Lord's day, and every day perform'd my due taskes of reading and praying, that then I was free to anie thing that was not sin, for I was not at the time convinc'd of the vanity of conversation which was not scandalously wicked. I thought it no sin to learne or heare wittie songs and amorous sonnetts or poems, and twenty things of that kind, wherein I was so apt that I became the confident in all the loves that were managed among my mother's young weomen, and there was none of them but had many lovers.' Lucy Apsley herself, who states that she was considered to be beautiful when she was a young girl, seems to have fallen in love, though she tore out of the manuscript of her unfinished memoirs several pages in which she had written about it, and left in only a passage expressing her more sober attitude towards it in later years. 'When any one mention'd him to me, I told them I had forgotten those extravagancies of my infancy, and knew now that he and I were not equall; but I could not for many yeares heare his name without severall inward emotions.'

When she was eighteen she met John Hutchinson, who was five years older than she. He was the son of Sir Thomas Hutchinson of the village of Owthorpe in Nottinghamshire. He had been brought up as a Puritan, and after going to Cambridge University had come to London to study law at the Inns of Court. He became friendly with the Apsley family. One day he was shown a sonnet which Lucy Apsley had written, and was astounded when he was told that it was written by a woman. He was very eager to meet her, and was not discouraged when he heard that she had no interest in men and was bored by the attentions of her many suitors. When he saw her, he fell in love at first sight, although she took no pains with her clothes or with the adornment of her person.

Many years later, Lucy wrote about their meeting in her biography of her husband. 'I shall passe by all the little amorous relations, which if I would take the paynes to relate, would make a true history of a more handsome management of love than the best romances describe; for these are to be forgotten as the vanities of youth, not worthy mention among the greater transactions of his life. There is only this to be recorded, that never was there a passion more ardent and less idolatrous; he loved her [Lucy] better than his life, with unexpressable tendernesse and kindnesse, had a most high oblieging esteeme of her, yet still consider'd honour, religion, and duty above her, nor ever suffer'd the intrusion of such a dotage as should blind him from marking her imperfections.' They were married on 3 July 1638 at St Andrew's church in Holborn. She immediately conceived twins, but lost them, and nearly lost her own life, four months after the marriage. Next year, in September 1639, she gave birth to twin boys. Her third son, John, was born in 1641. He was an intelligent and lively child, 'but death soone nipt that blossome', and he died at the age of six.

When the Civil War broke out, John and Lucy Hutchinson were living with their children at Owthorpe in Nottinghamshire. Lucy, like her husband, saw the issue in the simple terms in which she viewed the whole struggle between Puritanism and Popery. For her, Mary Queen of Scots was 'a wicked Queene, daughter of a mother that came out of the bloody house of Guize, and brought up in the Popish religion'. Queen Elizabeth was 'not only glorious in the defence of her owne realme, but in the protection she gave to the whole Protestant cause in all the neighbouring kingdomes'. James I was a King under whom the country saw 'the Protestant interest abroad deserted and betrey'd, the prelates att home dayly exalted in pride and pomp, and declining in vertue, godlinesse, and sound doctrine. Arminianisme crept in', and 'secret treaties were entertain'd with the Court of Rome.' King James's court was 'a nursery of lust and intemperance'. Charles I, on the other hand, 'was temperate and chast and serious', but 'the example of the French king was propounded to him, and he thought himselfe no Monarch so long as his will was confin'd to the bounds of any law.'

On 22 August 1642 King Charles raised his standard at Nottingham, and the Civil War began. Three weeks later he left Nottingham, and never again did the town fall into Cavalier hands. This was largely because of the energy and courage of Colonel Hutchinson, who raised a local force, like his Puritan relative and neighbour Ireton, to fight for Parliament. Hutchinson's uncle Sir John Byron of Newstead in Nottinghamshire, who afterwards became the first Lord Byron, and Byron's brother Sir Richard Byron, fought for the King. While Hutchinson was in command of the Roundhead garrison at Nottingham, Sir Richard Byron held Newark for the Cavaliers. Some of the local Roundheads, seeing that Hutchinson's uncle was commanding the enemy forces in the area, had doubts about Hutchinson's loyalty, and Lucy Hutchinson states that because of this, Hutchinson was compelled, against his instincts, to be more hostile to Sir Richard Byron than to any of the other Cavalier commanders. Lucy wrote that 'whether it were that the dissension of brethren is allwayes most spitefully persued, or that Sir Richard Biron, as 'twas reported, suffer'd under the same suspitions on his side, it is true they were to each other the most uncivill enemies that can be imagined.' On one occasion when Hutchinson was in action against Byron, he ordered his men 'to take him or shoote him . . . and not let him scape though they cut his leggs off.'

At the beginning of the war, Owthorpe was occupied by Prince Rupert's army. Hutchinson escaped into Northamptonshire, but Lucy and the children remained at Owthorpe. Fortunately Lucy's brother, Colonel Sir Allen Apsley, was serving in the Cavalier army at Owthorpe, and he took up his quarters in the house next door to Lucy's, so that he was in a good position to protect her and her property. On one occasion, his attempts to help her led to unfortunate consequences. A Cavalier officer, Captain Welch, who had occasion to call on Lucy, began paying her compliments and passing strictures on Hutchinson for having deserted so charming a wife. This annoyed Lucy, and she asked Apsley to pretend to be Hutchinson, in order to make Welch believe that her husband was at home. When Welch reported this to Rupert's headquarters, he was ordered to arrest Hutchinson as a Roundhead combatant, and he seized Apsley, and took him as a prisoner to Rupert. It was only with considerable difficulty, and with the help of the Byrons, that Apsley was able to prove his identity.

In the last campaign of the First Civil War, in 1646, Apsley held out at Barnstaple for the King. He eventually surrendered, being granted terms which guaranteed his immunity from prosecution or punishment. He was nevertheless vexed by a woman who, according to Lucy Hutchinson, 'was handsome in her youth, and had very pretty girles to her daughters, whom, when they grew up, she prostituted to her revenge and mallice against Sir Allen Apsley.' She had lived in Barnstaple when Apsley was in command there, and after the surrender of the town she complained to the Roundheads that Apsley had destroyed her house as part of his measures for the defence of Barnstaple, and she demanded that he should be punished for it. Apsley took shelter in the Hutchinsons' house at Owthorpe, and Hutchinson successfully used his influence with the Roundhead authorities to protect Apsley. After the Restoration, Apsley met this woman at Whitehall, when she was claiming her reward from Charles II, and he discovered that she had been a secret agent of the Cavaliers throughout the whole period of the Commonwealth, and had apparently denounced Apsley as a cover for her spying activities.

Hutchinson's firm belief in religious toleration, and his relationship and friendship with Ireton, led him to support the Independents and the army against the Presbyterians and Parliament. Lucy herself became an Anabaptist as a result of meeting an Anabaptist gunner during the siege of Nottingham. He raised serious doubts in her mind about the efficacy of baptism. When her next child was born, she searched assiduously in the Bible, but could find no text which prescribed the baptism of infants, and she refused to allow her child to be baptized.

Hutchinson disapproved of Pride's Purge, but he believed that Charles I should be brought to justice for the blood that he had shed, and he sat as a Commissioner at the King's trial and signed the death warrant. He was not happy about Cromwell's dissolution of the Rump, and suspected Cromwell of personal ambition, while Lucy Hutchinson disapproved of the frivolity of Cromwell's daughter Elizabeth Claypole and thought that Cromwell permitted too much gaiety at his court. Lucy was particularly censorious about Frances Lambert, and considered that Lambert and the Major-Generals were seeking to establish a military dictatorship. Hutchinson therefore withdrew with his family to Owthorpe and lived there quietly throughout the Protectorate.

The Hutchinsons placed the blame for the disturbances of 1659 on Lambert, and, like Hazelrig and Scot and other republicans, relied on Monck's army to protect them and the authority of the Rump against Lambert. When Monck restored Charles II to the throne, Lucy Hutchinson described him as 'that vile Traytor who had sold the men that trusted him'. Hutchinson was in danger of punishment as a regicide. Lucy set out to save his life by all the means at her disposal. Her brother Sir Allen Apsley used his influence on Hutchinson's behalf, as did the Marquis of Dorchester who was Lord Lieutenant of Nottinghamshire. But Clarendon, the Lord Chancellor, who as always thought only of the interests of the State, was working against him.

Despite all Lucy's efforts to persuade him to do so, Hutchinson refused to express penitence for his part in the King's death. Lucy drafted a petition to Parliament for him to sign, in which he asked for mercy, expressed his repentance for his part in Charles's execution and threw the blame for it on to Cromwell, pretending, like most of the regicides did, that Cromwell had compelled them against their will to sit as Commissioners at the King's trial and sign the death warrant. As Hutchinson refused to sign this petition, Lucy forged his signature, and gave it to her brother to present to the House of Commons. As a result of this, Hutchinson was one of a group of regicides who were disqualified from holding any public office for the rest of their lives, but was exempted from all other punishment.

As the trial of the regicides drew near in October 1660, Hutchinson, who had retired to Owthorpe, was ordered to come to London to be examined by the Attorney-General, Sir Geoffrey Palmer. Palmer wished to call Hutchinson as a witness for the prosecution at the trial of the regicides, and asked him to identify the signatures of his fellow-signatories on Charles I's death warrant. The warrant had been given to the authorities by Mrs Hacker, the wife of Hutchinson's Nottinghamshire friend and neighbour Colonel Hacker, who had commanded the troops at the King's execution, because Mrs Hacker hoped that it would show that Hacker had only acted in obedience to the authority of his superiors. It did not save Hacker, who was executed as a regicide, but it provided damning evidence against the signatories. Hutchinson was unwilling to incriminate his colleagues; he identified the signatures of Cromwell, Ireton and Lord Grey, all of whom were dead, but of no living regicide. The Attorney-General warned him that his attitude would make a very bad impression, and when Charles II heard of it he commented that 'they had sav'd a man meaning Colonel Hutchinson, who would doe the same thing for him he did for his father, for he was still unchang'd in his principles and readier to protect than accuse any of his associates.'

Hutchinson was present at the trial of the regicides in case the Attorney-General decided to call him as a witness for the prosecution; but when he saw, sitting among the judges, such old Roundheads as Monck, Ashley-Cooper, and Denzil Holles, who had 'openly sayd he abhorr'd the word "accommodation" when moderate men would have prevented the warre', he was so angry that he decided that if he were called as a witness 'he was resolv'd to have borne testimony to the Cause and against the Court'. But he was not called. Clarendon was very angry at Hutchinson's attitude, and told Apsley that they should never have allowed Hutchinson to escape punishment.

Hutchinson retired to Owthorpe and lived there quietly for three years. To his annoyance, his son married the daughter of Sir Alexander Ratcliffe, a prominent Cavalier in Essex; but though Hutchinson's first reaction was to threaten to turn his son out of the house, he forgave him when he met his charming daughter-in-law, and was greatly saddened when she died in childbirth a year after the marriage.

The government had not forgiven Hutchinson for his refusal to give evidence against his old comrades. Apsley and Lucy Hutchinson's Cavalier friends warned him that he would be well-advised to leave England, but he refused to go, and incurred fresh suspicion by sending alms to Nonconformist preachers who were imprisoned in Nottinghamshire for unlawful preaching under the Clarendon Code. Suddenly, on the evening of 11 October 1663, a band of soldiers arrived at the house in Owthorpe and arrested Hutchinson on a charge of plotting a rising against the government. Hutchinson was ill, but although it was a very stormy night the guards refused his request to be allowed to stay at home until next morning, and carried him to Newark, where he was confined under guard at the local inn. A week later he was interrogated by the Marquis of Newcastle, who treated him with great courtesy and wished to release him, as he found no evidence

against him; but Newcastle received orders from the Duke of
Buckingham that Hutchinson was to be sent as a prisoner to
London. There he was examined by Sir Henry Bennet, the
Secretary of State—afterwards the Earl of Arlington—and was
asked to give the names of his associates in the plot. He said that
he knew of no plot, and so could name no associates. Bennet
warned him that he had done himself no good by his attitude, and
sent him to the Tower.

Lucy Hutchinson hurried to London to try to help her husband.
Sir Allen Apsley again exerted all his influence on his brother-in-
law's behalf, but the Lieutenant of the Tower was hostile, and
used his position—which thirty years before had been held by
Lucy's father—to extort money from the Hutchinsons for every
favour accorded to him. With some difficulty Apsley arranged for
Lucy to see Hutchinson, and also to have an interview with
Bennet; but Bennet was hostile, and as soon as she had left the
room he told Hutchinson's Cavalier cousin, Sir Robert Byron,
that God was now punishing Hutchinson for his part in Charles
I's death, even though Charles II had pardoned him for this.
Clarendon explained to Apsley that it would be dangerous to
release Hutchinson, because Hutchinson had not attended church
in Owthorpe in the last few years before his arrest. The government planned to ship him off as a prisoner to the Isle of Man.
Apsley prevented this by pretending that he had a claim against
Hutchinson in connection with a property transaction which
made it necessary for him to see Hutchinson in the Tower.

In the spring of 1664 Hutchinson was taken to Sandown
Castle near Deal. Lucy Hutchinson was not allowed to live there
with him, but she took up residence in Deal with her children,
and was allowed to see him every day, and walk along the seashore with him accompanied by an escort of guards. In September
she returned to Owthorpe for a few weeks to deal with matters
there. While she was at Owthorpe Hutchinson caught a chill
from walking on the seashore, and died after a few days' illness
before Lucy could come to him, though his brother was with
him when he died.

Lucy was allowed to take his body back to Owthorpe for
burial. The authorities insisted on holding an inquest on his body
in order to show that they had not poisoned him. 'But if they did
not that way dispatch the Collonel,' wrote Lucy, 'it is certaine

their unjust and barbarous usage of him did occasion his death, whose murther the Lord will not forget when he makes inquisition for the blood of his saints.'

Lucy Hutchinson lived on for at least another eleven years, but the date of her death is unknown. She was still living in 1675 when she sent to Arthur Annesley, Earl of Anglesey—who was one of the influential Cavaliers who had helped her husband at the Restoration—the English translation of Lucretius which she had compiled in her 'vainly curious youth', though she now hated 'the atheisms and impieties in it', and thought that the study of pagan poets and philosophers was 'one great means of debauching the learned world'. She wrote two books on Christian theology; but her chief work was her biography of her husband, which she wrote for her children, and not for publication.

Her admiration for her husband was unbounded. 'To number his vertues is to give the epitome of his life, which was nothing elce but a progresse from one degree of vertue to another.' As long as he lived, he was the centre of her existence; after his death, she lived only to write about him for the children. 'The greatest excellence she had,' she wrote about herself, 'was the power of apprehending and the vertue of loving his. Soe, as his shaddow, she waited on him every where, till he was taken into that region of light which admits of none, and then she vanisht into nothing.'

18

James Nayler

From the battles and controversies of the Civil War, from the
debris of the seventeenth-century doctrines of Presbyterians,
Independents, Anabaptists and Fifth Monarchy Men, there
emerged the sect known as the Quakers, who were to achieve so
much in two continents during the next three hundred years. In
July 1643, when the Cavaliers were driving the Roundhead
forces out of the south-west and defeating Waller at Roundway
Down, while Cromwell was clearing Lincolnshire of the enemy,
and the north was still held firmly by the Cavaliers, a young man
aged nineteen, George Fox, after going to a fair in his native
village in Leicestershire, felt the call to proselytize, left home, and
first began to preach the doctrines which later became those of
his followers in the Society of Friends, whom their opponents
called Quakers. By 1647 Fox had established a small group of
followers on the borders of Lancashire and Westmorland.

It was in Lancashire, in Wigan, that Gerrard Winstanley was
born in 1609, and this connection with Lancashire, as well as the
similarity between Winstanley's doctrines of social equality and
the Quakers' objections to titles, caused their orthodox critics to
identify Winstanley and the Quakers. Winstanley went to
London, where he became a clothier and an established tradesman in the City; but before 1649 he had gone bankrupt. By 1648
he had begun writing a succession of pamphlets in which he not
only wrote in the most extreme and incoherent language about
the significance of the passages in the Book of Revelation, but
also put forward the doctrine that goods should be owned in
common.

In the spring of 1649, directly after the establishment of the
republic and at the time of the Leveller mutinies in the army,
Winstanley and a band of supporters, who called themselves

Diggers or True Levellers, began to cultivate waste land at St George's Hill at Walton-on-Thames in Surrey. The Diggers set up huts on the land, cultivated it by their labour and lived on the crops that they had sown. The local landowners considered this to be a violation of property-rights and a menace to the established social order. They attacked the Diggers, burned their huts and pulled up their crops; and though the Diggers did not retaliate, the landowners complained to the newly-established republican Council of State, and asked the Lord General Fairfax to send troops to disperse the Diggers.

Winstanley was summoned before the Council of State, and after pointing out that the local landowner who was instigating the attacks on the Diggers had been a Cavalier during the Civil War, he defended the right of freeborn Englishmen to cultivate land that was not put to useful purposes by the landowner. Fairfax did not think that the Diggers constituted a threat to the republic, and refused to intervene; but the persecutions of the local landowners and JPs made life unbearable for the Diggers, who eventually dispersed. Winstanley, after publishing his last pamphlet in 1652, resumed his career as a business man, and in October 1660, when the regicides were being tried for having murdered King Charles the Martyr, Winstanley brought a lawsuit in the King's courts in connection with a commercial transaction. This is the last thing which is known about him.

It is doubtful whether the Quakers, who refused to take off their hats to magistrates and to their social superiors, or to address them by any title other than 'Friend', had in fact any connection with Winstanley. But Fox and Winstanley had at least one thing in common: they had both opted out of the Civil War and the political controversies of the time in order to put forward doctrines, and to pursue a way of life, which seemed to them to be of greater importance than the issues which excited most of their contemporaries. James Nayler, on the other hand, fought in the Civil War on the Roundhead side, and is a direct link between the sectaries of Cromwell's army and the Quakers.

Nayler was born about the year 1617, the son of a yeoman farmer of Ardsley near Wakefield in Yorkshire. He was twenty-five when the Civil War began and, filled with Puritan zeal, he immediately volunteered as a private soldier in Lord Fairfax's army. He served in the north throughout the Civil War, and by the time that Lambert had become commander of the army in Yorkshire, Nayler had been promoted to the rank of Quarter-Master-Sergeant. He would often preach sermons on the spur of the moment to his fellow-soldiers. He went with the army into Scotland in 1650, and attracted Lambert's attention by his courage and good service at Dunbar. A few days after the battle he preached a particularly passionate sermon to the soldiers. One of them said that he was more frightened by Nayler's sermon than he had been by the enemy during the battle of Dunbar.

After the final victory at Worcester, Nayler was discharged from the army, and returned to his farm in his native Yorkshire village of Ardsley. Early in 1652 George Fox came to the neighbouring parish of West Ardsley. As it was an offence to interrupt a religious service—Fox had already been imprisoned more than once for doing so—he waited until the service in the village church was over, and then preached to the congregation as they left. He was attacked by the people and imprisoned by the local JPs. Nayler was indignant at the way in which Fox had been treated, and made himself unpopular in the village by protesting about it. A few months later, while Nayler was ploughing on his holding, he received what he believed was a call from God to go forth and preach. Without saying good-bye to his wife and family, he left the village and made his way to the Quaker settlements in Lancashire and Westmorland, where he found Fox.

The Quakers believed that the only way to save the country from its ills, and win the forgiveness of God, was through the personal salvation of the individual. They taught that man was capable of achieving perfection, as Christ was in every man. They were given the name of 'Quaker' because they periodically went into paroxysms of religious frenzy during which their knees knocked together and their limbs shook. They declared that only those who had had this quaking experience had felt the fear of the Lord as Moses and David had felt it. Many of their preachers were women. One of them, Mary Fisher, after being imprisoned for her sermons in Yorkshire, stoned and savagely whipped in Cambridge, and imprisoned, stripped naked, and robbed of all her meagre possessions in Massachusetts, made her way to Turkey to convert the Sultan, and was listened to with more patience by Mohammed IV than by the Christian authorities in England or in America.

The Quakers were repeatedly arrested and prosecuted in the courts. They were prosecuted under the statutes which prohibited travelling on Sundays, and for refusing to take oaths of allegiance when ordered to do so and to swear to speak the truth in the courts of law. Above all, they were prosecuted for preaching their doctrine of the perfectibility of man and that Christ was in every man, under a statute of the Rump Parliament of 1650 which made it blasphemy to assert that any man could be the equal of God. In January 1653 Nayler and Fox were prosecuted at Appleby Assizes for preaching that Christ was in every man, and were sentenced to imprisonment. Nayler was released after five months and went to London, where he preached to Quaker gatherings and built up a body of devoted followers, many of whom were women. He had allowed his brown hair and beard to grow full, and in his physical appearance resembled the traditional pictures of Christ. Many of his followers worshipped him, kneeling to kiss his feet. One of the women claimed that he had resurrected her from the dead by his touch.

In the summer of 1656 Nayler heard that Fox had been arrested at Launceston in Cornwall, and he set off for Launceston with some of his followers. On his way, he and his friends were arrested and imprisoned at Exeter. While he was in prison he received a letter from one of his followers in London, telling him that henceforth he should no longer be called James, but Jesus. On his release from prison in Exeter he went with his followers to Bristol, and on 24 October 1656, in heavy rain, he rode into Bristol on an ass. His followers walked beside him, strewing branches before him, and calling out: 'Holy, holy, holy, Lord God of Israel!' He was arrested, and sent to London to be dealt with by Cromwell's Parliament.

He was accused of blasphemy, of having claimed to be Christ and of having accepted from his followers the honours due only to God. Nayler claimed that his followers were not worshipping him, but the Christ within him. Many MPs denounced him strongly, though Lambert spoke in his favour and recalled his good service in the army, and especially at Dunbar. A resolution was moved that he should be put to death for his blasphemy, but was defeated by ninety-six votes to eighty-two. Parliament then sentenced him to be pilloried in Palace Yard and whipped to the Exchange, to be pilloried again two days later at the Exchange, when his tongue was to be bored through with a hot iron and he was to be branded on the forehead with the letter B for blasphemy, then to be whipped in Bristol, and finally to be imprisoned during the pleasure of Parliament.

The first part of the sentence was carried out on 18 December 1656. After being placed for two hours in the pillory at Palace Yard he was whipped to the Exchange with such savagery that it seemed impossible to proceed to the second part of the sentence two days later. On the petition of his friends, the further punishment was postponed for a week; but though several Quakers petitioned for a reprieve, and Cromwell questioned the power of Parliament to sentence Nayler, the second part of the sentence was carried out on 27 December. The London Quaker merchant, Rich, stood beside Nayler when he was in the pillory, and raised a notice 'This is the King of the Jews' over Nayler's head; but one of the officers tore it down. Nayler eagerly put out his tongue to be bored by the hot iron, but shrank when the branding iron was applied to his forehead, though Rich tried to suck out the fire. Nayler was then taken to Bristol, and on 17 January was forced to ride through the city on a horse, bareback and facing the tail, and was then whipped through the city. He was taken back to London and imprisoned in Bridewell, where Parliament ordered that he was to be denied pen and ink, was to perform the heaviest manual labour in solitude and to be given the minimum amount of food.

He remained in prison for nearly three years, but after the fall of Richard Cromwell the Rump Parliament ordered his release in September 1659. He immediately went to Reading to see Fox; but Fox, who had condemned his ride into Bristol and was ill, refused to see him. Nayler, however, had repented of his action. He published a pamphlet admitting his offence, and went to Bristol, where he preached along the same lines, and asked the foregiveness of the people. Fox forgave him, and authorized him to resume his preaching on behalf of the Quakers.

At the Restoration, 700 Quakers were released from prison under an amnesty, though they were soon to be persecuted more savagely than ever under the Quaker Act of 1662, when over 4,000 were arrested. In October 1660 Nayler decided to leave

London and return to his native village in Yorkshire. Although he was in poor health, he set out on his journey, on foot. He was seen and recognized by a Quaker acquaintance near Hertford; but he refused his friend's offer to give him food and shelter in his house, and pressed on to the north. On the road between Huntingdon and Peterborough he collapsed, and as he lay exhausted he was set upon by footpads and robbed of his possessions and his clothes. He was found lying in a field by a farm labourer, and carried to a house in the village of Holme, where a Quaker doctor was called to care for him; but he died a few days later, at the age of forty-three.

19

George Monck,
Duke of Albemarle

Twice during the lifetime of George Monck, the ruler whom he was serving—in the first case Charles I, in the second Cromwell —received information that Monck was a traitor who was planning to desert to the enemy. On both occasions the accusation was untrue; both Charles I and Cromwell disbelieved it, and affirmed their trust in Monck; and on both occasions Monck did in fact soon afterwards betray the cause and go over to the enemy.

Monck had his principles—the simple principles of a professional soldier. He believed in the duty of a soldier to be brave on the battlefield and to carry out his duties conscientiously; and his sense of discipline led him to oppose religious toleration and all forms of libertarianism and anarchy. But apart from this, he thought only of his own self-advancement. In an age when so many of the other leading figures were religious zealots and political theoreticians, Monck devoted himself single-mindedly to the aim of winning power and wealth for himself.

He was born on 6 December 1608 in the village of Potheridge near Torrington in Devonshire, where his father, Sir Thomas Monck, was a respected but impoverished landowner. Though his background and education were not basically different from those of Pym, Blake and Prynne, his character was very different. He grew up to be, not the Puritan scholar of the Universities and the Inns of Court, but that other specimen of Jacobean England—the gallant, boisterous, bullying gentleman of Shakespeare's plays.

Monck, who was his father's second son, decided to seek adventure and to pursue a military career. An unexpected incident precipitated his decision. He was sixteen when King Charles I succeeded to the throne in the spring of 1625 and made his first royal 'progress' by visiting the West Country. Sir Thomas Monck, like all the Devon gentry, was preparing to meet the King at Exeter, when one of his creditors instructed the Under-Sheriff of Devonshire to arrest him for debt. Young George Monck contacted the Under-Sheriff and offered him a bribe on condition that the Under-Sheriff did not arrest his father until after he had received the King. The Under-Sheriff accepted the bribe, and then arrested Sir Thomas Monck before the King arrived. George Monck went to the Under-Sheriff's lodgings in Exeter and gave him a sound thrashing. This attempt to bribe the Under-Sheriff, the indignation at the breach of faith, and the resort to physical violence, were typical of Monck's character throughout his life.

Charles I had decided to send a fleet to capture Cadiz and the Spanish treasure-fleet in an attempt to win his subjects' goodwill by a limited intervention on the Protestant side in the Thirty Years War. The expedition was on the point of sailing from Plymouth, and Monck joined it, enlisting in the company of his cousin, Richard Grenville, the brother of Sir Bevill Grenville of Kilkhampton in Cornwall. Monck was out of the country before the Under-Sheriff of Devonshire could take proceedings against him for assault.

The expedition to Cadiz was a disaster. Owing to corruption and inefficiency in the military administration, supplies of food ran out, and by the time they reached Cadiz the soldiers were half-starved. The English landed, captured a fort, and marched a little way inland, but within a week they had re-embarked and left Cadiz in search of the Spanish treasure-fleet. They did not find it, and the starving and mutinous troops returned to England having accomplished nothing. Two years later, Monck went on his second military campaign when, at the age of eighteen, he joined the Duke of Buckingham's expedition to the Ile de Ré to relieve the French Huguenots threatened by Richelieu's armies in La Rochelle. This expedition, too, proved to be a disastrous failure, thanks to Buckingham's incompetence and bad luck; but Monck had an opportunity to show his courage and resourcefulness when Buckingham entrusted him with a despatch which he was to carry to King Charles in England. Monck sailed right under the guns of the French fleet off the Ile de Ré, and was lucky to get through. After four months' ineffectual operations, the English troops returned to England, leaving La Rochelle to fall a year later.

In 1629 Monck joined the English volunteers who had enlisted in the armies of the Prince of Orange to fight in the Netherlands for the Protestant Cause in the Thirty Years War. Monck had no particular interest in the Protestant Cause, but welcomed the military experience and adventure, and unlike his unfortunate experiences when fighting in the English army, he was often on the victorious side in Holland. He particularly distinguished himself at the siege and capture of Breda. After nine years' successful service he had risen to the rank of Lieutenant-Colonel and was highly thought of by the Prince of Orange when an unfortunate incident put an end to his career in Holland. One of his soldiers was arrested by the Dutch civilian authorities at Dordrecht and charged with some criminal offence. Monck offered to try the man by court-martial and punish him, but denied the right of the Mayor and corporation of Dordrecht to exercise a criminal jurisdiction over his troops. Both the Mayor and Monck appealed to the Prince of Orange, and Monck threatened to resign from the Prince's service if the Prince decided against him. The Prince did not wish to lose the services of an able commander, but thought that this was preferable to antagonizing his civilian subjects by interfering with their municipal privileges. He held in the Mayor's favour, and Monck left the Dutch service.

He returned to England, and made preparations to take part in a colonizing expedition to Madagascar, but he changed his plans on the outbreak of King Charles's second war against the Scottish Covenanters in 1640. While the people of England were rising against the government, and many of the King's troops were mutinying against their Roman Catholic officers, Monck was prepared to serve the King with the non-political loyalty of the professional soldier. He joined the King's army and took part in the only battle of the war, when the Scots forded the Tyne and defeated the royal troops at Newburn. Monck's regiment was almost the only one in the King's army that did not run away, and he was able to hold off the Scots and save the artillery, and retreated with his men in good order to Newcastle. He was disgusted at the cowardice of the King's soldiers and the incompetence of their commanders, and was equally angry when the King capitulated to the Scots and to his English subjects and agreed to all the Covenanters' terms at Ripon. Monck, looking at the position in purely military terms, was certain that they could have defeated the Scots and crushed the rebellion if the King had shown sufficient resolution.

After the outbreak of the Irish Catholic rising in 1641, when the forces in Ireland divided into the three parties—the Catholic rebels, the King's garrisons, and the English Parliamentary expedition—Monck joined the King's army in Ireland, and took part in the operations which the Earl of Ormonde was conducting against the Irish rebels. Monck showed great energy and ruthlessness, capturing many towns and fortresses from the rebels and hanging many prisoners.

He was occupied in Ireland during the first year of the English Civil War, but in the autumn of 1643 the King and Ormonde decided to use the army in Ireland in the Civil War in England. Ormonde asked all his officers if they would be prepared to fight for the King in England. Monck was one of two officers who were unwilling to give this undertaking, because he was always slow to commit himself politically. Pym, who had been impressed by Monck's record as a soldier, wrote secretly to Monck in Ireland inviting him to join the Roundhead armies in England. Some of Monck's Cavalier colleagues found out about the letter, and told Ormonde that Monck was not to be trusted; and when the army which Ormonde had raised in Ireland sailed to England to fight for the King, Ormonde arrested Monck and sent him in custody to Bristol. Monck asked for an audience with the King. When he met Charles at Oxford, he convinced him of his loyalty, and he was sent to join his comrades in the regiments which had come from Ireland and were besieging Nantwich in Cheshire.

In January 1644 the Roundheads sent a force from Yorkshire and Lincolnshire under the command of Sir Thomas Fairfax to fight the Anglo-Irish Cavaliers in Cheshire. Fairfax surrounded them at Nantwich, and to Monck's disgust the Anglo-Irish infantry surrendered, and Monck was taken prisoner. The Roundheads, in accordance with the usual practice, gave the prisoners the opportunity of changing sides and enlisting in the Roundhead armies. Many of them accepted, but Monck refused.

He was brought before the House of Commons on a charge of high treason for having fought against Parliament, but the charge was not proceeded with and he was held as a prisoner in the Tower, though Prince Rupert tried unsuccessfully to arrange for him to be exchanged for a Roundhead prisoner-of-war.

He remained in the Tower for more than two years, and was only released after the end of the war in November 1646. He suffered some hardship in the Tower, as he was short of money, and had difficulty in buying provisions and in bribing the jailers to give him privileges. His brother Thomas, who had inherited his father's impoverished estate and was fighting for the King, sent him £50, which was all he could afford to send; and King Charles himself sent him £100.

While he was in the Tower, he met his laundress, Mrs Anne Radford, who washed and repaired his clothes. She came from the lowest ranks of society. Her father, Thomas Clarges, was a farrier who shod horses, and she had been married before she was fourteen years old to Radford, another farrier, who was in the service of Charles, Prince of Wales. In 1644 she was aged twenty-five. Her contemporaries described her as being vulgar and plain, but from her portrait she seems to have had not unattractive features and much strength of character. She was a formidable personality, and exercised a strong influence over Monck, who was devoted to her. She probably became his mistress at this time, though she did not leave her husband until 1649. In 1653, after Radford's death, she married Monck.

Like many other working-class women, she was an enthusiastic and intolerant Cavalier, and very different in outlook and temperament from the devoted and submissive Puritan wives. If Monck annoyed her, she sometimes slapped his face. There is no evidence that he was ever unfaithful to her, and no reason to believe the allegations made by the Roundheads—after he had betrayed them at the Restoration—that he led a grossly immoral life, though his chaplain and biographer, Gumble, may have exaggerated when he wrote that Monck never cast amorous glances at women.

He spent his time in the Tower writing a military manual for officers. His book, which was published twenty-seven years later after his death under the title *Observations upon Military & Political Affairs*, was written at the same time, in 1644 and 1645, that Prynne, Peters, Lilburne and Milton were writing their pamphlets for and against religious toleration and freedom from censorship. The difference between their writings and Monck's book, both in style and content, could not be greater. Monck's work, which contains hardly a single reference to God, is reminiscent of the writings of Machiavelli in its brevity and clarity of style and its short chapters, as well as in its basic approach and philosophical outlook. Much of it is concerned with purely military matters, such as the best hour of the night for laying a mine when besieging a castle, the best kind of timber to use for building a stockade, and how, when choosing bivouacs on the march, the infantry should be quartered in houses in the valleys and the cavalry in those on the hilltops.

Monck also touches on broader political issues, though always from the point of view of a military commander. He urges a general not to employ enemy aliens as mercenaries to fight against their own country, unless their religion is different from their government's. In advising a general on how to govern enemy territory which his armies have occupied, he urges him to make every effort to conciliate the native population, especially by allowing them to maintain their own laws and customs; but if it is impossible to avoid antagonizing the natives and a spirit of resistance develops among them, Monck suggests that all the inhabitants of the conquered territory should be expelled and deported to a foreign country. If a ruler is confronted with a danger of revolution among his own subjects, it is a good idea to adopt the well-known policy of going to war with a foreign state in order to distract his subjects' attention; but the ruler should be very careful, in these circumstances, to attack a weaker state, and not a strong one which will involve him in a long and costly, and perhaps unsuccessful, war.

When Monck was released from prison in November 1646, he asked permission to leave England, as he wished to enlist in some foreign army; but the Parliamentary authorities were eager to employ him in their own forces. As the Civil War in England was over and the King was a prisoner in the Parliament's hands, Monck was prepared to enlist in the Roundhead army, and sub-scribed to the Solemn League and Covenant which was obligatory on all officers in the armed forces. He was appointed to command the Parliamentary forces in Ulster, where he was confronted both with the Anglo-Irish Cavaliers under Ormonde and with the native Irish Catholic rebels under Owen Roe O'Neill. For two years Monck conducted successful, if defensive, operations against both Ormonde and the Papist rebels; but after the execution of Charles I in 1649 his position became very difficult, because the Scottish Presbyterian settlers in Ulster, like the Covenanters in Scotland, rose in support of Charles II. Many officers of the republican army in Ireland, who were indignant at the King's execution, deserted to Ormonde; but Monck refused all invitations to rejoin the Cavaliers.

Ormonde had made peace with O'Neill's Irish rebels, and captured a number of towns and castles from Monck's republican forces. Monck became alarmed that Ormonde and O'Neill would unite against him. He therefore concluded an armistice with O'Neill for three months. From a military point of view, this was sound sense, but politically it was very embarrassing for the republicans in England who had always claimed that the Cavaliers were secret sympathizers with the Papists, and were now themselves making a truce with these Papists; and it angered many of Monck's officers and soldiers. The desertions from his army increased, and nearly all the towns and fortresses held by the republic in Ireland, except Dublin, surrendered to Ormonde. Monck was not surprised when the English government repudiated his truce with O'Neill, and summoned him home to receive a public reprimand from the Rump Parliament; but the House exonerated him from all accusations of disloyalty. The danger to the republican cause in Ireland was relieved when Cromwell landed in Ireland with his army in August 1649.

Monck served under Cromwell in Scotland in 1650, and fought at Dunbar. His friends afterwards claimed that it was he who thought out the tactic which enabled Cromwell to defeat the Covenanters at Dunbar, though his opponents gave the credit for the idea and the victory to Monck's future enemy, Lambert. When Cromwell and Lambert marched south in August 1651 in pursuit of Charles II and the Covenanters in the campaign which ended at Worcester, Cromwell left Monck behind as Commander-in-Chief in Scotland. Monck continued the war against the Cavalier and Covenanter forces. He captured Stirling, Aberdeen and Dundee, where his troops looted the town and massacred many of their opponents. Soon after the capture of Dundee he was crippled with a violent attack of rheumatism, and was recuperating at Bath when the last pockets of Cavalier and Covenanter resistance in Scotland surrendered in the spring of 1652.

Monck's next command was at sea. He had never served in the navy, but it was the usual practice to appoint commanders of land forces, like Blake and Deane, to serve as admirals, or, to use their official title, as 'General-at-sea'. The war with Holland had broken out in the summer of 1652, and Blake had won two victories and suffered one defeat at the hands of Tromp. Monck joined Blake, Deane and Penn in command of the fleet in December. On 18 February 1653 he was lying with his ships in the middle of the English Channel when Blake and Deane were attacked off Portland by a greatly superior Dutch fleet under Tromp. Penn brought reinforcements to his colleagues later in the day and thus relieved the situation, but they were still hard-pressed by superior Dutch forces while Monck, battling against a strong wind, sailed north in an attempt to reach Portland and join in the battle. His arrival in the late afternoon of 18 February saved the situation, and he was able to take part in the fighting during the next two days when the combined English fleet drove the Dutch to Cape Gris-Nez and completely defeated them.

When Cromwell dissolved the Rump in April 1653, Monck immediately declared his support for the new government. As Blake was still suffering from the wound which he had received off Portland in February, Monck and Deane were appointed to command the fleet which blockaded the Dutch coast. On 2 June Tromp engaged them in a battle off Nieuport. Early in the battle Deane was killed by a musket shot as he stood beside Monck on the deck. Monck immediately threw his cloak over Deane's face so that the men should not see that the Admiral had been killed, and ordered that his body be carried below. Monck continued to command the action until reinforcements arrived under Blake, who had insisted on sailing himself with the relieving ships although he was still suffering from his wound. Soon afterwards, Blake fell ill and had to return to England, leaving Monck in command of the fleet which continued the blockade of Holland and won the final naval battle of the war, in which Tromp was killed, on 31 July 1653.

Soon after the end of the war, a group of sailors came to Monck and protested against the delay in paying them their prize-money. Monck promised to do what he could to expedite the payment, but to his annoyance the sailors returned later in the day with a considerable number of supporters and staged a demonstration outside his office at Charing Cross. He charged into the demonstrators, striking at them with his sword, and scattered them. In the course of doing this, he cut the nose of a peaceful passer-by. Monck sent the man £10 as compensation, and commented: 'What did Jack-Daw do among Rookes?'

Monck was sent back to Scotland to deal with a Cavalier rising in the Highlands in 1654. There were no roads in the district, and the terrain was very difficult. The cavalry were forced to dismount and go on foot, and Monck was unable to cover more than six miles a day; but he marched as far north as Inverness, and suppressed the rising and pacified the Highlands. Next year, Cromwell thought of appointing him to command the naval expedition against the Spanish colonies in the West Indies, but decided to send Penn instead, and kept Monck in Scotland. Monck ruled Scotland for six years. The executive power was nominally in the hands of the Scottish Privy Council, in which Scottish collaborators like Warriston took their place; but Monck, who sat in the Council as Commander-in-Chief of the armed forces, was in practice dictator of Scotland, though the system of the military dictatorship of the Major-Generals was not officially extended to Scotland. The old Scottish Parliament was abolished, and Scotland sent MPs to Cromwell's Parliaments at Westminster, where they sat in the single chamber side by side with MPs from England and Ireland in the first Parliament of the whole United Kingdom.

In 1655 Charles II, who periodically tried to enter into contact with influential leaders in England, wrote secretly to Monck. Monck sent a copy of the letter to Cromwell. But rumours were circulating about Monck's disloyalty to the Protector, which was not surprising in view of the repeated conspiracies with which Cromwell was confronted. The rumours were increased by the attitude of Mrs Monck. She openly expressed her Cavalier sympathies at dinner at Monck's headquarters. Monck tried to get her to keep quiet. When his chaplain Price, who also had Cavalier sympathies, said that Mrs Monck had only spoken the truth, Monck quoted the proverb 'that he who follows Truth too closely upon the Heels, will, one Time or other, have his Brains kicked out.'

In 1657 Cromwell was informed that Monck was in secret communication with Charles II and Cavalier agents. He promptly wrote to Monck himself, and after dealing with other matters added a postscript: 'There be that tell me that there is a certain cunning fellow in Scotland called George Monk, who is said to lye in wait there to introduce Charles Stuart; I pray you, use your diligence to apprehend him, and send him up to me.' After the Restoration, Monck's biographers quoted this letter to prove that Monck had always been a loyal subject of Charles II, but that Cromwell was blinded by Divine Providence so that he took no action against Monck; but in fact, Monck was undoubtedly loyal to Cromwell in 1657.

During his government of Scotland, Monck maintained law and order, and succeeded in winning the respect and affection of the population, particularly of the merchant class, because of the prosperity which he brought to the country. He not only defeated the risings and plots of the Cavaliers, but also discovered and suppressed a Leveller conspiracy in the army which was organized by his second-in-command, Colonel Overton.

When Cromwell died, Monck, along with all the other generals, immediately declared his allegiance to Richard Cromwell as Lord Protector. He took no action in Scotland in April 1659, when Fleetwood and Desborough overthrew the Protector, or a few weeks later when the republicans and Lambert re-established the Rump. He simply carried on the government of Scotland under the new régime. In the summer of 1659, just before the outbreak of the Cavalier rising led by the Presbyterian, Sir George Booth, in Cheshire, the Cavaliers made a secret approach to Monck. Monck's younger brother, Nicholas Monck, who had gone into the church, had been appointed to the living at Kilkhampton in Cornwall by the local landowner, his cousin Sir John Grenville, later the Earl of Bath, the son of Sir Bevill Grenville. Sir John Grenville was one of Charles II's chief agents in England. At the suggestion of General Monck's brother-in-law, Thomas Clarges—who, like his sister Mrs Monck, was a secret Cavalier—

Nicholas Monck and Grenville went to Monck's headquarters at Dalkeith, with a letter to Monck from Charles II. They stayed for several days at Dalkeith, where they enlisted the support of Mrs Monck and Price. They urged Monck to pledge his loyalty to Charles II, and on Charles's behalf offered Monck £100,000 if he would restore the King when the opportunity presented itself. Monck refused to commit himself or to send any reply to the King, but he did not tell the government in London, or any of his colleagues in Scotland, about Grenville's mission and the King's letter. He now let it be known that he was a devout Presbyterian, although hitherto it had always been assumed that he was not particularly committed in religion.

In October 1659 Lambert overthrew the Rump, and Hazelrig appealed to Monck and to the army generals in Ireland and the provinces to support the Rump against Lambert. The other generals did not respond, but Monck issued a declaration of support for the Rump, and pledged himself to restore its authority. It was an uncharacteristic departure from Monck's usual policy of supporting the men in power, and it is impossible to know what his intentions were at this time. He may already have been planning the restoration of Charles II; he may have been contemplating the possibility of making himself Lord Protector and dictator; or he may have seen himself as the effective power in the land as Lord General of the army under the rule of the Rump. His declaration won the support of all the gentry and merchants who hated military rule, and of the Presbyterians in Scotland to whom Lambert and the rule of the army Grandees had always represented Independency and religious toleration, even though the Presbyterians disliked the republicans of the Rump for the same reason. Monck was suppressing Anabaptists and the extreme sectaries in the army in Scotland, while the Anabaptists and sectaries in England were joining Lambert's forces. Monck also pleased the Presbyterians by taking firm measures against the Quakers in Scotland, although two Quakers who came to Dalkeith to preach pacifism to Monck's soldiers were received with an amused and contemptuous tolerance by Mrs Monck.

For a time it seemed as if Monck had miscalculated. He wrote to the army commanders in Ireland and to the admirals in charge of the fleet and asked for their support against Lambert; but they all refused to side with Monck. This made Monck adopt a defensive posture, and when Lambert marched against him and reached Newcastle, Monck played for time. He proposed to Lambert that Lambert should not advance north beyond Newcastle, while he himself would not march south of Berwick. Lambert unwisely agreed to this proposal, and agreed also to open negotiations with Monck's representatives in Newcastle, who drew out the negotiations for as long as possible and then agreed to terms which Monck afterwards refused to ratify. Meanwhile Lambert, who had no money with which to pay his troops, was faced with desertions from his army, while Monck, who had £70,000 in the Scottish treasury at his disposal and the support of the Scottish merchants and taxpayers, knew that he had time on his side. He spent it in purging the army in Scotland of officers and men who were sympathetic to Anabaptists, Quakers, and Independent sectaries. When Lambert sent Colonel Cobbet to Monck's army to make propaganda among the soldiers, Monck arrested him; and when Lambert sent Colonel Zanchy to protest against the arrest, he arrested Zanchy too.

In November Monck moved his army forward from Dalkeith to the Border, and on 9 December, after a night march from Berwick through wind and rain, he established his headquarters at Coldstream, on the north side of the River Tweed. It was an exceptionally cold winter, and the men at Coldstream, looking out for many miles across the valley of the Tweed, could see nothing except a great expanse of snow and ice, so that it was impossible to distinguish land from water. The soldiers huddled around the fires in the barns, and were grateful that they were well supplied with large stocks of food and ale. Monck himself lived in a small, smoky cottage, with two great dunghills in front of the door. Here he continued to lead his usual austere life, sleeping for only four hours at night, and taking only one light meal a day, standing and walking around the room to take some exercise as he dictated his letters, and as usual chewing tobacco and spitting it out on the floor.

He waited at Coldstream while Lambert's army disintegrated. By the end of December, Hazelrig and the republicans in London had restored the Rump, and Lambert was on the point of hurrying south to ask the Rump for his pardon. On Sunday 1 January 1660 Monck began his march on London, sending his vanguard across the frozen Tweed. Next morning he crossed himself with the main body of his army. By 3 January he was at Morpeth, by the 4th in Newcastle, by the 5th in Durham, and by the 11th in York. Between Durham and York he rode through the scattered and leaderless remnants of Lambert's army, straggling along the roads through the snow. Monck's officers feared that some Anabaptist zealot among them might attempt to assassinate Monck, but Lambert's men merely stared at him as he rode past. In York he found that Fairfax and the Yorkshire gentry had seized the city from Colonel Robert Lilburne, whom Lambert had left in command there. Fairfax urged Monck to restore Charles II, but Monck merely told him to go home. In York, one of Monck's soldiers announced that they would restore Charles II. Monck indignantly repudiated the statement, and gave the soldier a severe thrashing with his own hands.

He marched on south from York, by Nottingham, Leicester and Market Harborough, through snow and ice all the way; his chaplain, Price, wrote that they had not once trodden on the bare earth during the whole of their month's march. On 28 January they reached St Albans. Monck was greeted on his journey by several republican leaders who had come from London to meet him; two of them, Thomas Scot and Hugh Peters, were to be executed as regicides before the year was out. Monck received them all with a cool and noncommittal politeness. On 3 February he marched into London and took up his residence in Whitehall Palace, where he was surrounded by suitors asking for favours, and by republicans and Independents who, braving the insults of Mrs Monck, hoped to be reassured about their growing fears that Monck would restore the King. On 6 February he received an address of thanks from the Rump Parliament. In his speech in reply, he called on the nation to unite against the fanatical sectaries on the one hand and the Cavaliers on the other. On that evening, one of Charles II's agents in London wrote that Monck had betrayed the hopes of the Cavaliers, having thrown off the mask and revealed himself as a convinced republican.

The Presbyterians were campaigning for the readmission to Parliament of the MPs who had been expelled in Pride's Purge, and again expelled by the Rump Parliament in May and December 1659. The City authorities in London, who had always supported the Presbyterians, announced that they would not pay taxes until the Presbyterian MPs were readmitted. The Rump ordered Monck to march into the City, to arrest eleven leading citizens, and to remove the City gates and portcullises, which was a traditional way of punishing the rebellious citizens of a town. Monck carried out these orders, but his wife and brother-in-law and many of his friends left him in no doubt about the indignation with which his action had been received in London and throughout the country. Monck realized that he could delay no longer if he did not wish to remain as the Rump's general for the rest of his life. Two days later, on 11 February, he published a letter to the Rump in which he demanded that the Presbyterian MPs be readmitted to Parliament. On the same day he addressed the Lord Mayor and the City Council at the Guildhall, and said how much he regretted that he had been ordered to remove the City gates.

Monck's action, and the joy with which it was received, added greatly to the momentum in favour of a restoration of Charles II. The excluded Presbyterian MPs took their seats in Parliament and voted for the dissolution of the Long Parliament and for elections to be held for a new Parliament. The Presbyterians were now openly discussing the possibility of inviting Charles II to return as King on the terms of the treaty which they had offered to Charles I at Newport in 1648—that England should became a Presbyterian state. Monck decided to outbid them. He now for the first time made secret contact with Charles II at Breda, and offered to restore the King without any conditions; but in his public proclamation, he ordered his officers to arrest any agents of Charles Stuart who disturbed the peace of the Commonwealth.

On 4 April Charles wrote to Monck praising his loyalty and his recent actions and inviting him to restore his rightful sovereign to the throne. Monck showed the letter to a selected group of his officers, but told them to keep it secret for the time being. On 10 April Lambert escaped from the Tower, and Monck sent Colonel Ingoldsby to crush him in Northamptonshire. After Lambert had been brought as a prisoner to London on 24 April, Monck's officers suggested that Monck could safely call for the restoration of Charles II; but even now Monck urged them to be cautious and to make no public statement, though he had fully committed himself secretly to the King.

On 1 May he showed his hand at last. He sent the King's letter of 4 April to the newly-elected Parliament, and recommended to them that they should invite the King to return. They enthusiastically accepted his advice, and King Charles II was proclaimed in London on 8 May, the proclamation emphasizing that he had become King on the day of his father's death, and not by virtue of any decision of Parliament. Monck was feasted by several of the City livery companies at great banquets at which odes were recited hailing him as the saviour of his country, as a second and greater St George, because St George had merely saved the life of one Princess when he killed his dragon, whereas George Monck had saved a whole nation when he slew the Dragon Regicide.

The King landed at Dover on 25 May. Monck was the first to greet him, on his knees, as he came ashore. He accompanied the King on his journey to London. At Canterbury the King and the Duke of York invested Monck with the Order of the Garter. At Blackheath the army was drawn up in some bewilderment to receive the King. The popular rhyme told the story;

> Hey ding a ding
> I heard a bird sing,
> The Parliament soldiers have gone for the King.
> Some did laugh and some did cry
> To see the gallant King go by.

On 29 May, the King's thirtieth birthday, he rode into London with Monck at his side amid the cheers of the people.

The King appointed Monck Captain-General of the army— that is to say, Commander-in-Chief under the King—and Master of the King's Horse, a Gentleman of the Bedchamber, a member of the Privy Council, and one of the Commissioners of the Treasury. At the beginning of July, he created him Duke of Albemarle, Earl of Torrington, and Baron Monck of Potheridge, Beauchamp and Tees. Monck was also granted a pension of £7,000 a year. When he took his seat in the House of Lords, he was acclaimed by the peers, and a resolution was moved that a statue of him should be erected in Palace Yard; but the proposal was reluctantly withdrawn after Monck had demurred, and had pointed out that there was no precedent for such a proposal. His brother Nicholas, who had played his part in bringing about the Restoration, was appointed Bishop of Hereford and Provost of Eton, though he only lived to enjoy these offices for a few months.

The defeated Puritans considered that Monck was a traitor, and particularly resented his attitude towards the regicides and others of his old comrades-in-arms. He was one of the judges at the trial of the regicides; having been in Ireland in January 1649, he had no share in the King's death. He is said to have intervened behind the scenes in favour of Hazelrig and Milton and others. He was not vindictive, or consumed by a principled desire for vengeance or justice, like Prynne; he thought only of his own interests, and was prepared to use his influence in favour of petitioners, particularly if they offered suitable gifts, unless it was more to his advantage to win the favour of the government by helping to secure the conviction of his old comrades. He watched happily while the corpse of his former leader, Cromwell, was outraged at Tyburn, and those of his old fellow-admirals, Blake and Deane, were removed from their graves in Westminster Abbey and thrown into a pit.

He caused most indignation by his conduct at the trial of the Marquis of Argyll. Argyll, who had fought for Charles II against Cromwell and Monck in Scotland in 1650-1, and had crowned the King with his own hands at Scone, was tried for high treason in 1661 for having submitted to the authority of the usurper Cromwell after the battle of Worcester. The court was presided over by Argyll's bitter enemy, Middleton, whose Cavalier revolt in the Highlands in 1654 had been suppressed by Monck. Despite all Middleton's efforts to obtain a conviction, it seemed as if Argyll would have to be acquitted for lack of evidence. But when Monck had been Commander-in-Chief of Cromwell's army in Scotland, Argyll had written him letters of support and pledges of loyalty. Monck now sent these letters to Middleton in the closing days of Argyll's trial for them to be produced as evidence of Argyll's treasonable collaboration with Cromwell. They were sufficient to convict Argyll, who was sentenced to death and beheaded. He commented that he had placed the crown on the King's head, but that the King was now helping him gain a better crown than his own.

In January 1661 Monck used the army to suppress a revolt in London of a small group of Fifth Monarchy Men under the leadership of a crazy cask-maker, Venner. The revolt was easily suppressed, and was followed by a large number of executions and by intensified persecution of the Republicans and sectaries. Monck's old Roundhead colleague, Edward Montagu, now Earl of Sandwich, who had ordered the navy to support the Restoration and had brought Charles II from Holland to Dover, was shocked at the severity with which Monck rounded up the humbler members of the rank-and-file of Venner's followers and marched them endlessly through the City as prisoners. Soon afterwards, to the relief of most of the people of England, the army was disbanded, only one regiment being retained as a standing army. This regiment was given the name of the Coldstream Regiment, which was later changed to the Coldstream Guards, in honour of Monck's march from Coldstream in January 1660.

In 1662, Monck was employed in the unpopular task of negotiating the sale of Dunkirk to France. The capture of Dunkirk from the Spaniards by Cromwell's soldiers four years before had been hailed by the people as a great national triumph, which, in the centenary year of the loss of Calais in 1558, gave England once again a bridgehead on the Continent. But Charles II preferred to gain the friendship of Louis XIV and the money, and after Monck and his fellow-Commissioners had engaged in much hard bargaining with the French representatives, Dunkirk was sold to France for 2,500,000 French *livres*.

In the summer of 1665 Monck was given the duty of maintaining order in London with a small body of troops during the Great Plague, when the King and court retreated to Oxford and many citizens left London. Monck encamped the soldiers in tents in Hyde Park so that they would not come into contact with the infected people in the plague-ridden city; but he himself took up his residence unconcernedly in his house at the Cockpit in Whitehall. Next year he was again at sea, in action against the Dutch in a new Dutch war, in which the English navy suffered a series of disasters that in the eyes of many Englishmen compared unfavourably with the naval victories over the Dutch in the days of the Commonwealth. Monck was appointed to command the naval forces together with the Duke of York and Prince Rupert, who had had experience of naval warfare in his campaign against Blake.

Monck, sailing in Blake's ship *The Naseby*—now renamed *The Royal Charles*—fought the four-day battle against the Dutch between the North Foreland and Dunkirk on 2-6 June 1666. His daring tactics in attacking eighty Dutch ships with fifty-four of his own proved unsuccessful, and he was saved from disaster only by the timely arrival of Prince Rupert's fleet. During the most critical moment of the battle, Monck alarmed the young courtiers who were serving as officers under him by informing them that he intended to blow up his ship rather than allow her to fall into enemy hands. Monck and Rupert had their revenge when they defeated the Dutch off the Dutch coast at the end of July.

Monck was back in London by the beginning of September, taking charge of the administration of the city during the chaos which followed the Great Fire. Next year he was again in action against the Dutch, who sailed into the Thames. Monck was sent to stop them at Chatham, but on 8 June 1667 the Dutch broke through his defences, captured *The Royal Charles*, and sailed up the Medway, inflicting further humiliations on the English Navy. Many people blamed Monck for the disaster, but he succeeded in exculpating himself, because men respected him for his abilities and liked him for his bluff, genial personality. Meanwhile his wife, who was relishing to the full her new position as Duchess of Albemarle, was shocking Pepys by her outrageous remarks at the dinner-table about her husband's colleagues at the Admiralty, and enriching herself by accepting gifts from suitors and petitioners and candidates for office, and sharing in the corruption of Charles II's court.

In 1668 Monck's health began to fail, though he was not yet sixty, and he withdrew to his house at Newhall in Essex. Now for the first time in his life, unable to work or to take exercise, he acquired a hobby, indulging in gambling at cards as the only form of excitement available to him. Although his strength was failing, he managed to attend his son's wedding on 30 December 1669, but next day he had to retire to bed, and it was realized that he was dying. On New Year's Day the King and the Duke of York visited him, but they left sooner than they intended because Monck insisted on rising to his feet and standing in their presence. Two days later, on 3 January 1670, he died, sitting up, or half-standing, in his chair, and surrounded by a group of his old officers, 'like a Roman General or soldier'. The Puritans, who had believed that God would punish him for his betrayal of 1660 by striking him down with some terrible death, had foretold that he would not die in his bed. They now claimed that their prophecy had been fulfilled, as he had died, not in his bed, but in his chair.

He was given a great state funeral, at the King's expense, and buried in Westminster Abbey from which the bodies of his old comrades had been ejected. His wife did not live to see it. She died twenty-six days after Monck, and was buried in the Abbey on 28 February, whereas Monck's funeral, because of the administrative incompetence of Charles II's government, did not take place until 30 April, four months after his death. A spate of newspaper articles and street ballads sang his praises, and his obituaries repeated the eulogies of ten years earlier in honour of the hero who had restored the King.

Next year his chaplain Gumble published his biography of Monck, in which he wrote that just as Monck had always been an Anglican at heart and had only supported the Presbyterians because they were better than the Independents, so he had never been a republican. Gumble claimed that throughout the whole period when he had served Cromwell, he had been a secret sympathizer with the Cavaliers, and was only biding his time till he had the opportunity to restore the King. Gumble described him as 'a great, yet not a blazing Star, that borrowed his light, not from the elementary breath of popular applause, but from Majesty it self, to whom he always was a sure, though for some time but a secret, servant.' Another biographer, his physician Dr Skinner, praised his skill in having used the Independents of the Rump to destroy the Anabaptists and sectaries, then the Presbyterians to destroy the Independents and the Rump, and finally sweeping away the Presbyterians to restore the King without conditions. 'And now', he concluded, 'may the Imperial Crown of England never want any thing to support it, besides its own Majesty and Greatness; But if ever it should, may there never be wanting a Duke of Albemarle.'

The King and the Cavaliers had reason to be grateful to Monck. In the spring of 1660, the fate of Britain depended on him alone.

With the support of his loyal soldiers and the goodwill of most of the civilian population, he could have made himself dictator, but instead he brought back Charles II, not only because of the influence of his Cavalier wife, but also because of his temperament. He was self-seeking, but not wildly ambitious, and usually adopted the more cautious policy. He did not aspire to a position which even Cromwell had only held with difficulty, and did not wish to become absolute ruler at the cost of having to face endless assassination plots, Cavalier risings, and attempts to seize power by rival generals. He preferred to gain a dukedom, great wealth, and personal and political security under England's lawful King.

20

Edmund Ludlow

The modern reader who turns from the speeches and writings of the leading Roundheads to the memoirs of Edmund Ludlow will feel that he is moving from a strange and distant world into modern surroundings. After the Aristotelian logic and sixteenth-century theology of Prynne and Milton, the mystical meanderings of Cromwell and the participants in the Putney debates, the indignant self-pity of Lilburne and the incomprehensible writings of Winstanley, Ludlow's rational approach, his straightforward, clear and unpretentious style of writing, seem several centuries in advance of most of his contemporaries. Only by referring to the portrait of Ludlow, in his seventeenth-century periwig and costume, will the reader remember that he is not reading the autobiography of some twentieth-century statesman or general. While the Levellers and Diggers were groping their way towards ideas of modern democracy and socialism by way of Foxe's *Book of Martyrs* and the Book of Revelation, Ludlow, like Algernon Sidney and a small handful of 'Commonwealth's men' were rationally advocating the merits of modern republicanism as compared with the Tudor and Stuart concepts of royal despotism and 'Sacred Majesty'.

Ludlow was born in 1617, the son of Sir Henry Ludlow, the leading landowner of the village of Maiden Bradley, near Mere in Wiltshire. He was educated at Blandford Grammar School, and in 1634 went to Trinity College, Oxford. In 1636 he took his degree and went on to the Inner Temple in London. His upbringing had been Puritan, but a little different from that of most of his Puritan contemporaries because his father believed in the abolition of monarchy and the establishment of a republic. Sir Henry Ludlow had arrived at this conclusion as a result of his study of classical history and by his ideas of commonsense, despite the fact that there was nothing about a republic in the Bible.

Sir Henry was elected MP for Wiltshire to the Long Parliament in 1640, and joined the small group of MPs under the leadership of Henry Marten who shocked even the most radical of their fellow-MPs by advocating the deposition of King Charles I and the establishment of a republic. When the Civil War began, Edmund Ludlow, who was aged twenty-five, joined Essex's Roundhead army. He took part in the first engagement of the war at Worcester in September 1642, and a few weeks later fought at Edgehill. In the spring of 1643 he was sent into his native Wiltshire to organize the Parliamentary forces in the county for service in the armies of Waller, the general commanding in the south.

In May 1643 Ludlow served under Lord Hungerford at the siege of Wardour Castle near Shaftesbury, which was defended by Lady Arundell, the wife of its Papist Cavalier owner. Lady Arundell held out gallantly for a week, but after the Roundheads had bombarded the castle, she surrendered. Hungerford ordered Ludlow to hold the castle against attempts by the Cavaliers to recapture it. Ludlow soon realized that this would be a formidable task, because after the advance of Hopton's Cavaliers from Cornwall to Wiltshire in the spring and summer of 1643, and Waller's defeat at Roundway Down in July, the whole area was in the hands of the Cavaliers and there was no other Roundhead garrison within twenty miles of Wardour Castle. But the Cavaliers were in no hurry to besiege it, and Ludlow had plenty of time in which to destroy the breastworks which the Roundheads had erected when they were besieging the castle, and to stock up with a big supply of ammunition, food and ale in preparation for a long siege. By the autumn Cavalier forces had begun to 'gather around', but still did not lay siege to the castle. Ludlow was visited at Wardour by his cousin, Sir Robert Phelips, who was fighting for the Cavaliers and afterwards played a leading part in organizing the escape of Charles II after the battle of Worcester. Phelips warned him that Wardour Castle would shortly be besieged and urged him to surrender it, as he would not be able to hold it. But Ludlow replied that he would do his duty and hold it for the Parliament.

In December 1643 the castle was at last besieged by a Cavalier force under Lord Arundell, who had recently succeeded to the title when his father died at Oxford immediately after the first siege of Wardour Castle, and Sir Francis Doddington, who was a distant relative of Ludlow. Doddington was hated by the Roundheads on account of his cruelty, and was often accused of atrocities by the Roundhead newspapers in London, though the charges were repudiated as lying propaganda by the Cavalier newspaper in Oxford. Ludlow was to find Lord Arundell a much more honourable opponent during the siege than his cousin Doddington.

Ludlow held Wardour Castle for three months, hoping that Waller would send an army to relieve him. The Cavaliers tried every means to take the castle. They bribed a fourteen-year-old kitchen-boy to poison the garrison and sabotage the cannon, but he was discovered by the defenders in time. They forcibly enlisted some miners from the Mendips and made them tunnel under the castle, where they laid and exploded a mine. Once one of Ludlow's men was severely wounded in a sortie and was buried under some debris in front of the castle. Doddington refused Ludlow's request for a cease-fire during which the Cavaliers could either go and capture the wounded man, or allow Ludlow's men to fetch him and hand him over to them, so that he could receive medical treatment. This angered Ludlow, because on more than one occasion he had agreed to a truce while the Cavaliers carried away their dead and wounded. The man died under the debris after three days' suffering.

The Cavaliers repeatedly sent envoys to the castle to summon Ludlow to surrender. Ludlow took the opportunity, by various subterfuges, to make the envoys believe that his stocks were twice as large as they really were and he refused the demands for surrender, even when Doddington offered him the last opportunity to surrender before he stormed the castle, giving no quarter to the defenders. But by the middle of March 1644 Ludlow's supplies were almost exhausted, his surgeon was seriously wounded and unable to perform his medical duties, and there was no prospect of any Roundhead force being sent to his relief. He now received another letter from Doddington, in which Doddington, after reminding him of their family connections and deploring the fact that Ludlow was fighting for so evil a cause, again summoned Ludlow to surrender. Ludlow replied: 'Sir, As I may not omitt my thankefull acknowledgement for the expression of your respects unto our family, soe may I not passe by the cleareing of mine innocency touching any offence committed against my leidge Soveraigne. I shall never seeke by-paths (by deserting my Saviour, who is the way, the truth, and the life) to attaine the haven of peace, and happynesse. Yet shall I not bee soe presumtuous upon the mercys of the Almighty, to draw downe his justice upon my head, for the guilt of so many men's blood, as are now with me, by an obstinate resolution to withstand all opposers without hopes of releife.' He therefore offered to surrender on terms, and yielded up the castle to Doddington five days later, on 18 March 1644.

Doddington treated Ludlow with great courtesy, holding him prisoner in his own lodgings, but to Ludlow's indignation he broke the terms of surrender. He had promised quarter to all Ludlow's soldiers, but after capturing the castle he discovered that two of them had deserted from the Cavalier army, into which they had been conscripted against their will. Despite Ludlow's protests, and after lengthy arguments with him about the inter-pretation of the surrender terms, he insisted on court-martialling the two men and executing them as deserters. Doddington had also promised Ludlow that he would not be sent as a prisoner to Oxford, but this condition was also broken. Ludlow was, how-ever, favourably impressed by the attitude of Doddington's second-in-command, Lord Arundell. Nine years later, under the Commonwealth, Ludlow interceded in favour of Arundell when the government was intending to confiscate his estates. He wrote to the authorities telling them that it was Arundell who had persuaded Doddington to grant quarter to the defenders of Wardour Castle, although Doddington had intended to put them all to the sword.

The Roundhead newspapers in London were full of stories about the ill-treatment of their prisoners-of-war in Oxford. Ludlow found that although he encountered several instances of ill-treatment, some of the inhabitants of Oxford gave relief to the prisoners and showed kindness to them in other ways. He was visited in prison at Oxford by Lady Byron. Her husband Sir Nicholas Byron, who was a Cavalier officer, had been taken prisoner by the Roundheads and she suggested to Ludlow that he and Sir Nicholas should be exchanged. Ludlow wrote a letter to the Parliamentary authorities in London proposing an exchange, and gave it to Lady Byron, who arranged for it to be taken to London, and the exchange was agreed. Ludlow was led blindfold through the defences of Oxford and left outside the city to find his way back to Roundhead territory.

He took part in the second battle of Newbury in October 1644, and in several minor engagements in Hampshire and Wiltshire. On one occasion he took part in a skirmish with a band of Cavaliers in Winchester. He saw an old school-friend of his among the Cavaliers. 'I called to him,' wrote Ludlow, 'telling him, that I was sorry to see him there; but since it was so, I offered to exchange a shot with him.' The Cavalier retreated among his infantry, and called to Ludlow to come on. Ludlow did so, and was struck on the breastplate by a bullet from a musket, while another bullet wounded his horse. The horse carried Ludlow safely back to the Roundhead lines, but died that night.

In December 1644 he took part in the expedition which was sent to relieve Blake, who was holding Taunton deep in Cavalier territory. As they approached Taunton, the Cavaliers raised the siege, and Ludlow and his comrades were able to deliver fresh supplies to Blake in preparation for the next siege. Ludlow took part in the final mopping-up operations in Devon and Cornwall in February and March 1646. His father had died, and in the by-election of May 1646 he was elected to replace him as one of the county MPs for Wiltshire. As he was waiting in the lobby before taking his seat for the first time he met Blake, who had also just been returned at a by-election, and the two men walked into the chamber together and took their seats in the House.

Ludlow was at first a little uncertain as to what policy to pursue in the conflict between the army and Parliament in 1647. He did not approve, in principle, of military rule, and was suspicious of Cromwell's negotiations with Charles I; but he soon realized that the army was the only force that could resist Presbyterian intolerance and would proceed to the establishment of a republic and defeat the Presbyterians' plans to restore Charles to power. When the army demanded the expulsion of the eleven Presbyterian MPs, and the London apprentices rioted and forced the House to reinstate them, Ludlow was one of the fifty-seven Independent MPs who withdrew from the House and fled to the army headquarters on Hounslow Heath. Ludlow was largely responsible for persuading the Speaker, Lenthall, to accompany the fifty-seven MPs to Hounslow. He supported the army's march on London and Westminster, and returned to the House after the final expulsion of the eleven MPs.

Ludlow did not serve in the army during the Second Civil War, but remained in London pursuing his Parliamentary duties and viewing with alarm the negotiations of the Presbyterian majority in Parliament with the King in the Isle of Wight. The moment had come for Ludlow to play a decisive part in English history. In September 1648, while Cromwell was marching into Scotland and Ireton was with Fairfax at the siege of Colchester, Ludlow went to Colchester and warned Ireton that the Presbyterians were about to sign a treaty with Charles by which they would re-establish him in power as a Presbyterian King. He urged Ireton to act at once and use the army to stop the treaty from being signed. Ireton was in a difficult position. He was unable to consult Cromwell, he knew that Fairfax would take no responsibility, and he was being urged by Lilburne to do nothing against the King until a new Parliament had been elected by popular suffrage. He told Ludlow that he thought they should do nothing until the treaty was actually signed, though Ludlow was adamant that preventive action should be taken by the army to forestall it. Ludlow failed to persuade Ireton, but as Charles refused at the last moment to sign the treaty with the Presbyterians, it did not matter.

On 20 November, with Cromwell still absent in the north, Ireton acted, sending the army's Remonstrance to Parliament against the negotiations with the King. On 30 November he sent Colonel Ewer to take the King from the Isle of Wight to Hurst Castle, and on 2 December the army occupied London and Westminster. Ireton had decided to dissolve Parliament and establish a military dictatorship. Ludlow persuaded him not to do so, but instead to expel the Presbyterian MPs from the House of Commons, leaving the Independent minority to continue as a Parliament and to govern in collaboration with the army.

On the morning of 5 December, after an all-night debate, the House of Commons passed a resolution approving of the negotiations with the King. During the afternoon, Ludlow met Ireton and drew up the plans for Pride's Purge which were put into operation next day. He afterwards described in his memoirs how 'three of the members of the House and three of the officers of the army withdrew into a private room, to consider the best means to attain the ends of our said resolution, where we agreed that the army should be drawn up the next morning, and guards placed in Westminster Hall, the Court of Requests, and the Lobby; that none might be permitted to pass into the House but such as had continued faithful to the publick interest. To this end we went over the names of all the members one by one, giving the truest characters we could of their inclinations, wherein I presume we were not mistaken in many; for the Parliament was fallen into such factions and divisions, that any one who usually attended and observed the business of the House, could, after a debate on any question, easily number the votes that would be on each side, before the question was put. Commissary-General Ireton went to Sir Thomas Fairfax, and acquainted him with the necessity of this extraordinary way of proceeding, having taken care to have the army drawn up the next morning by seven of the clock. Colonel Pride commanded the guard that attended at the Parliament-doors, having a list of those members who were to be excluded, preventing them from entring into the House, and securing some of the most suspected under a guard provided for that end; in which he was assisted by the Lord Grey of Grooby and others who knew the members.'

On the evening of the next day, Cromwell arrived in London. 'He declared that he had not been acquainted with this design; yet since it was done, he was glad of it, and would endeavour to maintain it.' Ludlow played a leading part in the King's trial, sitting as a judge at all the sessions of the court, signing the death warrant, and urging the waverers to do the same. A fortnight after the King's execution he was appointed as a member of the Council of State. Soon afterwards he married Elizabeth Thomas, the daughter of a gentleman of Glamorgan. Mrs Ludlow's uncle, Sir Henry Stradling, had fought for the Cavaliers in the Civil War.

In the summer of 1650 Cromwell returned from his campaign in Ireland and prepared to march against Charles II and the Covenanters in Scotland. He had left Ireton in command of the army in Ireland, and asked Ludlow to go to Ireland as Ireton's second-in-command. Ludlow arrived in Ireland in January 1651, with the rank of Lieutenant-General, and spent the next ten

months campaigning with Ireton against the Irish rebels. He
became close friends with Ireton, and greatly admired him for his
devotion to duty. He also thoroughly approved of Ireton's
ruthless methods against the rebels. After the capture of Limerick,
Ireton died from the plague or some other form of fever brought
on by fatigue and overwork, and Ludlow took over as commander-in-chief in Ireland. He was not, however, appointed to
succeed Ireton as Lord Deputy of Ireland, because the post, after
being promised to Lambert, was eventually given to Fleetwood,
who married Ireton's widow, Cromwell's daughter Bridget.
Perhaps Ludlow, away in Ireland, could not compete with the
men and women in London who were intriguing to get the
office for themselves or their husbands; but for a year before
Fleetwood arrived he acted as Lord Deputy and commander-in-
chief in Ireland.

He conducted operations against the Irish Papist rebels in the
same spirit as all the English officers in Ireland, with a determination to avenge the Catholic atrocities of 1641. But even in
this matter, his attitude was surprisingly modern, for he seems to
have acted more in the spirit of a nineteenth- or twentieth-
century conqueror than of a seventeenth-century Puritan fanatic.
His description of smoking out a group of Irish guerrillas who
had taken refuge in a cave, and then killing the survivors, has a
painfully modern ring, and he mentions only very briefly the fact
that he found in the cave 'the priest's robes, a crucifix, chalice, and
other furniture of that kind'. Although he was ruthless in suppressing resistance, he censured Colonel Axtell, who had commanded the guards at Charles I's trial and was afterwards executed
as a regicide, when Axtell killed some rebels who had surrendered
on a promise of quarter; and on one occasion, when Ludlow's
soldiers were massacring every Irishman whom they met as they
marched through the country, he ordered them to stop the
killing, and talked in a friendly manner to the Irish while he
drank a pot of sour milk which they offered him.

In principle he favoured a policy of severity in Ireland, and
supported the forcible deportation of the Irish Catholic gentry
beyond the River Shannon into Connaught and the expropriation
of their lands for the benefit of the English soldiers and settlers.
In May 1652 he and a group of his brother-officers sent a letter to
the Rump Parliament, urging that some summary procedure

should be adopted for punishing the rebels who had been guilty of atrocities against Englishmen, even though it was impossible to obtain evidence of their guilt. He and his fellow-signatories deplored the tendency of the authorities in England, and of soldiers newly-arrived in Ireland from England, to be over-merciful to the Irish, and pointed out that the people in England, unlike those who had served in Ireland, did not realize the enormities of the crimes which the Irish had committed.

Ludlow was not unduly perturbed when he heard in April 1653 that Cromwell had dissolved the Rump Parliament, and he welcomed the attempts of the Barebones Parliament to reform the law and curtail the privileges of the lawyers and tithe-holders. But he was incensed when Cromwell dissolved the Barebones Parliament and became Lord Protector in December. He refused to sign the proclamation which was issued by the government in Dublin proclaiming Cromwell as Protector, and resigned his civilian offices in Ireland as a protest. He did not resign his position in the army, either, as his opponents claimed, because he wished to retain his salary, or, as he stated himself, because he hoped to use his position to overthrow Cromwell when the opportunity arose. Fleetwood was anxious to retain Ludlow's services in the army, and Ludlow remained as second-in-command of the army in Ireland.

In January 1655 Fleetwood discovered that Ludlow was using his position in the army to encourage the distribution among the soldiers of revolutionary pamphlets attacking Cromwell. Ludlow was immediately dismissed from his post and from the army. He asked leave to go to England to see Cromwell, but he was refused permission to go and was detained in Ireland for nine months until the revolutionary disturbances in England in the spring of 1655 had been suppressed. In October 1655 he was permitted to sail for England, but on landing at Beaumaris in Anglesey he was arrested and imprisoned in Beaumaris Castle. After being held there for six weeks, he was taken to London and was examined by Cromwell and the Council. He refused Cromwell's request that he should give an undertaking not to oppose the government's policy; but Cromwell was in a friendly mood and allowed Ludlow to go free.

In the summer of 1656 Ludlow was again summoned to appear before Cromwell and the Council, and was again closely interrogated; but again Cromwell was friendly, and allowed him to go free. On this occasion Cromwell sent Strickland, one of his Councillors, to argue with Ludlow and persuade him to support the government, but Ludlow told Strickland that he would never submit to the rule of the sword. Strickland reminded Ludlow that he had held Wardour Castle by the sword. Ludlow replied that there was a difference 'between a sword in the hands of a Parliament to restore the people to their antient rights, and a sword in the hands of a tyrant to rob and despoil them thereof'.

Ludlow spent the next two years living quietly in Essex. This satisfied Cromwell, who was anxious to prevent him from going to his native Wiltshire and making trouble there for the government. On two occasions his friends in Wiltshire wished to nominate him as an MP for Cromwell's Parliaments, but on both occasions Cromwell forced them to withdraw the nomination.

After Cromwell's death, Ludlow was elected as MP for Hindon in Wiltshire in Richard Cromwell's Parliament of January 1659, and took his seat after he had avoided, by a skilful manoeuvre, the obligation to take the oath of allegiance to the new Protector. He spoke against the Protectorate in Parliament, explaining that although he respected Richard Cromwell as a person, he wished to return to the rule of the Rump and a free Commonwealth. His chance came after Fleetwood and Desborough had overthrown Richard Cromwell in April 1659. He was the leading spirit in the negotiations of the republicans with Colonel Robert Lilburne and Lambert, as a result of which Fleetwood and Desborough were forced to restore the Rump and reappoint Lambert to his command in the army. Ludlow was very satisfied with the state of affairs in England when he sailed for Dublin in the summer of 1659 to take up his new office as Commander-in-Chief of the army in Ireland. He purged the army of corrupt and conservative officers, and promoted Anabaptists and other sectaries to important military positions.

When Hazelrig impeached Lambert after the presentation of the Derby petition by the army officers in September 1659, Ludlow immediately realized that there was a grave danger that the split between the republicans and the army would let in the 'common enemy', Charles Stuart. His anxieties increased after Lambert dissolved the Rump in October. He came to England

and tried to reconcile Hazelrig and Lambert, urging Lambert to reinstate the Rump and attempting to deter Hazelrig from appealing to Monck for support against Lambert. He put forward a compromise plan by which both the Rump and the army should govern in their respective spheres, neither body having power over the other, with a committee of twenty-one members, to be known as the Conservators of Liberty, who would settle any dispute between the republicans and the army leaders; but neither Lambert nor Hazelrig would agree to this. As the conflict developed, Ludlow drew closer to Lambert, because he was very suspicious of Monck. He accepted Lambert's invitation to become a member of the Committee of Safety which acted as the government in London when Lambert marched against Monck.

In December he heard that in Ireland Sir Charles Coote and Sir Hardress Waller, whom he had left in command there, had declared their support for Monck and were purging from the army the Anabaptists and sectaries whom Ludlow had appointed to important positions in the previous summer. He hurried over to Ireland to try to retrieve the situation. Coote refused to allow him to land at Dublin, so he sailed to Duncannon on the south coast, where he landed and fortified the town, intending to hold it as his headquarters while he rallied the more radical elements in the army against Coote and Sir Hardress Waller. But in January 1660 he heard that Hazelrig and the Rump Parliament, which had reassembled in London after the disintegration of Lambert's army, had dismissed him from his office as Lord Deputy of Ireland. He returned to London to attempt to stop the rot at the centre of power; but by the time that he reached London, Monck and his army had arrived from Coldstream.

Ludlow had an interview with Monck, but though Monck was friendly, Ludlow feared the worst. At the new elections which were held after the dissolution of the Long Parliament, Ludlow stood as a candidate for Hinton. His local influence in Wiltshire was sufficiently strong to secure his election, although the tide was running strongly in favour of the Cavaliers; but when Parliament issued an order for the arrest of all the regicides who had sat in judgment on Charles I, he went into hiding. He was given shelter by a friend in lodgings in Southampton Buildings in Holborn, and from a window in the house, on 29 May 1660, he watched the troops and the people returning from the celebrations to welcome Charles II on his arrival in London from Dover.

In view of the leading part which Ludlow had played in Pride's Purge and the decision to try and execute Charles I, it is surprising that he was not included among the seven regicides who were first selected for death by the House of Commons in May; but he was personally liked by many influential Cavaliers. On 6 June Charles II issued a proclamation which ordered all the regicides to surrender themselves to the authorities on pain of being charged with high treason if they failed to do so. This was widely interpreted as implying that those who did surrender would not be put on trial; but as Clarendon was afterwards to point out, the proclamation did not expressly say so, and several of the regicides who surrendered were afterwards executed or sentenced to life imprisonment. On the advice of some of his friends who were in contact with the Cavaliers and the court, Ludlow gave himself up to the authorities, and was released on bail provided for him by his wife's Cavalier uncle, Colonel Thomas Stradling.

For the next two months, Ludlow faced the terrible dilemma of whether to try to escape or to wait calmly in London till his fate was settled. His wife made great efforts on his behalf, contacting Annesley and Ormonde, both of whom treated her with great courtesy and kindness. Like others in his position, he had more to fear from former friends than from old enemies, for while Annesley and Ormonde did their best to help him, Sir Charles Coote wrote to the King to inform him that Ludlow had told him that Cromwell would never have executed Charles I if Ludlow had not persuaded him to do so. Ludlow heard that Monck had told the King that Ludlow was the most dangerous man in the kingdom; and Lady Vane told Mrs Ludlow the unlikely story that Mrs Monck had gone on her knees to the King to beg him for Ludlow's head. From time to time one of Ludlow's contacts at Court sent him word that the King and Clarendon were quite determined to take his life, and that his only chance was to escape from England at once. Then he would hear from other contacts that it had definitely been decided to pardon him, but that an unsuccessful attempt to escape would ruin everything.

Meanwhile Ludlow, who had taken a house at Richmond,

waited in complete uncertainty as to the future, but for the moment remaining at liberty. One day he went to Wimbledon and passed Lambert's house, which had been empty since Lambert's arrest. He wandered through the deserted grounds, and came to a banqueting house. On the outside walls of the building the words were written: 'The way to ruin enemies is to divide their councils.' Ludlow reflected bitterly that the present disasters might have been avoided if Lambert had paid heed to this warning.

At the end of August, Ormonde's son, Lord Ossory, told Mrs Ludlow that the King had decided to have Ludlow tried and executed, and that his only chance was to escape from England at once. After a brief hesitation, Ludlow decided to follow this advice. One evening he went in a coach to Southwark, where there were many Roundhead supporters, and in front of St George's Church he met a man who was waiting with two horses. They rode all night by the by-ways to Lewes, where he planned to take ship for France. When they arrived there early in the morning, he found a ship waiting in the River Ouse which was ready to sail but was held back by contrary winds. He made arrangements with the captain to take him, but he did not go on board, perhaps because he was afraid that he might be recognized by some member of the crew or by one of the other passengers. Seeing a barge drawn up on the beach a little distance away, he entered the barge and waited there, out of sight, until his ship was ready to sail. While he was in the barge the coastguards came and searched the ship for escaping regicides and other criminals. They noticed the barge drawn up on the beach, but as it was obvious from her position that she would not put to sea in the immediate future, they did not search her. Ludlow had to wait all day and all night for the wind to change, but the ship sailed next morning with him on board. During the voyage the captain asked him whether he knew if there was any truth in the rumour that Lieutenant-General Ludlow had been arrested. Ludlow casually answered that he had heard nothing about it. Within a few days the news of his escape had been published, and he was being searched for everywhere; and in the course of the next few months the newspapers continually reported that he had been seen in Devon, at Canterbury and elsewhere.

Ludlow landed safely at Dieppe, and stayed in the house of a

French lady to whom he had been recommended by his friends in England. But he discovered that there were always many Irish sailors in Dieppe. It occurred to him that he might be recognized by some Irishman who had seen him when he was Lord Deputy of Ireland, and he knew that if he were denounced to the French authorities, the government of Louis XIV would extradite him to England. He therefore accepted his hostess's suggestion that he should move to her house in the country, and soon afterwards he decided to go to Switzerland. He set off for Paris, which he reached after a three-day journey. He made arrangements at a bank in Paris to draw bills of exchange at a bank in Geneva, and spent a day calmly sightseeing at the Palace of the Louvre and noticing the dirt in the King's stables, which were open to the general public. Then he went on to Switzerland. He was stopped and searched by the French authorities in Lyons and at the frontier, but was allowed to proceed, and felt great relief when he crossed the Rhône and entered the territory of Geneva.

In Geneva, he stayed at the house of a Swiss who had fought for the Roundheads in the English Civil War and had married an English woman, and to his delight he was immediately offered a drink of beer by his English hostess. He remained in Geneva for two years, and was joined by several other English republican refugees, including John Lisle, who had been one of Charles I's judges. The Swiss cantons had been the only governments in Europe who had acclaimed the establishment of the English republic in 1649, and Ludlow felt sure that he would be granted asylum there. But the Protestant city of Geneva, which had been menaced for over a century by its powerful Catholic neighbour, the Duke of Savoy, relied on the protection of the King of France, with whom it had a permanent military and political alliance. Some of the members of the City Council assured Ludlow that he and his colleagues would be safe in Geneva, but others objected to granting asylum to a fugitive from justice from the King of England, whose sister Henrietta had married Louis XIV's brother, and who was on very friendly terms with the King of France. The refugees feared that if Louis XIV were to demand their extradition at some time in the future, it would be impossible for the government of Geneva to refuse, and thought that they would be safer in the canton of Berne. The government of Berne not only granted them asylum but also received them as honoured guests. They settled first at Lausanne, which like all the modern canton of Vaud was then in the territory of Berne; but after a few months, Ludlow and Lisle and some of the other refugees moved to Vevey.

At the trial of the regicides in October 1660, the Attorney-General, Sir Geoffrey Palmer, had declared that the regicides who had escaped would be hunted down wherever they might be. 'Some Eighteen or Nineteen have fled from Justice, and wander to and fro about the World with the Mark of Cain upon them, are perpetually Trembling lest every Eye that sees them, and ev'ry Hand that meets them, should fall upon them.' News reached the authorities in Berne that Charles II's sister, Henrietta Duchess of Orleans, had hired assassins to avenge her father's death by murdering the English regicides in Switzerland, and above all Ludlow. Some of the assassins took advantage of the annual fair at Vevey to go there in order to murder Ludlow, but they were identified and made a hasty escape. The authorities advised Ludlow and his colleagues to move from Vevey to Lausanne or Yverdon, because a murderer could easily cross the lake from Savoy or France and land at Vevey without being noticed, whereas it would be more difficult for him to reach Lausanne or Yverdon without being arrested on the way. Ludlow decided to take the risk of staying at Vevey, because he had made friends there, though Lisle and some other refugees moved to Lausanne. In 1663 Mrs Ludlow joined her husband at Vevey.

On 11 August 1664,* as Lisle was on his way to church in Lausanne, he was shot dead in the churchyard in full view of the other members of the congregation by a man who shouted '*Vive le Roi d'Angleterre!*' and escaped before he could be arrested, thanks to the incompetence or connivance of the local officials in Lausanne, which greatly angered the government of Berne. The murderer was Sir James FitzEdmond Cotter, an Irish gentleman in the pay of the English government, and his feat was acclaimed in the English newspapers, though his identity was kept secret until it was revealed in 1700 a few years before his death. Some years after Lisle's murder, the English government made two other attempts to kill their chief target, Ludlow. A French assassin, Deprez, was sent to Switzerland to murder him, but on

---

* By our modern New Style calendar, which was already in force in the canton of Berne. In England the date was 1 August.

the way he murdered his own brother-in-law in Savoy, and when he reached Bernese territory he was arrested and executed on a charge of rape and for the attempted murder of the English refugees. Soon afterwards the English government sent another Frenchman in their service, Roux, to Berne with instructions to arrange for the extradition, or perhaps the murder, of Ludlow and his colleagues. Roux was also instructed to organize espionage against Charles II's ally, Louis XIV. The French government discovered this, and sent agents who kidnapped him in Vaud and took him to France, where he was condemned to death and broken on the wheel.

Ludlow remained in Vevey for twenty-seven years. Although he had been attainted as a traitor in England by Parliament in his absence, and his property had been confiscated, he was not in financial difficulties in Vevey and was able to keep five Spanish horses and a pack of hounds with which to indulge in his favourite recreation of stag-hunting. After the execution of Roux, he was not troubled by any further attempt on his life. Some of his fellow-fugitives were not so fortunate. Thomas Scot, who had fled to Flanders in April 1660, returned to England in response to the King's proclamation in June, and was tried and executed as a regicide. Colonel Okey and two of his colleagues, who had escaped to Germany, were lured into Holland by a promise of safe-conduct from Charles II's Ambassador to Holland, George Downing, who had formerly been a zealous Roundhead preacher and a chaplain in Okey's own regiment. They were then arrested with the consent of the Dutch government, extradited to England and executed in 1662, while Downing was rewarded with a baronetcy and in due course had Downing Street named after him. Two of Cromwell's Major-Generals, Whalley and Goffe, escaped to Massachusetts in 1660, but were pursued there by the English government, and though the colonists gave them shelter for a time, they were forced to flee from one English settlement to another, and sometimes to hide in caves in the forests until the King's agents had returned to England. Colonel Joyce, who as Cornet Joyce had seized Charles I at Holmby House in 1647 and taken him into the custody of the army, and who was wrongly believed by many people to have been the masked headsman who had cut off the King's head, was spotted by English agents in Rotterdam in 1670, but was warned of his danger. He disappeared, and was never heard of again.

Ludlow, in Vevey, took every precaution to avoid falling into the hands of his enemies. When the Dutch went to war with England in 1665, they contacted the English republican exiles and invited them to come to Holland to discuss the possibility of using their services against Charles II's government. They approached Ludlow, but he refused to go to Holland, remembering how the Dutch had handed over Okey and his companions to the English government. He also refused a suggestion by the Dutch that he should meet their agents in France, because he thought that he might well be arrested by Louis XIV's government and extradited to England if he set foot in France.

Ludlow wrote his memoirs in Vevey, and this gave him the opportunity to reflect on the course of events in England and the reasons for the failure of republicanism there. He had no hesitation in attributing the chief blame to Cromwell, and now remembered a number of conversations that he had had with Cromwell when walking in the park and on other occasions between 1646 and 1648, and thought that some of Cromwell's remarks on these occasions had been indicative of his future intentions. Ludlow believed that Cromwell, by overthrowing the Rump and establishing a military dictatorship, had been responsible for the restoration of Charles II.

Soon after he arrived in Vevey, the government of Berne invited him and the other English refugees to attend a banquet in their honour in the city of Berne on 3 September 1663.* After dinner Colonel Weiss, a member of the Council of Berne, asked Ludlow to explain how it was possible that the Commonwealth in England, which had seemed to be so strong at the time of Cromwell's death, had collapsed in less than two years without one drop of blood being shed. Ludlow said that to explain this, he would have to start at the beginning. Most of the Roundhead leaders who had begun the war had hesitated to defeat the King, though they had many opportunities to end the war by a decisive victory, but had tried to make peace with the Crown on terms favourable to themselves. This was shown by the conduct of the Earl of Essex and the Earl of Manchester, who on several occasions refused to fight the King, with Manchester 'giving this at a Council of War for the reason of his refusing to fight, That if

* New Style. The date was 24 August in England.

the King were beaten twenty times by us, he would be still King; but if he should once beat us, we should be all treated as traytors.' So the House of Commons removed Manchester and Essex and the rest of the nobility from their commands, and replaced them with commoners 'whose interest they knew it was to take away the monarchy it self. By these means they soon put an end to the war, sentenced the King to die for the blood that had been shed, establish'd a free Commonwealth, brought their enemies at home to submit to their authority, and reduced those abroad to accept such terms as they would give. In the midst of all this prosperity they were betray'd by Oliver Cromwell,' whom they had appointed as their general, but who overthrew his masters and made himself ruler. After Cromwell's death and the downfall of his son Richard, it seemed for a moment as if a free republic would be re-established; but the officers whom Cromwell had appointed to the army again overthrew the Rump, and Monck, 'who had been a creature of Cromwel and advanced by him', took advantage of the situation, pretending to save the republicans from the army, but betraying them and bringing back the son of the late King.

Ludlow was not forgotten in England. In 1683 a group of extreme Whigs and republicans plotted to assassinate Charles II and the Duke of York at Rye House in Hertfordshire. Ludlow was contacted by the plotters, but did not take any active part in the attempt. Two of the plotters escaped and visited Ludlow in Vevey, where they urged him to lead an insurrection in the West of England; but they found Ludlow 'in no wayes disposed to the thing, saying he had done his work he thought in the world, and was resolved to leave it to others.'

In November 1688 William of Orange landed at Torbay, drove James II into exile, and was proclaimed by Parliament as King William III. He was supported by a coalition of republicans, Whigs, Presbyterians, and Anglican Tories, who were all determined to get rid of a Roman Catholic King. In the summer of 1689 Ludlow was approached by someone in the English government and informed that King William wished to use his experience of Irish affairs in his campaign against James II and the Catholics in Ireland. The old Leveller, John Wildman, was Postmaster-General in King William's government. Alice Lisle, the widow of Ludlow's murdered friend John Lisle, had been sentenced to death by Judge Jeffreys at the Bloody Assize at Winchester and executed in 1685 for giving shelter to a government spy who pretended to be a fugitive from Monmouth's rebel army, and she was now acclaimed as a martyr and declared to be a victim of a miscarriage of justice by an Act of Parliament which reversed her conviction. The moment seemed propitious for Ludlow to return. But many of King William's supporters were old Cavaliers and High Church Tories, who still revered the memory of King Charles the Martyr, and had only turned against James II when he granted religious toleration to the Roman Catholics.

Ludlow left Vevey on 25 July 1689. He was aged seventy-two, but was in excellent health. In a farewell speech to the authorities at Vevey, he said that he felt obliged to go back to England to serve the new Gideon who had been raised up to lead the English nation out of the house of bondage. He had reached London by the middle of August, and was enthusiastically greeted by the republicans, who flocked to his house. The Tories were indignant. None of them were as indignant as Sir Henry Seymour, MP, who had been granted Ludlow's forfeited lands in Wiltshire. He did not raise the matter himself in the House of Commons but seems to have instigated several of his friends to do so. In November 1689 the matter was raised in the House by several Tory MPs, who claimed that Ludlow was planning a republican insurrection against King William, and in any case was a regicide who had been condemned as a traitor by an Act of Parliament in 1660. The House agreed to petition the King to arrest Ludlow and prosecute him for high treason for his part in the murder of the King's grandfather, King Charles the Martyr, in 1649.

A delegation from the House of Commons called on King William; it was headed by Sir Henry Seymour. This put the King in a difficult position. He did not wish to anger his Tory supporters by protecting and favouring Ludlow, or to antagonize his Whig and republican supporters by executing or imprisoning him. He pursued the policy which he had adopted the year before when he was confronted with the problem of what to do with James II, and had solved it by allowing him to escape abroad. He told Seymour and the House of Commons delegation that he thought their request was very proper, and issued a proclamation for Ludlow's arrest, offering a reward of £200 for anyone who apprehended him. But he almost certainly warned

Ludlow and allowed him to escape. The Tories were convinced
that the King had connived at Ludlow's escape, and pointed out
that Ludlow was safe in King William's principality of Holland
before the proclamation for his arrest was issued in England.

Ludlow returned to Vevey, and lived there for another three
years. He had at least been able to enjoy a sight of his native land,
and felt at home in Vevey after nearly thirty years' residence. He
erected an engraving over the door of his house in Vevey—
'*Omne solum forti patria quia patris*' ('To him to whom God is a
father every land is a fatherland'). His last surviving English
colleague at Vevey had died in 1687, but Mrs Ludlow was still
alive, and survived him by a few years. He died at Vevey in the
autumn of 1692. Unless Cornet Joyce was still alive in some part
of the world, Ludlow was the last surviving regicide.

Conclusion:
After the Restoration

The Restoration was a black day in British history. It was a victory for pornography, corruption, and—surprising though it may seem—for the worst kind of Puritan intolerance.

It was victory for pornography, because the King's return caused a spate of street-ballads and pamphlets in which the defeated Roundheads and sectaries were vilified in language so obscene that they cannot be quoted today, even in our modern permissive society.

It was a triumph for corruption, because the most unscrupulous individuals gained most and the most upright ones suffered most. The Roundheads who were loyal to their principles, or who refused to betray their friends, were executed, imprisoned, or otherwise penalized; the most loyal Cavaliers, who had sacrificed everything for the King during the previous twenty years, were in most cases unrewarded, and were often unable to recover their confiscated estates. The turncoats thrived, especially if they were willing to give untrue evidence which would lead to the conviction of their former comrades.

It was also a victory for the worst elements in Puritanism. The most bigoted and pleasure-hating Puritans, like the actors' scourge, Prynne, and the Scottish Presbyterians, were enthusiastic supporters of the Restoration, even if they soon found that they were doublecrossed by the King and the Cavaliers. It was the more tolerant and artistic Puritans, like Milton, and the rationalists like Vane and Ludlow, who were suppressed at the Restoration.

Above all, the Restoration brought back religious persecution. Under the republic and the protectorate there had been some religious persecution of both Roman Catholics and Quakers, but there had been religious toleration for the Protestant sects. After the Restoration, the Roman Catholics and the Quakers were persecuted even more savagely than they had been under the Commonwealth, and all the Nonconformist sects, including the Presbyterians, were also persecuted.

The Restoration is usually seen today as a victory for a happy, pleasure-loving people over dismal Puritan saints, and is supposed to have been hailed by the people as a liberation from the restrictive rule of the Puritans, a return to the pleasures of the theatre, the maypole, dancing, and village fairs. This feeling may have been present, and theatres, maypoles and fairs were again permitted after the Restoration; but no trace of this attitude appears in the pamphlets and street-ballads of 1660. They contain nothing about Puritan killjoys and a return to popular pleasures. Apart from their main theme—a hysterical and morbid fascination with the real and imagined sufferings of King Charles the Martyr, and a denunciation of those who carried 'the Guilt of that Sacred Blood'—they denounce the Puritans for their hypocrisy, for over-eating and getting drunk, and indulging in coarse jests, fornication and adultery in secret. It was not for suppressing the theatre that the pamphleteers vilified the arch-Puritan, Hugh Peters, but for having once acted the part of the Clown in Shakespeare's plays.

According to all the contemporary observers, the great majority of the people welcomed the Restoration. We who have experienced the results of Public Opinion Polls, to say nothing of the political forecasts of journalists and other expert observers, may be a little sceptical about believing this. The people of England never had the opportunity of expressing their wishes in 1660 in a general election or referendum, for not more than two per cent of the people were entitled to vote in the election which returned the Cavalier Parliament. But in the absence of evidence to the contrary, we should doubtless accept the fact that the majority of the people in 1660, tired of the rule of the saints, preferred to live under the rule of the sinners. If so, their hopes were disappointed, because the standard of living of the people fell sharply in the forty years which followed the Restoration.

In practical terms, the Civil War really achieved nothing at all. The objects for which the Puritans, the gentry, the lawyers and the House of Commons began the struggle under James I and Charles I were fulfilled; but this victory had been won before the

Civil War began. The elimination of Laud's High Church ritual and the renunciation of his attempt to impose Anglicanism in Scotland, the abolition of the Court of Star Chamber and the other prerogative courts with their use of torture and the punishment of mutilation, the recognition of the principle that only Parliament could enact new laws and impose new taxation, the abolition of wardships and monopolies, had all been gained by 1641. For the Roundheads, the war may have been necessary to prevent the loss of these gains; but all the further advances made after the start of the Civil War—the abolition of bishops and the establishment of Presbyterianism as the state religion in England, the grant of religious toleration to Nonconformist Protestant sects, the creation of the republic, the establishment of the principle that a King, like any subject, should be brought to justice and punished for his crimes—were rejected at the Restoration, though the principle that a tyrant might lawfully be put to death by his people was to serve as a precedent for France and other countries in the more distant future. The Restoration put the clock back to 1641, but no further. The Revolution of 1688, which won religious toleration for the Protestant sects, moved it a little further forward.

The Restoration inaugurated that era of crude selfishness and complete lack of social conscience which marks the period which is generally known today, a little inaccurately, as the eighteenth century. The destruction of an independent peasantry, the impoverishment of the agricultural labourer, the beginnings of the evils of industrialization, the bondage of the indentured coal-miners, the increase in the African slave trade, the class domination of the landed aristocracy, the corruption in public life, the savage discipline in the army and navy, all of which had existed and begun to develop earlier in the century, were greatly accelerated after the Restoration with the destruction of both the older patriarchal concepts and the religious idealism of the Civil War period. It was not until more than a hundred years later, towards the end of the eighteenth century, that a social conscience began to reassert itself in public life.

Bibliography

ABBOTT, W. C., *The Writings and Speeches of Oliver Cromwell*, Cambridge, Mass, 1937–47.

ADAIR, JOHN, *Roundhead General: a military biography of Sir William Waller*, London, 1969.

An Advertisement As touching the Fanaticks Late Conspiracy . . . in the City, London, 1661.

AGREEMENT OF THE PEOPLE, *Foundations of Freedom: Or an Agreement of the People*, 1648.

ALLEN, W., *Killing Noe Murder*, 1657.

Animadversions upon a Declaration of the Proceedings against the XI Members of the House of Commons . . . By His Excellency Sir Thomas Fairefax, and the Army under his Command, Cambridge, 1647.

An Answer to a Proposition In order to the proposing of A Commonwealth or Democracy, London, 1659.

The Army Harmlesse, London, 1647.

Articles of High Treason . . . Against The Lord Kymbolton, Mr Danzill Hollis, Sir Arthur Haslerig, Mr John Pym, Mr Iohn Hampden, Mr William Strode, London, 1641/2.

Articles of Impeachment Agreed upon by the Army . . . Against Sir John Clotworthy, Sir Wil. Waller, etc, London, 1647.

ASHLEY, MAURICE, *Oliver Cromwell: the Conservative Dictator*, London, 1937.

—*The Greatness of Oliver Cromwell*, London, 1957.

BOWEN, CATHERINE DRINKER, *The Lion and the Throne: the Life and Times of Sir Edward Coke*, London, 1957.

BRETT, S. REID, *John Pym*, London, 1940.

A Brief Iustification of the XI Accused Members, London, 1647.

Britains Triumph, for her Imparallel'd Deliverance, And her Joyfull Celebrating the Proclamation Of her most Gracious, Incomparable King Charles the Second, London, 1660.

Bumm-Fodder or Waste-paper Proper to wipe the Nation's Rump with, or your Own, 1660.

Calendar of State Papers (Domestic), 1649–60 (ed Mary Anne Everett Green), London, 1875–86.

Calendar of State Papers of the Reign of Charles II (ed Mary Anne Everett Green, etc), London, 1860–1938.

The Case is altered, Or, Sir Reverence the Rumps last Farce, 1660.

CHARLES I, *The Kings Majesties Desires to His Excellency Sir Thomas Fairfax*, London, 1647.

—*The Kings Majesties Most Gratious Letter to his Sonne, his Highnesse James Duke of York*, London, 1647.

—*Charles I in 1646: Letters of King Charles I to Queen Henrietta Maria* (ed John Bruce), London, 1856.

CLARENDON, EDWARD HYDE, EARL OF, *State Papers collected by Edward, Earl of Clarendon*, Oxford, 1786.

—*The History of the Rebellion and Civil Wars in England*, Oxford, 1858 ed.

CLARKE, W., *The Clarke Papers* (ed C. H. Firth), London, 1891–1901.

[COMBER, THOMAS], *Christianity no Enthusiasm: or, The Several Kinds of Inspirations and Revelations Pretended to by the Quakers*, London, 1678.

A Conference betwixt the Kings most Excellent Majesty, and Mr Peters, the Minister, at Newmarket, London, 1647.

Conflict in Stuart England: Essays in honour of Wallace Notestein (ed W. A. Aiken and B. D. Henning), London, 1960.

A Copie of a letter sent From the Agitators of his Excellency Sir Thomas Fairfax's Armie, to All the honest Sea-men of England, 1647.

A Copie of that Letter Mentioned in a Letter printed July 12. written out of Lancashire, 1647.

The Copy of a Letter Printed at New-Castle, July the 6, 1647, Sent From the Adjutators of the Army, London [1647].

CURTIS, C. D., *Blake*, Taunton, 1934.

DAVENANT, SIR WILLIAM, *A Panegyric to His Excellency The Lord Generall Monck*, London, 1659.

DAVIES, GODFREY, *The Restoration of Charles II 1658–1660*, San Marino, Calif, and Oxford, 1955.

DAWSON, JOHN HARBUTT, *Cromwell's Understudy: the life and times of General John Lambert*, London, 1938.

The Declaration and Proposals of the Citizens of London concerning the Lord Generall Fairfax and the Armies entring, and quartering within the Walls of the said City, London, 1648.

A Declaration From the Kingdom of Scotland Concerning the apparent danger of his Majesties Royall person, London, 1648/9.

A Declaration from the People called Quakers, To the Present Distressed Nation of England, London, 1659.

A Declaration of The Proceedings of His Excellency The Lord General Fairfax In the Reducing of the Revolted Troops, London, 1649.

A Declaration to the Kingdome, Of The Armies generall Survey of the Income of the Excize, London, 1648.

The Demands, Resolutions and Intentions, Of the Army, 1648.

Dictionary of National Biography, Oxford, 1885–1900.

A Discovrse Betwixt Lieutenant Colonel Iohn Lilburne Close Prisoner in the Tower of London, and Mr Hugh Peter: Upon May 25. 1649, London, 1649.

EDWARDS, THOMAS, *Gangroena*, London, 1646.

FAIRFAX, LORD, *Short Memorials of Thomas, Lord Fairfax*, London, 1699.

The Famous Tragedie Of the Life and Death of M^{ris} Rump, London, 1660.

FELL, JOHN, *The Interest of England Stated*, London, 1659.

FRASER, ANTONIA, *Cromwell: Our Chief of Men*, London, 1973.

A full Vindication and Answer of the XI Accused Members, London, 1647.

GIBB, M. A., *The Lord General: a Life of Thomas Fairfax*, London, 1938.

The Glory of these Nations . . . being a brief Relation of King Charles's Royall progresse from Dover to London [1660].

The Glory of the West . . . Being an unparallel'd Commemoration of General Monck's coming towards the City of London, London [1660].

The Grand Informer . . . Being A cleare and iust Vindication of the late proceedings of the Army, Oxford, 1647.

The Grand Memorandum, or A true and perfect Catalogue of the Secluded Members of the House of Commons, sitting 16 March 1659, London, 1660.

GREGG, PAULINE, *Free-born John*, London, 1961.

GUMBLE, THOMAS, *The Life of General Monck, Duke of Albemarle*, London, 1671.

HALLER, W., *The Rise of Puritanism*, New York, 1938.

—*Liberty and Reformation in the Puritan Revolution*, New York, 1955.

HEATH, JOHN, *Flagellum: or The Life and Death, Birth and Burial of Oliver Cromwell, The late Usurper*, London, 1663.

HILL, CHRISTOPHER, *Puritanism and Revolution*, London, 1958.

—*Society and Puritanism in Pre-Revolutionary England*, London, 1964.

—*Intellectual Origins of the English Revolution*, Oxford, 1965.

—*God's Englishman: Oliver Cromwell and the English Revolution*, London, 1970.

The History of the Life and Death of Hugh Peters that Arch-traytor, London, 1661.

HOLLES, LORD, *Memoirs of Denzil, Lord Holles*, London, 1699.

The holy Sisters Conspiracy against their Husbands, and the City of London, [1661].

House of Commons Journal (vol. II, 1640–3), London, 1803.

HULME, H., *The Life of Sir John Eliot*, London, 1957.

The Humble Answer Of the General Councel of Officers of the Army, London, 1648/9.

The Humble Petition of Many Thousands of young Men, and Apprentices of the City of London, London, 1647.

The Humble Petition of Those well affected to Government, both young men and Apprentices of the City of London, London, 1647.

HUTCHINSON, LUCY, *Memoirs of the Life of Colonel Hutchinson* (ed James Sutherland), Oxford, 1973 ed.

The Hypocrites Vnmasking Or A Cleare Discovery of the grosse Hypocrissy of the Officers and Agitators in the Army, London, 1647.

Independency stript & whipt, 1648.

The Indictment, Arraignment, Tryal, and Judgment, at Large, Of Twenty-Nine Regicides, the Murtherers Of his most Sacred Majesty King Charles I Of Glorious Memory, London, 1714.

JAMES, MARGARET, *Social Problems and Policy during the Puritan Revolution*, London, 1930.

The Kingdomes Weekly Intelligencer . . . Number 217. from Tuesday 6 July to Tuesday 13 July 1647.

KINGSTON, ALFRED, *Hertfordshire during the Great Civil War and the Long Parliament*, London and Hertford, 1894.

KNAPPEN, M. M., *Tudor Puritanism*, Gloucester, Mass, 1963.

LAMONT, W. A., *Marginal Prynne*, London and Toronto, 1963.

The Lawfulness of the Celebration of Christs Birth-day Debated, London, 1649.

A Letter from the Lord General Monck And the Officers here to the . . . Forces in England, Scotland and Ireland, London, 1659/60.

LILBURNE, JOHN, *The Poor Mans Cry Wherein Is shewed the present miserable estate of mee Iohn Lilburne Close prisoner in the Fleete*, 1639.

—*Innocency and Truth Justified First against the unjust aspersions of W. Prinn*, London, 1645.

—*Ionahs Cry out of the Whales belly*, 1647.

—*An Impeachment of High Treason against Oliver Cromwel, and his Son in Law Henry Ireton Esquires*, London, 1649.

—*The Upright Mans Vindication*, 1653.

LILLY, W., *A peculiar Prognostication Astrologically predicted . . . Whether, or No, His Majestie Shall suffer Death this present Yeere 1649*, 1648/9.

The Loyall Scout, Numb. 36 . . . From Friday Decem. 30 to Friday January the 6. 1659, 1659/60.

LUDLOW, EDMUND, *The Memoirs of Edmund Ludlow* (ed C. H. Firth), Oxford, 1894.

MACLURE, MILLAR, *The Paul's Cross Sermons 1534–1642*, Toronto, 1958.

MASARES, F., *Select Tracts relating to the Civil Wars in England in the reign of King Charles the First*, London, 1815.

MASSEY, R., *The Examination and Correction of a Paper . . . Intituled A Relation of the Discourse between Mr Hugh Peters and Lieut. Collonel Iohn Lilburne in the Tower of London*, London, 1649.

MASSON, D., *The Life of John Milton*, London, 1859–80.

MAYNE, JOSEPH, *Oxao-Maxia Or The Peoples War Examined According to the Principles of Scripture & Reason*, 1647.

MCGRATH, PATRICK, *Papists and Puritans under Elizabeth I*, London, 1967.

Mercurius Elendicus. Numb. 5 . . . From Monday 21 May to Monday 28 May, 1649.

Mercurius Impartialis: or, An Answer to that Treasonable Pamphlet, Mercurius Militaris, 1648.

MILTON, JOHN, *The Complete Prose Works of John Milton*, New Haven and London, 1953–73.

The Mirrour of Allegiance Or a looking-glasse for the English, 1647.

MITCHELL, W. M., *The Rise of the Revolutionary Party in the English House of Commons 1603–1629*, New York, 1957.

A Moderate and Clear Relation of the private Souldierie of Colonell Scroops and Colonel Sanders Regiments: concerning the Parliaments proceedings in these our late daies, London, 1648.

MONCK, GEORGE, DUKE OF ALBEMARLE, *Observations upon Military & Political Affairs*, London, 1671.

Mr William Prynn, His Defence of Stage-Plays, or A Retractation of a former Book of his called Histrio-Mastix, London, 1649.

Mrs Rump brought to Bed of a Monster, 1660.

A New Declaration Concerning the King, From the Commons of England, assembled at Westminster, London, [1649].

A New Remonstrance from the Souldiery, To his Excellency the Lord General Fairfax, London, 1648.

NICHOLAS, SIR EDWARD, *The Nicholas Papers: Correspondence of Sir Edward Nicholas* (ed G. F. Warner), London, 1892.

The Northern Intelligencer: Communicating the Affayres of those Parts: and particularly The Agitations of Mr Hugh Peeters in five several Counties, 1648.

NUGENT, LORD, *Some Memorials of John Hampden*, London, 1832.

On the Death of His Grace The Duke of Albemarle, London, 1670/1.

An Ordinance of the Lords and Commons Assembled in Parliament: For the chusing of Common-Councell-men And other Officers within the City of London, London, 1648.

OVERTON, RICHARD, *An Appeale From the degenerate Representative Body the Commons of England*, London, 1647.

The Parliament under the power of the Sword with A briefe Answer thereunto By some of the Army, London, 1648.

The Pedigree and Descent of His Excellency, General George Monck, London, 1659/60.

PEPYS, SAMUEL, *The Diary of Samuel Pepys* (ed Henry B. Wheatley), London, 1893–9.

The Perfect Weekly Account, 6–13 December 1648.

PETERS, HUGH, *Milke for Babes, And Meat for Men*, London, 1641.

—*Church–Government and Church–Covenant discvssed*, London, 1643.

—*The full and Last Relation, Of all things concerning Basing-House*, London, 1645.

—*Gods Doings, and Mens Duty: Opened in a Sermon Preached before both Houses of Parliament . . . April 2*, London, 1646.

—*A Dying Fathers last Legacy to an Onely Child*, London, 1660.

—*The Case of Mr Hugh Peters, Impartially Communicated to the View and Censvre of the Whole World*, London, [1660].

The Petition of the Jewes For the Repealing of the Act of Parliament for their banishment out of England, London, 1649.

PHILLIPS, C. E. LUCAS, *Cromwell's Captains*, London, 1938.

POWELL, J. R., *Robert Blake*, London, 1972.

PRICE, JOHN, *The Mystery and Method of his Majesty's Happy Restauration laid open to Publick View*, London, 1680.

A Proclamation of his Excellency Tho. L. Fairfax . . . Requiring all Persons who have engaged for the King . . . to depart the City, London, 1649.

PRYNNE, W., *Histrio-Mastix, The Players Scovrge, or Actors Tragedie*, London, 1633.

—*Newes from Ipswich*, Ipswich (?), [1636].

—*A new discovery of the Prelates tyranny*, London, 1641.

—*The Soveraigne Power of Parliaments and Kingdomes*, London, 1643.

—*The Treachery and Disloyalty of Papists to their Soverajgnes*, London, 1643.

—*A Breviate of the life of William Laud Arch-bishop of Canterbury*, London, 1644.

—*Hidden Workes of Darkenes Brought to Publike Light*, London, 1645.

—*The Levellers Levelled to the very Ground*, London, 1647.

—*Articles of Impeachment of High-Treason exhibited by the Commons of England in a Free Parliament against Lieutenant-General Oliver Cromwell Esquire, etc*, London, 1648/9.

—*A Breife Memento to the Present Vnparliamentary Ivnto Touching their present Intentions and Proceedings to Depose and Execute Charles Steward, their lawfull King*, London, 1648/9.

—*Mr Pryn's last and finall Declaration To the Commons of England Concerning the King, Parliament, And Army*, London, 1648/9.

—*A Briefe Polemicall Dissertation, concerning the true Time of the Incohation and Determination of the Lords Day-Sabbath*, London, 1655.

—*The Quakers unmasked, And clearly detected to be but the Spawn of Romish Frogs, Jesuites, and Franciscan Freers*, London, 1655.

—*A New Discovery of Free-State Tyranny*, London, 1655.

—*A Seasonable, legal and Historicall Vindication . . . of the Good, Old, Fundamentall liberties . . . of all English Freemen*, London, 1655.

—*A Short Demurrer to the Jewes long discontinued Remitter into England*, London, 1656.

—*Pendennis and all other standing Forts Dismantled*, London, 1657.

—*A Brief Narrative Of the manner how divers Members of the House of Commons . . . Coming Vpon Tuesday the 27ᵗʰ of December 1659 . . . were again forcibly shut out*, London, 1660.

—*The Case Of the old Secured, Secluded, and now Excluded Members, Briefly and truly Stated*, London, 1660.

—*An Exact History of Popes intollerable Usurpations Upon the liberties of the Kings, and Subjects, of England & Ireland*, London, 1666–8.

Puritan Manifestoes (ed W. H. Frere and C. E. Douglas), London, 1907.

The Quarrel between the Earl of Manchester and Oliver Cromwell (ed John Bruce and David Masson), London, 1875.

RAMSAY, ROBERT W., *Henry Ireton*, London, 1949.

Rebels no Saints, Or A Collection of the Speeches . . . of those Persons lately Executed, London, 1661.

A Relation of the ten grand infamous Traytors who . . . were Arraigned, Tryed, and Executed in the Moneth of October 1660, 1660(?).

The Re-Publicans and the other spurious Good Old Cause, briefly and truly Anatomized, 1659.

The Resolution of his Excellency the Lord General Fairfax and His Generall Councell of Officers Concerning Major Generall Brown . . . With a Remonstrance from the Navie, touching the Army, London, 1648.

The Resolution of the Army concerning the King, Lords, and Commons, London, 1648.

The Riddles Unriddled . . . Written for Vindication of the Army, 1647.

ROGERS, EDWARD, *Some Account of the Life and Opinions of a Fifth-Monarchy Man*, London, 1867.

ROGERS, JOHN, *Jegar-Sahadvrtha: an Oiled Pillar Set up for Posterity Against the present Wickednesses . . . of the Serpent Power (now up) in England*, 1657.

ROGERS, THOROLD, *History of Agriculture and Prices*, Oxford, 1872.

ROWE, VIOLET A., *Sir Henry Vane the Younger*, London, 1970.

The Rump Dockt, 1659/60.

SABINE, GEORGE H., *The Works of Gerrard Winstanley*, New York, 1941.

Salus Populi, Desperately ill Of a languishing Consumption . . . By Theophilus P, London, 1648.

SKINNER, THOMAS, *The Life of General Monk: late Duke of Albemarle*, London, 1723.

SNOW, VERNON F., *Essex the Rebel*, Lincoln, Neb., 1970.

A Song to his Excellency The Lᵈ General Monck, at Skinners-Hall on Wednesday, Aprill 4. 1660, London, 1660.

SPALDING, RUTH, *The Improbable Puritan: A Life of Bulstrode Whitelocke*, London, 1975.

The Speech and Confession of Hugh Peters . . . With the manner how he was taken on Sunday Night last in Southwark, London, 1660.

A Speech made to His Excellency the Lord General Monck . . . At Fishmongers-Hall in London. The Thirteenth of April 1660, London, 1660.

A Speech made to the Lord General Monck at Clotheworkers Hall in London The 13. of Marche 1659, [London, 1660].

A Speech spoken to his Excellency the Lord General Monk . . . at Drapers-Hall, Wednesday the 28. of Marche [London, 1660].

SPRIGG, JOSHUA, *Anglia Rediviva* London, 1647.

STEARS, R. P., *The Strenuous Puritan: Hugh Peter*, Urbana, Ill., 1954.

The Tales and Jests of Mr Hugh Peters, (London, 1660,) London, 1807 ed.

THOMAS-STANFORD, C., *Sussex in the Great Civil War and the Interregnum*, London, 1910.

THURLOE, JOHN, *A Collection of the State Papers of John Thurloe Esq*, London, 1742.

To His Excellency General Monck. The Humble Petition of the Lady Lambert, London, 1659/60.

TREVOR-ROPER, H. R., *Archbishop Laud*, London, 1940.

The Triall of Mr John Lilburn . . . upon Wednesday, Thursday, Friday and Saturday the 13. 14. 15 and 16 of July 1653, London, 1653.

A True and ful Relation of the Officers and Armies forcible seising of divers Eminent Members of the Commons House, Decemb. 6 and 7, 1648, London, 1648.

VICARS, JOHN, *The Pictvre of Independency Lively (yet Louingly) Delineated*, London, 1645.

Vox Populi Suprema Rex Carolus, Or, The Voice of the People for King Charles, London, 1660.

WALLER, SIR WILLIAM, *Recollections, by General Sir William Waller*, published in *The Poetry of Aunt Matilda*, London, 1788.

—*Vindication of the Character and Conduct of Sir William Waller, Knight*, London, 1793.

WARNER, OLIVER, *Hero of the Restoration: a life of General George Monck first Duke of Albemarle*, London, 1936.

WARRISTON, LORD, *The Diary of Sir Archibald Johnston of Warriston*, Edinburgh, 1911–40.

WEDGWOOD, C. V., *The King's Peace*, London, 1955.

—*The King's War 1641–1647*, London, 1958.

—*The Trial of Charles I*, London, 1964.

—*Oliver Cromwell*, London, 1973.

The Weekly Intelligence of the Common-Wealth, 1655.

The whole proceedings of the barbarous and inhumane demolishing of the Earle of Essex Tombe on Thursday night last, November 26. 1646, 1646.

WINSTANLEY, GERRARD, *The Mysterie of God Concerning the whole Creation*, 1648.

—*Truth Lifting up its head above Scandals*, London, 1649.

WINTHROP, JOHN, *Winthrop's Journal, 'History of New England' 1630–1649* (ed James Kendall Hosmer), New York, 1908.

WODROW, ROBERT, *The History of the Sufferings of the Church of Scotland*, Glasgow, 1838 ed.

A Wonderfull Plot . . . Being a Parallel between a Jesuite . . . And a petty Independent, London, 1647.

A Word to Mr Wil. Pryn Esquire and two for the Parliament and Army, London, 1649.

YONGE, WILLIAM, *Englands Shame: or the Unmasking of a Politick Atheist*, London, 1663.

Index

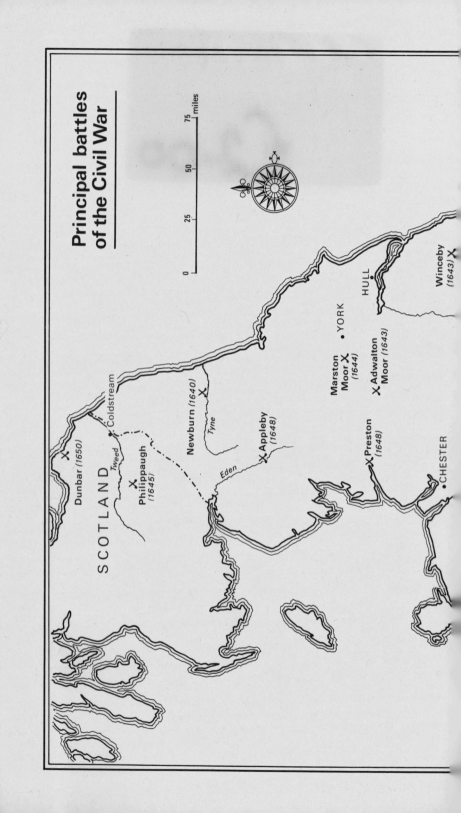

Principal battles
of the Civil War

0   25   50   75
miles

SCOTLAND

Dunbar *(1650)*

Coldstream

Tweed

Philippaugh
(1645)

Newburn *(1640)*

Tyne

Eden

Appleby
(1648)

Marston
Moor X
(1644)
• YORK

Adwalton
Moor *(1643)*

HULL

Winceby
(1643)

Preston
(1648)

• CHESTER